Learners with Special Needs

Editor

M.L. Dhawan

ISHA BOOKS
DELHI-110 033

Learners with Special Needs

ISBN: 81-8205-159-2

Published in 2007 in India by
Isha Books,
B-63, Ist Floor, New Gupta Colony,
Near DDA Market, Delhi-110 009
Phone : 9212142040
Email : ishabooks@hotmail.com
Laser Typesetting at: Shree Vaishnavi Creations, Delhi
Printed at: Rajdhani Printers, Delhi

PREFACE

Teachers in inclusive classrooms regularly face the difficult task of having to modify the curriculum to reach all of their students, many of whom have special needs. There will be different categories of learners with special needs in a classroom including gifted students, students with average abilities and students with disabilities—whether physical, emotional, or cognitive. These different categories of students respond to the curriculum differently.

The needs of the gifted students are totally different to that of a disabled students. Students who have intellectual, creative, leadership, or physical gifts need to be in settings at least part of the time where they can be challenged by their peers and can have opportunities to develop their capacities even further. Depending on the ability itself and other factors affecting their ability to succeed academically, disabled students may need modifications such as advance and graphic organisers, instructional scaffolding, additional practice and time to complete assignments, and/or alternative media.

To meet the goal of equal access to the curriculum for everyone, to enable each student to engage with his or her lessons in a meaningful way, teachers must be prepared to provide useful alternatives in terms of both curricular materials and instructional delivery. Well-adapted materials without an effective method of teaching are practically useless, but with the proper tools and instructional methods, a good teacher encourages each member of the class to participate directly in the learning experience. Caring teachers can assist students to "own" and develop their talents by understanding and responding to adjustment challenges and coping strategies. They should develop special strategies to evaluate the abilities of each categories of students. Effective guidance and counselling programmes can also play an important role in the mental, physical and academic growth of students.

This book provides a good description of the special educational needs of different categories of students. The challenges confronted by special education teachers and specific strategies they have to develop to help the students are described elaborately. It is hoped that this work will serve as a highly beneficial reference tool for teachers, counsellors, school administers, parents and child care-givers.

Editor

CONTENTS

Preface — *v*

1. Learners with Special Needs — 1
2. Helping Children with Special Needs — 30
3. Role of Guidance and Counselling — 74
4. Evaluation — 130
5. Tools of Evaluation — 171
6. Construction of Tests — 191
7. Elementary Concept of Normal Distribution Curve and Correlation — 232
8. Statistical Analysis — 263
9. Standardised and Teacher-made Tests — 277

Index — 291

1

LEARNERS WITH SPECIAL NEEDS

A teacher, school counsellor and involved school personnel need to be knowledgeable about specific disabilities for several reasons:

— To be able to deal with the student with a disability with comfort and safety.

— To be able to know what to expect from the student in terms of their disability.

— To feel that they have some accurate information and not be functioning from misconceptions.

INDENTIFICATION OF DISABILED CHILDREN

For the purposes of this chapter, the term physically disabled will be used to describe individuals who are basically nonsensory physically impaired, resulting in limitations of mobility. Although loss of sight and hearing are certainly physical disabilities, they will not be discussed on their own, but only as they are associated with or secondary to mobility disabilities.

A physical disability may or may not be a handicap to a person. Disability refers to an objective measurable organic dysfunction or impairment. Loss of a hand, paralysis of legs or arms are examples of physical disabilities. A disability may be the medical diagnosis. A handicap is the effect of a disability on an individual's functioning in specific circumstances. Someone who uses a wheelchair for mobility, due to cerebral palsy for example, has a physical disability but that person may not he handicapped — except when the environment (lack of ramps, accessible washrooms) prevents normal functioning.

Even within a specific disability grouping, such as cerebral palsy or spina bifida, no two individuals are alike in their abilities or their needs. Functional impairments range from mild to severe. Individuals with the same medical diagnosis may be as different as day and night in their ability to function. Educators should be aware of the various disabling conditions they may deal with in order to understand the nature of the disability and any educational implications of the disability. Teachers should also be aware of the medical jargon used by other professionals who work with physically disabled children, and not be afraid to have another professional clarify their meanings.

Physical disability interrupts normal development, on many levels. Some individuals who have a physical disability may experience pain; some may have difficulty with motor control, with speech impairments, etc..

The child with a disability which was existing at birth may have experienced disruption of consistent mothering due to repeated hospitalization, and feel helpless to make any effect on their lives.

There are special stresses and fears connected with disabilities — fear of pain, of bodily mutilation, abandonment, and of death. Repeated hospitalizations, some planned and some unexpected, disrupt a secure and continuous home life. A disability is sometimes a frustration and often a nuisance.

An individual with a disability grows up with a feeling of always being different, unique. They may learn that their body cannot be depended upon and may even have a sense that their body can betray them. Some physical conditions require that activity levels need to be reduced — such as during hospitalization or when the condition leaves a child open to injury. Medical treatments such as a cast or brace can restrict movement and activity and contribute to the feeling of uniqueness and isolation.

Disability often causes ongoing crises, and these crises can cause stress and emotional changes within the family. Parents are called on for extra attention and care during medical crisis. The emotional state of the family may go up and down with an often unrealistic hope that a cure will be found, or the right treatment will make the child normal. These stresses often effect a child's psychological growth. If there is little structure or limit setting in the home (perhaps the parents feel guilty about rules) the child with a physical disability may continually test the limits of the rules at school.

— A child may withdraw, due to fear, and become lethargic, nonresponsive.

— Adolescents with a physical disability have a strong need of acceptance of peers, to be like their friends. They may refuse necessary medical treatments, refuse to use special equipment needed for mobility, or the use of any aid which makes them look different.

— The stress of having a disability may cause or aggravate emotional and behavioural deviations. Stress may cause or aggravate physical symptoms such as ulcers, eczema, or aggravate symptoms of asthma and arthritis.

— Some psychological symptoms which an individual can exhibit may be overdependence, insecurity, undirected hostility.

Teachers must first identify their own biases and negative attitudes to disability. Classroom teachers unfamiliar with physical disabilities may have many concerns and fears. A regular classroom of 25 or more students is a heavy demand on an individual teacher. It becomes even more pressing when a student with a disability enters the classroom. The teacher has many questions, and needs accurate answers as well as support. They may have fears about saying the wrong thing or doing something which can harm the student. Some disabilities may require that the student refrain from rough housing or extreme physical exercise. The teacher may fear for the physical safety of the student. The response on the teacher's behalf may be defensiveness and a wish to avoid the problems.

Invisible Handicaps

Some children will be in the regular classroom with handicaps which are less obvious, even invisible, but which result in some mobility impairment. The classroom teacher who has such children needs to be as informed about these invisible disabilities as well as the visible, obvious disabilities. The teacher's role is the same with children with invisible handicaps as with visibly handicapped students or non-handicapped students — to assist them to achieve their full potential. Some of these invisible illnesses or disabilities have the same effect on development, social interaction and how the individual student copes with life on a daily basis as would a visible handicap.

Some illnesses, disabilities and chronic conditions which may be counted as 'invisible' are:

- — Asthma; a respiratory condition.
- — Diabetes; inability of body to break down sugar for energy.
- — Renal (kidney) diseases; requiring medication or dialysis.
- — Hemophilia; a condition where the person bleeds or bruises easily
- — Epilepsy; a transient spasm that causes disturbances of brain function.
- — Sickle cell anemia; a genetic defect of hemoglobin.
- — Cardiac problems which may cause weakness.
- — Cystic fibrosis; a lung condition needing drugs and causing weakness.

The commonality of these diseases is that they are invisible to the outside world. The child may Seem healthy until the symptoms of the condition become evident. The biggest problem for these children is that they appear normal and usually do not wish to have others know their condition. Each condition mentioned, as well as numerous others not mentioned, should have information which is available through physicians or community clinics. Knowing more about the condition helps the caregivers, parents or teachers become more comfortable with the effects and with the person who has the disability.

The teacher has to he able to help the student function during their good times and help the student cope with the problems of illness, hospitalization. Some allowances need to be made to accommodate far the effects of the illness without lowering expectations so far as to kill all motivation

Some chronic illnesses may require the administration of medication, or allow for self administration of medication. For example, diabetes often requires insulin which can be self administered, as well as the possibility of an emergency where medication may need to be administered quickly. An asthma attack, as well, may require self administration of medication or, in a severe attack, assistance from the adults around in properly administering drugs.

The classroom teacher is the main method of attitude of change or acceptance by peers of the student with a disability. An individual with an 'invisible' disability will usually strive hard to appear as normal as all the other students. Some may attempt to use their chronic conditions to avoid taking part in their events they would rather avoid, to attract spiel attention and sometimes just to get their way. A teacher, together with parents and perhaps a school psychologist, need to sort out which behaviours deserve attention and which behaviours are being used to obtain special but negative attention.

Mobility Disabilities

Following are several specific and common disabilities which result in mobility impairment. Some conditions result from accident, or illness, some are from birth. The age of onset of a condition may have some effect on the individual's response. There is no possible way to say this disability or condition results in this impairment, or this specific need, for each individual's reaction is unique. The author has also purposely not included suggestions as to teaching methods or suggestions on physical treatments. Specific teaching methods are available to interested teachers through their training. Physical treatment or considerations of positioning and handling a student with a specific disability is the concern of the professional health care worker — usually a physiotherapist or occupational therapist.

Amputation

Amputation or limb absences which are either acquired through trauma, or are congenital (from birth). The main common causes of traumatic amputation are motor vehicle accidents, accidents involving explosives, railroad accidents and farm accidents. The most common non-trauma cause of childhood amputation is malignant disease such as cancer. When cancer is the cause of amputation, other ongoing medical treatments may be necessary. Congenital amputations means that the child is horn with partial or complete absence of a limb or limbs. Causes of limb absence can be varied and occur during fetal development, usually in the first three months in utero. In congenital limb absence, there may be no normal Structures such as fingers. Commonly, the middle segment of the limb may be absent (the arm) but some form of finger or hand may exist attached to the shoulder. The individual may chose to use these rudimentary fingers over an artificial limb.

Since our image of ourselves is linked closely to our self esteem, there may be a strong focus on self acceptance, using what one has to full potential to achieve maximum self care.

The response of parents, siblings, teachers and society in general to how the individual functions is of greatest importance.

— Feeling "normal", looking "normal" may be the biggest problem for the individual.

— Traumatic loss through accident or disease may engender feelings of grief.

— Counselling support for the individual and their families may be of great importance, as the feelings of loss continue to reoccur as the individual grows.

— Learning to use a prosthesis may cause pain, limits some physical activity initially and may cause the individual some embarrassment.

— Doing things 'differently', such as eating or drawing with the feet, may be a matter of great interest to peers and great embarrassment to the individual. Each individual reacts differently.

Some children may learn to use the portion of the limb present, to manipulate pens, eating utensils. If this is not possible a prosthesis (artificial arm) may be used. Some persons born with lack of arms may, with training and physiotherapy, learn to use their feet to eat, write, etc. Those born with lack of legs may learn to propel themselves with their arms or use a power chair.

Individuals with missing limbs are the subject of stares, comments and teasing from peers. This attention is embarrassing and may make the individual desire to hide out. The classroom teacher needs to understand how the student functions, what the real limitations may be, and with support, challenge and encourage. One issue which may cause disagreement between the student with an amputation and the adult caregivers around him/her is refusal to use prosthetic devices. The individual may invent ways to accomplish tasks which are unique and do not involve the prosthesis, while adult caregivers are attempting to 'normalize' the individual to prosthetic use. A teacher may be caught in the middle of this battle, on one hand encouraging individuality and on the other enforcing the rules.

Arthrogryposis

Arthrogryposis is a congenital bone and muscle degeneration with unknown cause. Arthrogryposis is not hereditary.

Various parts of the body may be involved;

- shoulders, elbows or knees may be fixed in deformed positions. Muscles are involved, and may be stretched into awkward positions because of the bone deformity.
- The individual may be able to use writing tools, but would benefit from adapted computer use as well.
- With arthrogryposis, some limb, back and facial deformity is common, sometimes more pronounced than others.
- There are some associated physical problems such as heart malformation which may contribute to a general lack of energy. Some other associated health problems may be
  - urinary abnormalities
  - respiratory problems
  - hernias

The individual may be able to use a manual wheelchair, or may do better with a motorized chair .

Treatment mostly involves assisting the individual gain mastery over daily self care. Some radical surgery may be used to realign bones or increase muscle flexibility. Casts, splints and braces may be worn to extend limbs, correct deformities and allow increased flexibility.

As with any mobility disability school needs to provide as many aides as needed to allow the individual full participation in daily living. School may be the central point for socialization.

Cerebral Palsy

The term means brain (cerebral) paralysis (palsy). There are ancient references to the condition. It is not a progressive condition. Most occurrences of C.P. are from birth, though some occurrences of C.P. may be acquired through injury after birth. The incidence of diagnosed C.P. is three out of a thousand births. There may be more incidences of C.P. but diagnoses may often be delayed two or three years after birth.

There are many 'causes' of cerebral palsy, in fact, so many complications and events can lead to an individual having Cerebral Palsy that there is no one 'cause'. C.P. is brain damage, with too much or too little stimulation to muscles from the brain and spinal column.

Some medical terms used to describe the effects of C.P.:

— Ataxia. Rigidity and Tremor.

— Ataxia - lack of coordination and sense of balance.

— Rigidity - lack of voluntary movement - in combination with other types - resistant to movement.

— Hypotonia - lack of tone, floppy.

— Tremor - involuntary motion - shaking.

Combination or only one type. Each type effects movement in a different way.

— Mild C.P. - no speech problems, can walk without aid. Some surgery may help correct muscles.

— Moderate C.P. - speech and walking problems - self care possible with equipment such as wheelchair, braces, walker.

— Severe C.P. - prognosis poor for self care. Complete dependence for care.

Cerebral Palsy may be classified by the manner and number of limbs involved in the conditions.

— Monoplegia - one limb

— Triplegia - three limbs (one arm and both legs)

— Hemiplegia - one arm and one leg on same side of body

— Paraplegia - only legs

— Quadriplegia - all limbs and rest of body

— *Speech*

  — Spastic speech - slow, labored, uncontrolled volume.

  — Athetoid speech - from severe impairment to slight awkwardness in forming words/sounds.

  — Speech may he delayed due to neuromotor problems, limitations of concept developments, hearing loss or possible mental retardation.

  — Speech may also be delayed through frustration on the part of the individual. No one may have shown the patience to listen to the labored speech, and no feedback or positive response has been given. The individual with C.P. may have lost the motivation to try to be understood.

Prenatal Causes:

1. Cerebral Palsy is rarely inherited.
2. Rubella in the first 3 months, toxoplasmosis (a parasitic infection) and shingles (a virus) in the mother may cause C.P. in fetus.
3. Lack of oxygen to the fetus
   — separation of the placenta
   — hemorrhage in the mother (injury such as an auto accident or fall)
   — knotting of the umbilical cord in utero

4. RH incompatibility
   — mother's immune defence destroy infants red blood cells. This type is less prevalent due to advances in medical care

5. Prematurity
   — premature infant's lungs may be unable to supply oxygen needed to the brain

6. Metabolic disorders in
   — mother diabetes
   — toxemia

Perinatal Causes:

1. Birth injury
   — compression of skull during birth (forceps)

2. Lack of oxygen during birth process
   — lung collapse
   — medication delays lung action

Post Natal Causes:

1. Head injury
   — auto accidents
   — falls
   — physical abuse (severe shaking of infant, striking infant in head)

2. Brain Infections
   — meningitis
   — encephalitis
   — lead or chemical poisoning

3. Brain hemorrhages

   — blood clots block oxygen to brain (possible injury)

4. Lack of oxygen

   — carbon monoxide poisoning (cars or malfunctioning heating)

   — drowning (rescue efforts delayed)

   — electrocution (cardiac arrest)

6. Brain tumour

Associated Handicaps:

Sometimes a person with Cerebral Palsy will have other disabilities which are the result of the cerebral palsy. In the multihandicapped person, the Cerebral Palsy may be the least disabling condition. Other associated difficulties may be:

1. Difficulties in swallowing, partial paralysis of neck muscles may cause choking on solid food.
2. Drooling. This can be, in an older child and adult, messy and embarrassing.
3. Speech may be effected severely due to paralysis of speech muscles, or due to problems in organizing and selecting speech. Some persons with Cerebral Palsy may be somewhat hard to understand, speaking slowly and deliberately. Some may he almost impossible to understand without great Patience and close attention to the person.
4. Hearing problems may he present but it is rare.
5. Visual problems such as farsightedness, near-sightedness and crossed eyes may be present. Many visual problems are usually more problems of lack of control of head and neck muscles, requiring aides to hold head still and positioning reading material at eye level.

Sensory deficits may be present, such as loss of the ability to feel shape or texture. Convulsive disorders may be present with different kinds of Cerebral Palsy. These convulsions may or may not respond to medication.

Mental Retardation - Research has identified that a majority of children with Cerebral Palsy have some level of mental handicap. Persons with Ataxia or spastic Hemiplegia (types of C.P.) are less likely to have mental handicap.

Perceptual Disorder - Persons with Cerebral Palsy may have problems with spatial relationships or may simply he unable to copy what is perceived. The difficulties may be more a visual-motor disorder. A developmental lag may be present, where a child with Cerebral Palsy may not be performing up to the norm for their age but will improve with time.

The Place of physical therapy - Therapy is not a cure for Cerebral Palsy. Physical therapy for persons with Cerebral Palsy can include using a walker, crutches or wheelchair, exercises to keep muscle flexible and prevent body deformity, exercises to improve balance and strengthen walking muscles. Occupational therapy helps the person with Cerebral Palsy perform daily living activities — how to bathe, dress, move your own chair. Physical and occupational therapy should be designed to help the individual maximize their full physical potential.

Outside Classroom Involvement - Individuals with Cerebral Palsy may be involved in special programs to design appropriate seating, braces, mechanical aides to move or talk. They may be trained to use computers to communicate. They may also be involved in long term medical treatment and spend long periods of time in hospitals or at home recovering from surgical medical procedures designed to help muscles.

Though much of the life of the individual with Cerebral Palsy may be in the hands of physicians, therapists and parents, teachers have a role in the educational domain and are part of the team who all have goals for the individual. Teachers may get a report describing the student with Cerebral Palsy. This may be a description of the condition of associated handicaps — in medical or psychological terminology. These labels and descriptions do not give a picture of the individual's needs or abilities or desires. The classroom teacher will need to consult with physiotherapists and resource teachers who may be involved with the individual. Most importantly, the teacher needs to consult with parents to understand the student's abilities.

Many physiotherapists and occupational therapists are concerned about positioning and setting. The classroom teacher and other support staff need to understand how important it is for a growing body to sit well supported so that deformities don't happen or pressure sores are not created. This may mean a teacher will need to help the student be comfortable and Sit in a position which does not promote deformity of either muscle or bone. Consultation with therapists and parents will help the teacher understand and overcome this difficulty. The school's role with an individual who has a disability is to help the student achieve a full potential, in a least restrictive environment and an individual with C.P. is no different.

Osteogenesis Imperfecta

O.I. is caused by lack of calcium and protein in the hone, as well as other necessary bone forming materials, so the bones are weak and brittle. Joints may also be effected, often having greater range of movement than normal. A person with O.I. has thin, pale skin and blue "whites" of their eyes. They usually have a triangular face, very broad forehead and small chin, looking elfin like. About one in 40,000 persons has O.I.. Genetic testing in utero can identify it.

Children born with O.I. may live only a short time, as they are fragile and have many fractures. As they age, surgical strengthening of the bones with metal rods often is a treatment. Individuals with O.I. usually use a wheelchair, crutches and braces. In adolescence, bones may become stronger, but there may be many bone deformities which effect the self-image.

There are some possible body deformities including dwarfism, hearing loss, triangular facial structure and skull deformities. A feature of O.I. is that the individual may have blue whites in the eye. There are two types of O.I., one may be evident at birth with severe fractures before and during birth and infancy, resulting in excessive hospitalization in early childhood. The second type, tarda, becomes evident in early childhood, with fractures happening in early childhood, seemingly unexplained. In other words, sometimes the condition is very evident, with the individual having to use a wheelchair or crutches for Severe deformities. Sometimes only small clues such as facial features and small size may be evident, as well as unexplained fractures. The individuals have pale, thin skin and are delicate in appearance.

There is no Cure for O.I. but encouragement to full social participation and self care should be a priority. Surgery may be used to straighten and strengthen limbs. Treatment of fractures with casts, braces may require long term periods of hospitalization at any early age. These individuals may have gone through extensive surgery to correct bone deformities and they may wear special orthopedic devices to lengthen and/or strengthen bones. Because of repeated fractures and hospitalization they may be isolated and often are homebound for long periods of time. They may he quite 'adult' at an early age and seem precocious. They are usually highly verbal and if given stimulation can turn their energies toward specialized areas of learning, such as music or art.

Equipment such as wheelchairs, scooters, etc. allows complete mobility and they usually are able to manage the washroom as long as there are wheelchair units. Bladder or bowels are usually unaffected and normal persons with O.I. need social skills and mastery of day to day living. They can take part in adapted physical education — contrary to most warnings — such as referees, time keepers, coaches

The teacher should be aware of psychosocial factors such as family guilt for the disease, over involvement by mother in care and other family dynamics. The extended family may reject the child and due to the nature of O.I., the family may be under suspicion of child abuse due to repeated fractures of the child. If O.I. isn't diagnosed, abuse may seem to be the cause of unexplained fractures. Routine activities can be dangerous for the individual with O.I..

Juvenile Rheumatoid Arthritis

Juvenile Rheumatoid Arthritis (JRA) refers to a group of diseases characterized by chronic arthritis of unknown causes. It may occur in infancy or show up at any age in an older child. Joints swell, bone growth changes, there is pain and tenderness as well as internal problems.

JRA is an inflammation of joints through possible auto-immune related diseases. Antibodies in the blood attack the body's components. There is no known cause or specific cure, though various drug treatments may have a helpful effect.

Childhood arthritis is unpredictable and can vary from day to day, month to month. Remission may occur. There may be growth deformities and joint inflexibility, plus obesity due to inactivity may be a problem. There may also be a loss of vision from inflammation, as well as possible hearing loss.

Aspirin and aspirin products are helpful in the treatment of arthritis, but aspirin in high doses often causes a ringing in the ears and intestinal problems. Steroids also can be helpful, but can have hazardous side effects.

Constant pain from JRA can create feelings of punishment, and a fear of physical activity. The result may be prolonged dependency on parent care.

Enforced inactivity may result in excessive withdrawal from peers, and a feeling of being isolated from society.

Remissions in the disease's progress may cause confusion and depression, as well as anxiety around personal interactions.

Deformities and pain may result in the individual feeling as if they have a social stigma attached to them, and have many problems in self esteem and body image.

Schools may have to make physical changes in structure to accommodate the individual with JRA, and perhaps in classroom changes. Spiel support from teacher's aides may he necessary, as well as more leeway time for assignments and tests, hut this may hold true for many types of physical disabilities.

Muscular Distrophy

Muscular Dystrophy (M.D.) is a progressive weakness of all muscle groups; muscle cells degenerate and are replaced by fat and fibrous tissue. Duchenne type is moat common in boys, though some females are affected. The cause is unknown.

Before M.D. (Duchenne Type) is identified as a problem, symptoms may be evident:

— awkward running, clumsy

— tiptoeing as muscles are weak in foot onset between 2-5 years of age

Early symptoms undiagnosed may lead to labeling as learning disabled, or as educationally handicapped. It is the parents, usually, who notice something wrong. They usually request medical intervention, leading to testing by physicians and psychologists. Effect of Muscular Dystrophy on Body Usually the upper muscles weaken last, with initial weakness being in lower limbs first. As the child ages, they eventually use crutches, wheelchairs and finally a motorized chair. The muscle and nerve deterioration may lead to increased heart and lung problems. The outlook is usually early death through respiratory failure, between ages 20-35. Physiotherapy can be used to maintain flexibility and independence in daily living. Some medications may be necessary. Close physical attention is vital to maintain good health.

Teachers should not lower expectations or see future as hopeless, but keep in mind realistic goals, personally and vocationally. Schools should enhance day to day pursuits in a positive manner. School age individuals may exhibit despair and anxiety. Teachers need to consult with parents about abilities and expectations. Teachers and other adults need to be supportive. Counsellors can center on helping adolescents accept their feelings, and overcome a sense of helplessness and defeat. Since the general outcome of M.D. (Duchenne) is usually continuing degeneration and eventual death, families need support from all individuals involved with the student, and the individual themselves needs to be supported in their daily living to provide themselves with a quality of life as full and productive as possible. Grief counselling allows the individuals and family to come to terms with the eventuality of death.

Spina Bifida

Spina Bifida is a term used to describe a group of congenital defects of the formation of the spinal card. Statistically, spina bifida is presently the most prevalent cause of paraplegia, replacing polio. Early death may result from bacteria in the spinal fluid, but once the defect is surgically closed this is less of a possibility. Spina bifida is, simply, a failure of the lover end of the spinal cord to close over at birth. It varies in severity and inclusion of other disabilities. Excessive spinal fluid may accumulate in the head causing enlargement of the head, increased pressure on the brain (hydrocephalus), which if left untreated may cause mental involvement. This excess fluid can he drained with a shunt, a tube which carries excess fluid from the brain to another part of the body, where it is safely absorbed.

Spina bifida is a congenital abnormality often referred to as myelomeningocele, meningocele or spina bifida. In some cases, the spinal cord actually protrudes from the back bone, in some cases there is no bone formation to protect the spinal cord. The spinal defect occurs in the developing fetus, as early as the 30th day of pregnancy. The reason for this abnormal development is unknown.

There may be paralysis and lack of development in lower limbs, depending on the level of the deformity. There may also be muscle weakness in the lower trunk and legs as well as some lack of growth of legs. The spine may be deformed and there may be some inflexibility of joints, especially hips. Persons with spina bifida may be small and short in stature, but unless excess fluid on the brain is left untreated there is no mental involvement. There will usually be involvement of bowel and bladder, which often is a major difficulty for school-aged children.

Infections of bladder or kidneys are common and often prove to be the biggest cause of death when left untreated. Surgery may provide an alternate means of collecting urine through the abdomen wall. It is important for the individual with spina bifida to master bowel and bladder care so they may achieve independence. As the individual matures, they may master the technique of self catheterization. In a classroom, the student may need to leave every two hours to complete their self care.

Immediate surgery closes the birth defect. Shunts may be installed to drain fluids on the brain. Braces and mobility enhanced devices allow freedom of movement and to encourage interaction with the environment.

A miniature wheelchair, a caster cart, can allow an infant great mobility. A frame to assist in standing allows the individual to strengthen arm, trunk and leg muscles.

Braces, crutches and wheelchairs will be necessary as time goes on.

Some surgery may be necessary to correct hip dislocation, leg or spinal deformities, so intermittent hospitalization can be expected.

Ongoing physiotherapy will be necessary to strengthen limbs and occupational therapy will help the individual tackle tasks of daily living to the fullest extent possible.

During early school years, urinary and bowel control is a major issue for the individual with spina bifida. A teacher may need to gently remind and encourage the student to tend to self care needs, such as self catheterization. Individuals over the age of 12 are more likely to be socially adjusted and take part in normal community activity. As with other mobility disabilities, school is the best environment for individuals to be encouraged to reach their personal potential.

Spinal Cord Injury

Spinal Cord Injury through accident is more likely to happen during late adolescence and young adulthood then in early childhood. When the spinal cord is injured, there is an interruption of the messages sent along the nerves and pathways going to and from various parts of the body to the brain. Spinal cord nerves which have been completely severed will not regain function. Some paralysis and lack of sensation will result below the level of the injury. Functional loss depends on how complete the severing of the spinal cord and the level of the injury.

Before 1950, polio was the most common cause of spinal cord impairment. Conditions such as Cerebral Palsy, spina bifida, muscular dystrophy, occasional polio, arthrogryposis, multiple sclerosis (less likely in childhood) may all cause spinal cord disruption, but most commonly, Spinal Cord Injury (SCI) refers to injury through accident or tumour. The main causes of SCI in the last decade are motor vehicle accidents (usually involving alcohol), gunshot wounds, sports injuries — especially hockey, farm accidents and diving accidents. Fractures of the spine are the most common cause of SCI, though rarely is the spinal cord totally severed bruising, hemorrhage, twisting or swelling causes damage to nerve pathways. Damage is permanent as nerve cells do not regenerate and paralysis can vary in extent from individual to individual.

Injuries are identified by the area of the spine which is involved:

— (Cl-7) Cervical Vertebrae

— (Tl-6) Thoracic Vertebrae

— (Ll-5) Lumbar Vertebrae

— Cl-7 injuries may result in quadriplegia (all four limbs involved) and at the Cl-2 level, the individual who survives may need a respirator to assist breathing.

— Tl-6 injury may result in quadriplegia or paraplegia (legs and trunk only). Injury in this area can be very individualized, with no way to fully predict the outcome and amount of functioning.

— Ll-5 injury may involve legs, bowel and bladder, feet and knees.

Paralysis may include effects to sensations of pain, pressure and response to hot and cold, voluntary movement of arms or legs, breathing and bowel and bladder control. Some quadriplegics may depend on mechanical breathing aides (respirators).

Prompt treatment as soon as possible after injury may prevent some paralysis. Treatment after injury usually involves physiotherapy and occupational therapy to help strengthen muscles and limbs not involved. As important is support and counselling about future hopes and possible choices, and gaining control over all possible aspects of daily living. This rehabilitation needs to involve family as well as the individual.

Depending on the level of injury and the age of the individual, SCI, as does any physical disability, has effect on the following areas:

— self image and self esteem

— future goals and choices

— sexuality

— depression

— feelings of helplessness

Rehabilitation is a long process which takes a lot of physical and emotional strength. Often schooling is put aside while physical abilities are developed. Often, too, emotional maturity is delayed as all energy focuses on rebuilding the body. An adolescent injured at age 15 may, at age 20, be emotionally immature and need to be taught many social skills. There are complications of a physical nature which must be taken into considerations by schools and by the individual. Pressure sores on buttocks, or other bony pressure spots can cause hospitalization or being confined to bed. Pressure sores uncared for can be infected and cause severe complications. Bladder infections due to improper urinary management can cause hospitalization and death.

Schools are responsible for educating all individuals and should be accessible, and provide any aides necessary. Teachers can help an individual set realistic goals, gain social skills, and help individuals reach full potential. The school should support community involvement, and involvement by the individual in all possible school activities.

INDENTIFICATION OF GIFTED CHILDREN

A student is considered gifted when she/he possesses demonstrated or potential abilities that give evidence of exceptionally high capability with respect to intellect, creativity, or the skills associated with specific disciplines. Students who are gifted often demonstrate outstanding abilities in more than one area. They may demonstrate extraordinary intensity of focus in their particular areas of talent or interest. However, they may also have accompanying disabilities and should not be expected to have strengths in all areas of intellectual functioning.

Early identification of students who are gifted is an important element in planning and delivering appropriate educational programs for these students. Some gifted students whose abilities are not identified and addressed early may exhibit secondary emotional and behavioural difficulties. District screening and identification procedures should be in place to ensure consistency of access to programs designed to support gifted students. Every effort should be made to ensure that screening and identification procedures are unbiased with respect to language, culture, gender, physical ability, learning or other disability.

No single criterion should be established for access to or exclusion from services for students who are gifted. Rather, identification and assessment should be carried out using multiple criteria and information from a variety of sources, all of which are valid components for identification. These should include several of the following:

— teacher observations including anecdotal records, checklists, and inventories;

— records of student achievement including assignments, portfolios, grades and outstanding talents, interests and accomplishments;

— nominations by educators, parents, peers and/or self;

— interview of parents and students; and

— formal assessments to Level C of cognitive ability, achievement, aptitude and creativity. A student who is talented in areas other than academics should also have an assessment of intellectual abilities, as it is important information for educational planning.

Districts should provide differentiated services to meet the diverse needs of the exceptionally capable learner. Since students who are gifted form a heterogeneous population, their individual needs, experiences, aptitudes and interests vary. Programs for students who are gifted often require a blend of opportunities available both in the school and in the community. The more extraordinary the abilities of the student, the more necessary it becomes to expand the options beyond the regular classroom. Differentiated curriculum opportunities need to be designed and programming needs to be varied and flexible (classroom-based, school-based, district-based). Since no single program modification model can provide strategies that will apply to content, process, product, pacing, and learning environment, teachers of gifted students will need to draw from one or more models in order to provide an appropriate educational program that meets the individual needs of the student. This should be reflected in the student's IEP.

Regardless of how services are delivered, there are some common elements that characterize an individualized program appropriate for a student who is gifted:

— it is different in pace, scope, and complexity, in keeping with the nature and extent of the exceptionality;

— it provides opportunities for students to interact socially and academically with both age peers and peers of similar abilities;

— it addresses both the cognitive and affective domains;

— it incorporates adaptations and/or extensions to content, process, product, pacing and learning environment; and

— it goes beyond the walls of a school and into the larger community.

Supplemental services for a gifted student should contain some of the following elements, but are not limited to these:

— independent guided education;

— specialist teachers in resource centres or resource rooms;

— district and community classes;

— special groupings which provide opportunities for learning with intellectual peers;

— mentorships;

— consultative services to assist teachers in expanding experiences in the regular classroom;

— accelerating/telescoping/compacting some or all of the student's program;

— opportunities to challenge courses when appropriate; and

— opportunities to take enriched courses and to participate in Advanced Placement, International Baccalaureate, or honours courses.

It is important to recognize the individual characteristics of school districts and their communities in designing services for gifted students. For example, students who are gifted may benefit from the use of information technology, which will increasingly facilitate access to information sources not readily available in all communities.

With sufficient training and experience classroom teachers will be capable of including most students who are gifted, and providing a program in which they can be successful, provided that specialized support is available when needed. Inservice training opportunities and a collaborative team approach are recommended to support and encourage the development of the necessary skills and understandings which the classroom teacher may require. Support teachers with specialized training and experience in gifted education may serve as helping teachers/consultants, and may work in resource centres or with specialized cross-school groupings or special courses. Teachers with responsibility for supporting programs for gifted students should fulfill the qualifications described for learning assistance. In addition, these qualifications should include coursework in:

— the nature of giftedness and the needs of gifted students; and

— strategies for meeting the educational and affective needs of gifted students.

A student is considered to have a physical disability or chronic health impairment based on the need for special educational services due to one or more of the following:

— nervous system impairment;

— musculoskeletal condition; and/or

— chronic health impairment.

Medical diagnosis, by itself, does not determine the special educational services required by students with physical disabilities or chronic health impairments. Students are only eligible for funding in this category if their education is adversely affected by their physical disabilities or chronic health impairments. To be eligible for supplemental funding for a student in this category, the following conditions must be met:

— the student must meet one or more of the above criteria; and

— a current IEP must be in place; and

— direct, ongoing special education service(s) must be provided.

These services should be outlined in the IEP and directly related to the student's identified special need(s). The special education service(s) must be in addition to any services provided under formula funding based on total student enrolment (e.g., learning assistance, counselling). Reduction in class size is not by itself a sufficient service to meet the definition.

Assessments should integrate current, relevant information related to the student's intellectual, social/emotional, sensory, physical and communicative abilities as well as his or her ability to perform activities of daily living at school. Individual Education Plans should take into account specific health care and personal care needs, and outline specific strategies to address those needs. An extended school-based team would typically include medical professionals and consultation with parents in order to develop and implement an effective IEP.

Medical diagnosis, by itself, does not determine the special educational services required by a student with physical disabilities or chronic health impairments. It is the extent and impact of the physical/medical condition, and the consequent need for services which enable the student to access an educational program and participate in a meaningful way, that are the determinants. For some students, increasing dependence is expected due to degenerative conditions or terminal illnesses. It is important that these students be encouraged to maintain normal routines as long as possible. At the same time, it is essential that the educational system affirm the rights of students and families to participate meaningfully in the individualization of the student's educational program.

Health care plans will need regular updating and will need to include emergency procedures to meet individual needs and circumstances. Students with physical disabilities or chronic health impairments should have opportunities to participate in school activities to the greatest extent possible. Adaptations to facilities or equipment to allow access to school areas and programs should be made as quickly as possible where physical barriers exist. In all situations where there is contact with body fluids, personnel are advised to follow the "Universal Precautions", and to contact the medical health officer as laid out in the School Act where there is a concern about safety of others.

In most cases, students with physical disabilities or chronic health impairments will take part in the regular program with the necessary adaptations. Evaluation will be based on the regular standards (i.e., extent to which learning outcomes were achieved). The method of evaluation will be consistent with the IEP and with ministry reporting policies in respect to the use of comments and/or letter grades. Some students may require extensive modifications to parts of their program so that some of their learning outcomes will be substantially different from the regular curriculum. In these cases, evaluation will be based on the degree to which the individualized outcomes are achieved. Evaluation would be referenced to individually set standards.

Reports to parents should be provided on the same schedule used for all students. Progress should be reported with respect to all components of the program, and with reference to progress in relation to IEP goals. Reports should indicate the adaptations and modifications made to the student's educational program. All personnel directly involved in the ongoing educational program (e.g., classroom teacher, specialist teacher, speech- language pathologist) should report on student progress.

With sufficient training and experience, classroom teachers will be capable of including most students with physical disabilities and chronic health impairments and providing a program in which they can be successful, provided that specialist support is available when needed. Inservice training opportunities and a collaborative team approach are recommended to support and encourage the development of the skills required.

Teachers with responsibilities for supporting students with physical disabilities or chronic health impairments should fulfill the qualifications described for learning assistance. In addition, they should have advanced coursework in:

— the characteristics and needs of students with physical disabilities and chronic health impairments; and

— specialized instructional methodologies and technologies; and adaptation or modification of programs for students with physical disabilities or chronic health impairments.

There also may be a need for a qualified health professional to monitor the quality of the health services. Recent and ongoing technological advances in adaptive devices related to computer access, environmental controls, and augmented communication have greatly enhanced learning opportunities for students with physical disabilities. Staff will need to stay informed of current developments and introduce new technology as appropriate.

Teacher assistants who work in classrooms with students with physical disabilities or chronic health impairments should have sufficient skills and training for the duties they are assigned, including:

— an understanding of the social, emotional, and educational implications of dependent needs;

— functional life skills and career development; and

— technological support.

It should be noted that teacher assistants work under the general supervision of a teacher or administrative officer. Inservice training should include opportunities to further develop expertise in these and related areas.

2

HELPING CHILDREN WITH SPECIAL NEEDS

MAINSTREAMING CHILDREN WITH DISABILITIES

The term 'mainstreaming' is commonly defined as a belief which involves an educational placement procedure and process for exceptional children, based on the conviction that each child should be educated in the least restrictive environment in which his/her educational and related needs can be satisfactorily provided. According to Turnhull and Schulz: "Mainstreaming in the educational arrangement of placing handicapped students in regular classes with their non-handicapped peers to the maximum extant appropriate". It has become accepted practice to integrate both mentally and physically disabled students into the regular school setting.

Mainstreaming is not to be viewed as simply "dumping" students with handicapping conditions into a regular school, but requires the student he educated in "the least restrictive environment". This usually means the elimination of special or segregated classes to the greatest extent possible.

Teacher Attitudes

There are some necessary components to successful mainstreaming of both physically and mentally handicapped students:

— qualified teachers
— competent advisory/support serves
— appropriate facilities and transportation
— parental involvement
— advocacy and commitment on the part of the school principal

Teachers often have expressed concern over the integration of a handicapped child into the regular classroom, not because they disagree with the concept of mainstreaming, but because they often feel they are ill-prepared to teach handicapped children. They have concerns, as well, about the child's ability to function in the regular classroom, and may believe that a handicapped child will be a disruption in the classroom.

Unfortunately, when mainstreaming is thrust upon the classroom teacher without adequate preparation, there may he resentment. The way the teacher responds to the child's need is more important to the success of the program than are any administrative or curriculum considerations; the progress of the student depends largely on teacher expectations. Teachers have expressed ambivalent attitudes towards mainstreaming, though they may agree with the philosophy.

There is throughout the literature an expressed need for increased support through resource material designed for the classroom teacher's use and good quality inservicing. A recent study have found that considerable dissatisfaction on the part of the classroom teacher with both the quality and quantity of support services routinely provided. Teacher anxiety is raised when they feel they have little resource and innovative teaching methods are replaced with less effective conservative methods.

Teachers generally feel inadequately trained to deal with exceptionalities, and as a group feel that large infusions of resources are required within regular school if exceptional students are to be mainstreamed successfully. Our attitudes towards persons with disabilities are deeply rooted and widespread. There are many ways which these negative attitudes can be perpetuated in the classroom by a teacher who feels pressured, uncertain of their skills with the disabled or feels uninformed about the disability.

Lomhana suggests that certain attitudes on behalf of the teacher will affect the physically disabled student's peers as well. A negative teacher attitude is the single factor that would cause the most difficulty in mainstreaming successfully. Avoidance of the disabled student leads to isolation, anxiety on behalf of the teacher leads to embarrassment for the student, pity leads to self pity in the student with a disability and overprotectiveness leads to dependence.

Parental Involvement

Parents play a major role in the successful mainstreaming of students with disabilities, and the classroom teacher must be prepared to deal with the family of the integrated student. Parents need to be involved from the beginning of the process, and one of their major contributions can be providing background information for the student's needs and describing the major components of his or her handicapping condition.

School Counsellor's Role

One of the major support services in the school for both teacher and parents is viewed as the school counsellor. One major role for the school counsellor should he to learn the counselling needs of students with disabilities and their parents. Both the classroom teacher and the school counsellor need access to appropriate resource and support material to confidently perform their roles in successfully mainstreaming of students with physical disabilities.

Counsellor responsibilities are to focus on social integration, peer influence, sex role identity and general psychological health of the student with a disability. Another important role of the school counsellor is to provide inservicing for the school personnel regarding the various handicapping conditions, the availability of resources for student, teachers and parents, and an explanation of the appropriate psychosocial needs of disabled students.

HELPING DISABLED CHILDREN IN TRANSITION FROM PRESCHOOL TO THE GENERAL SCHOOL SETTING

The transition from preschool to school can be difficult for a child with disabilities. The preschool environment characterized by small groups and individual attention is replaced by classrooms with more children, fewer adults per child, and greater demand for adapting to general classroom procedures and working independently. Parents and teachers from both receiving and sending programs need to be involved in placement as well as scheduling and facilitating the move.

Family members play a key role in providing information about the child's abilities, strengths and weaknesses, and interests. Parental insights complement information obtained from preschool sources and provide a broader picture of the child's capabilities and needs. Identifying specific ways for parents to be involved in the process is essential to a good transition. Parents may act as teachers, partners, decisionmakers, and/or advocates. They are teachers when they reinforce the skills acquired in preschool, partners when they communicate needs with school personnel, and decisionmakers when they participate in the IEP process.

Parents can help prepare the child for the transition to public school by maintaining and generalizing skills necessary for the transition. They also serve as a bridge between the two programs, visiting the new program with their child, helping the child to become familiar with the new setting, and discussing concerns and fears connected with the upcoming change. They can also help bridge the gap by arranging visits with former preschool friends and teachers as well as with new classmates. Parents can help their child develop skills in following directions, playing independently, attending to task, and self-care. These skills will help prepare the child for the new setting.

Sending and receiving teachers both play important roles in the transition process. Teacher attitudes, instructional priorities, and communication with parents and other members of the transition team will determine the quality of the child's transition. Sending and receiving teachers may have different goals and priorities, but they play complementary roles in preparing the child for the move from preschool to the general school setting. The sending teacher should find out what skills the child will need in order to function adequately in the new setting and implement a program for preparing the child to develop those skills. Familiarity with the receiving program is essential in order to design an appropriate transition curriculum.

The sending teacher can gain a better understanding of prerequisite skills by visiting the receiving classroom. For children placed in an integrated setting, behavioral requirements for successful functioning have been assessed and are referred to as survival skills. These include being able to function independently during group instruction, following classroom routines, completing tasks within an allotted time period, and working in the absence of teacher direction. Teaching survival skills as part of the preschool curriculum helps prepare the child for the demands of the general school setting. Skill-building activities should be developmentally appropriate for each child.

The success of the transition preparation is ultimately determined by the child's adaptation to the new environment. The receiving teacher's attitude toward and experience with children with disabilities may be factors in the success of the child's placement. Some flexibility will probably be required on the teacher's part in order to adjust expectations and adapt to the child's special needs. The sending and receiving teachers will have the continuing role of acting as liaisons between programs and with parents. Good communication and clearly defined goals will facilitate the preparation for the child's move from preschool to the general school setting.

The Capstone Transition Process is one model that provides clear guidelines for the transition process. The first activity initiates long-range planning by establishing a "transition timeline." This timeline serves as a guide for accomplishing transition activities and can be set up in chart form to track activities. The Capstone Transition Process addresses specific activities beginning 12 months before the move to a new program. The process includes preparation, implementation, and evaluation activities. The initial steps of the process are designed to prepare the participants for their role in the transition. Steps include notifying and preparing parents and teachers from both the sending and receiving programs. Data on the child's needs are collected or updated.

A profile of communication procedures, available services, prerequisite skills, and teacher expectations is developed from existing information. The preparation phase of the process culminates with the development by the transition team of an IEP for use as the basis of educational programming in the new setting. Following the IEP meeting, the timeline provides reminders for the transfer of information and records to the receiving program. The final step calls for evaluation of the effectiveness of the process.

Develop the transition timeline.

— Notify appropriate administrators of the student's approaching transition.

— Inform parent(s)/primary caregiver(s) that the child will be making the transition and collect information on family transition needs.

— Determine the communication policy of the potential receiving program(s) and obtain a description of the program(s).

— Obtain information from teacher(s) in potential receiving program(s) regarding the program/classroom overview and skills perceived as important for transition into the classroom.

— Verify the receipt of transition information and/or followup request for the transition information or additional information.

— Reevaluate: verify the student's assessment and eligibility.

— Prepare the parents for the transition planning meeting.

— Hold the transition planning meeting.

— Hold the IEP meeting. Obtain permission from the parents to release information.

— Provide information to all transition team participants.

— Link the parent/primary caregiver of the transitioning child with a parent/primary caregiver of a child already attending the new program.

— Send the receiving program all pertinent records and verify the receipt of the records.

— Provide the receiving program with information about the child's current program.

— Evaluate the effectiveness of the process after completion.

HELPING GIFTED CHILDEREN IN CAREER DEVELOPMENT

Although parents and teachers may be concerned about academic planning for gifted and talented young people, they often assume that career planning will take care of itself. Students may have many choices available because of multiple gifts or a particular talent, and a career choice in that area seems inevitable. There is no need for career planning: The student is simply expected to make an occupational decision around the sophomore year of college and then follow through on the steps necessary to attain that goal. Unfortunately, evidence is mounting that youthful brilliance in one or more areas does not always translate into adult satisfaction and accomplishment in working life.

Studies with such diverse groups as Merit Scholars, Presidential Scholars, and graduates of gifted education programs have shown that the path from education to career is not always smooth, and it may be complicated by social-emotional problems and needs of gifted students that differ from those of more typical students. Recognition of these problems has produced counseling models that address student needs. Some factors that can contribute to problems with career planning are presented here, along with ways of preventing and intervening with career development problems.

Multipotentiality

Multipotentiality is the ability to select and develop any number of career options because of a wide variety of interests, aptitudes, and abilities. The broad range of opportunities available tends to increase the complexity of decision making and goal setting, and it may actually delay career selection. Multipotentiality is most commonly a concern of students with moderately high IQs (120-140), those who are academically talented, and those who have two or more outstanding but very different abilities such as violin virtuosity and mathematics precocity. Signs that multipotentiality is a concern include the following:

— *Elementary school:* Despite excellent performance in many or all school subjects, students may have difficulty making decisions, particularly when they are asked to make a choice on topics or projects from among many options. Multiple hobbies with only brief periods of enthusiasm and difficulty in finishing up and following through on tasks (even those which are enjoyable) are additional signs for concern.

— *Junior high:* Despite continued excellence in many or all school subjects, difficulty with decision making and follow through continue. Students may participate in multiple social and recreational activities with no clear preferences, and they may overschedule, leaving few free periods and little time to just think.

— *Senior high:* Decision-making problems generalize to academic and career decisions, resulting in overly packed class schedules and highly diverse participation in school activities. Students often accept leadership of a wide variety of groups in school, religious activities, and community organizations. Adults may notice occasional signs of stress and exhaustion (absences, frequent or chronic illness, periods of depression or anxiety, etc.), or they may see evidence of delay or vacillation about college planning and decision making. Students are able to maintain high grades in most or all courses taken. An important clue to continuing multipotentiality is the student's vocational interest test profiles. These tests often show interests and similarities to an unusually large number of occupations.

— *College:* Multipotential students often have multiple academic majors. Three or more changes of college major are not unusual for an individual who cannot set long-term goals. They continue intense participation in extracurricular activities and have outstanding academic performance but are concerned about selecting a career. They may make hasty, arbitrary, or "going-along-with-the-crowd" career choices. They may encounter the dilemma of opportunities lost in giving up some interests in favour of others.

— *Adulthood:* Some of the implications of multipotentiality can be seen in bright adults who, despite excellent performance in most jobs, hold multiple positions in short time periods and experience a general feeling of lack of fit in most jobs. Some experience feelings of alienation, purposelessness, depression, and apathy despite high performance and excellent evaluations. Some experience periods of unemployment and underemployment, or they fall behind same-age peers in career progress and sometimes social development (marriage, family, community involvement).

Possible intervention strategies for multipotentiality at different educational levels include the following:

- Elementary School
  - Provide realistic exposure to the world of work through parent sharing and exposure to parents' working places.
  - Encourage career fantasies through dress-up and plays.
  - Encourage focusing activities such as class projects or achievement of Scout merit badges, which require goal setting and follow-through.
  - Use biographies of eminent people as primary career education material.
  - As teachers or parents, carefully evaluate skills, talents, and interests in order to help children understand possible areas of greatest interest.
- Junior High
  - Discuss the meaning and value of work.
  - Discuss family and community values pertaining to work.
  - Provide for light volunteer work in several areas of interest.
  - Provide "shadowing" experiences in which students spend the day with an adult working in an area of greatest interest.
  - Discourage overinvolvement in social and recreational activities for the sake of involvement, prioritize and decide on a few extracurricular involvements.
- Senior High
  - Seek appropriate vocational testing from a guidance professional or psychologist.

- Encourage visits to college and university classes in a few areas of interest.
- Provide for more extensive volunteer work.
- Explore possibilities of paid internships with professionals.
- Insist on a solid curriculum of coursework in order to insure against inadequate preparation for a later career choice.
- Provide value-based guidance, which emphasizes choosing a career that fulfills deeply held values.
- Discourage conformist, stereotyped career choices.
- Expose students to atypical career models.

- College Students and Young Adults
    - Seek career counseling including assessment of interests, needs, and values.
    - Enroll in a career planning class.
    - Encourage careful course selection.
    - Avoid conformist and stereotyped major choices.
    - Seek a mentor.
    - Engage in long-term goal setting and planning.

Early Emergence

Early emergers are children who have extremely focused career interests. A passion for an idea and an early commitment to a career area are common childhood characteristics of eminent individuals in a wide variety of professions; thus, early emergence should not be thought of as a problem of career development, but rather as an opportunity that may be acted upon, neglected, or, unfortunately, sometimes destroyed. Acting upon early emergence means noticing an unusually strong talent or enthusiasm, providing training in skills necessary to exercise that talent, providing resources, and keeping an open mind about the future of the talent or interest. Neglecting early emergence means overlooking the talent or interest or failing to provide education and resources.

Destroying the early emerger's passion may not be easy, but belittling the talent or interest ("Who cares about someone who doodles and draws all the time instead of listening?" "What makes you think you can become an anthropologist?") may easily extinguish the flame. Insisting on well-roundedness or disallowing needed training (e.g., refusing to allow a mathematically precocious child to accelerate in math) may diminish the passion. Overly enthusiastic encouragement and pressure may also remove the intrinsic pleasure the child feels in the interest or talent area.

As with multipotentiality, there are signs of early emergence:

— *Elementary school*: Avid interest in one school subject or activity with only general liking for other subjects and activities and extraordinary talent in one area and average or above average performance in others are underlying signs of early emergence. (These students may be mistakenly labeled as underachievers). Students may also try to write more papers than required, choose too many subjects in the area of interest, and mention early career fantasies about success and fame in a particular area of interest.

— *Junior high*: Students continue highly focused interests and may express a strong desire for advanced training in an area of talent and interest. Development of adolescent social interests may be delayed because of a commitment to work in a talent area or because of rejection by others, yet performance in the talent area grows, while performance in other areas diminishes.

— *Senior high*: Students may develop a strong identity in the talent area (the "computer whiz," "artist," or "fix it person," for example). They may express a desire for help with planning a career in an area of interest. A desire to test skill in competition with or in concert with peers in the chosen talent area and continued high performance in the talent area to a degree that causes neglect of other school subjects or social activities are additional signs of a focused interest and passion.

— *College students and young adults*: These young people make an early, but not hasty or arbitrary, choice of career or major. They often show a desire for completion of a training period in order to "get on with work," seek out mentors, continue intense focus, and often neglect social and extracurricular activities.

— *Adulthood*: Adults may continue their intense focus, desire eminence or excellence in the talent area, and possibly forego or delay other aspects of adult development such as marriage, nurturing of a younger generation, social and community involvement, and personal development.

Possible intervention strategies for early emergers at different educational levels include the following:

— Elementary School

  — Provide for early identification of unusual talent or area of precocity.

  — Consult with experts on the nature and nurture of particular gifts or talents.

  — Consult with the school on ways of nurturing the talent or gift.

  — Encourage fantasies through reading of bibliographies and playing of work roles.

  — Provide opportunities to learn about eminent people in the talent area (attend a concert; visit an inventor's workshop; attend a math professor's class).

    — Relate necessary basic skills to the area of interest.

    — Provide opportunities to socialize with children with similar, intense interests through such activities as music camps, computer camps, and Junior Great Books.

    — Strike a careful balance between encouragement and laissez-faire; provide support for the strong interest along with freedom to change direction. Do not become so invested in the child's talent or interest that you fail to notice that the child has changed interests. (Early emergers most often change to a closely related interest; that is, they switch musical instruments or transfer an interest in mathematics to an interest in theoretical physics).

— Junior High

    — Provide support and encouragement during the intensive training that often begins at this point.

    — Allow for plenty of time alone.

    — Seek opportunities for job "shadowing" (following a professional throughout the working day) in area of interest.

    — Seek opportunities for light volunteer work in area of interest.

    — Avoid pressuring the student into social activities.

— Senior High

    — Continue support, encouragement, and time alone.

    — Seek opportunities for internships and work experiences in the areas of interest (internship on archaeological dig; job as camp counsellor at a fine arts camp; coaching younger people in musical or athletic skill).

    — Seek career guidance from a guidance counsellor who is familiar with the talent area or from a professional in that field.

- — Make a detailed plan of training and education leading toward the chosen career goal, including financial arrangements.
- — Explore higher education or postsecondary training early and thoroughly, with contacts and visits.
- — Help the student establish a relationship with a mentor in the area of interest. Early emergers often fare better in a less prestigious institution where they have access to an enthusiastic mentor than in an Ivy League or high status institution where they do not.

— College Students and Young Adults

- — Help provide support for extended education and training.
- — Encourage the development of knowledge of career ladders in the area of interest.
- — Encourage a continuing relationship with a career counseling or guidance professional for support in decision making and problem solving.

The career development problems discussed here are nearly opposite one another: The multipotential student seems unfocused, delaying, and indecisive, whereas the early emerger is focused, driven, and almost too decisive. Both types carry with them dangers and opportunities. Skillful career education and guidance can help ensure that neither multipotentiality nor early emergence leads to difficulty in career planning and development.

Minority Gifted Students

Minority gifted students have special career planning needs as well as needs related to multipotentiality or early emergence. Minority students from Black, Hispanic, and American Indian backgrounds are less likely to have been selected for gifted education programs and less likely to perform well on standardized achievement tests than their nonminority peers. In addition, they may have lower career aspirations because of lower societal expectations. Nevertheless, the patterns of leadership and out-of-class accomplishments of gifted minority students are very similar to those of nonminority gifted students. Minority gifted students are active leaders in other communities. Therefore, career counseling for these students may be most effective when it focuses on raising career aspirations and emphasizes out- of-class accomplishments as indicators of possible career directions. Career planning must also go hand in hand with building a strong ethnic identity if later conflict between ethnic identity and achievement in majority society is to be avoided. Colangelo and LaFrenz have provided suggestions for how this can be accomplished.

Gifted Girls and Women

Persisting sex role stereotypes and the continued socialization of girls for secondary roles means that, despite great gains in certain fields such as medicine and law, gifted girls are less likely than gifted boys to achieve their full potential. Although gifted girls outperform gifted boys in terms of grades, gifted boys achieve higher scores on college admissions examinations. Compared to gifted boys, gifted girls are underprepared academically, having taken fewer mathematics and science courses and less challenging courses in social studies. As a result, they have fewer options for college majors and career goals. Bright women apparently let go of career aspirations gradually, first through underpreparation and later through decisions that may put the needs of husbands and families before their own. Gifted women fall behind gifted men in salary, status, and promotions throughout their working lives.

In order to ensure that gifted girls have the greatest possible chance to fulfill their potential, career planning should emphasize rigorous academic preparation, particularly in mathematics and science; maintaining high career aspirations;

and identifying both internal and external barriers to the achievement of career goals.

HELPING ADOLESCENTS ADJUST TO GIFTEDNESS

Young gifted people between the ages of 11 and 15 frequently report a range of problems as a result of their abundant gifts: perfectionism, competitiveness, unrealistic appraisal of their gifts, rejection from peers, confusion due to mixed messages about their talents, and parental and social pressures to achieve, as well as problems with unchallenging school programs or increased expectations. Some encounter difficulties in finding and choosing friends, a course of study, and, eventually, a career. The developmental issues that all adolescents encounter exist also for gifted students, yet they are further complicated by the special needs and characteristics of being gifted. Once counsellors and parents are aware of these obstacles, they seem better able to understand and support gifted adolescents. Caring adults can assist these young people to "own" and develop their talents by understanding and responding to adjustment challenges and coping strategies.

Several dynamics of giftedness continually interfere with adjustment gains during adolescence. Buescher has found that, during the early years of adolescence, gifted young people encounter several potent obstacles, singly or in combination.

Ownership: Talented adolescents simultaneously "own" and yet question the validity and reality of the abilities they possess. Some researchers have identified patterns of disbelief, doubt, and lack of self-esteem among older students and adults: the so-called "impostor syndrome" described by many talented individuals. While talents have been recognized in many cases at an early age, doubts about the accuracy of identification and the objectivity of parents or favorite teachers linger. The power of peer pressure toward conformity, coupled with any adolescent's wavering sense of being predictable or intact, can lead to the denial of even the most outstanding ability. The conflict that ensues, whether mild or acute, needs to be resolved by gaining a more mature "ownership" and responsibility for the identified talent.

A second basic pressure often experienced by gifted students is that, since they have been given gifts in abundance, they feel they must give of themselves in abundance. Often it is subtly implied that their abilities belong to parents, teachers, and society.

Dissonance: By their own admission, talented adolescents often feel like perfectionists. They have learned to set their standards high, to expect to do more and be more than their abilities might allow. Childhood desires to do demanding tasks PERFECTLY become compounded during adolescence. It is not uncommon for talented adolescents to experience real dissonance between what is actually done and how well they expected it to be accomplished. Often the dissonance perceived by young people is far greater than most parents or teachers realize.

Taking Risks: While risk taking has been used to characterize younger gifted and talented children, it ironically decreases with age, so that the bright adolescent is much less likely to take chances than others. Why the shift in risk-taking behaviours? Gifted adolescents appear to be more aware of the repercussions of certain activities, whether these are positive or negative. They have learned to measure the decided advantages and disadvantages of numerous opportunities and to weigh alternatives. Yet their feigned agility at this too often leads them to reject even those acceptable activities that carry some risk (e.g., advanced placement courses, stiff competitions, public presentations), for which high success is less predictable and lower standards of performance less acceptable in their eyes. One other possible cause for less risk taking could be the need to maintain control—to remain in spheres of influence where challenging relationships, demanding coursework and teachers, or intense competition cannot enter without absolute personal control.

Competing Expectations: Adolescents are vulnerable to criticism, suggestions, and emotional appeals from others. Parents, friends, siblings, and teachers are all eager to add their own expectations and observations to even the brightest students' intentions and goals. Often, others' expectations for talented young people compete with their own dreams and plans. Delisle, in particular, has pointed out that the "pull" of an adolescent's own expectations must swim against the strong current posed by the "push" of others' desires and demands. The dilemma is complicated by the numerous options within the reach of a highly talented student: The greater the talent, the greater the expectations and outside interference.

Gifted adolescents consistently report dramatic episodes of being pushed to the point of doubt and despair by insensitive teachers, peers, and even parents. Teachers in secondary schools, in particular, have tried to disprove the talents of individual students, saying, in effect, "Prove to me you are as gifted as you think you are." Coping with the vagaries of adolescence while also proving oneself again and again in the classroom or peer group significantly drains energy allocated for the normal tasks of adjustment and leads to frequent frustration and isolation.

Impatience: Like most other adolescents, gifted students can be impatient in many ways: eager to find solutions for difficult questions, anxious to develop satisfying friendships, and prone to selecting difficult but immediate alternatives for complex decisions. The predisposition for impulsive decision making, coupled with exceptional talent, can make young adolescents particularly intolerant of ambiguous, unresolved situations. Their impatience with a lack of clear-cut answers, options, or decisions drives them to seek answers where none readily exist, relying on an informing, though immature, sense of wisdom. The anger and disappointment when hasty resolutions fail can be difficult to surmount, particularly when less capable peers gloat about these failures.

Premature Identity: It appears that the weight of competing expectations, low tolerance for ambiguity, and the pressure of multiple potentials each feed very early attempts to achieve an adultlike identity, a stage normally achieved after the age of 21. This can create a serious problem for talented adolescents. They seem to reach out prematurely for career choices that will short-cut the normal process of identity crisis and resolution.

Coping Strategies

How can talented adolescents cope with the myriad obstacles to developing their talents? A study of young adolescents who participated in a talent search program Buescher & Higham suggested various strategies. Table 1 depicts the strategies suggested by the adolescents, arranged according to their assessment of acceptablity for use.

Table 1. Coping Strategies Suggested by Adolescents (In Order by Weighted Ranking; 0 = Least Acceptable to Students; 10 = Most Acceptable):

(0) Pretend not to know as much as you do.

(1) Act like a "brain" so peers leave you alone.

(2) Adjust language and behaviour to disguise true abilities from your peers.

(3) Avoid programs designed for gifted/talented students.

(4) Be more active in community groups where age is no object.

(5) Develop/excel in talent areas outside school setting.

(6) Achieve in areas at school outside academics.

(7) Build more relationships with adults.

(8) Select programs and classes designed for gifted/talented students.

(9) Make friends with other students with exceptional talents.

(10) Accept and use abilities to help peers do better in classes.

The strategies were influenced by such factors as age, sex, and participation in programs for gifted students. For example, over the course of 4 years (ages 11 to 15), "using one's talent to help others" moved from second place to first, by way of third. "Achieving in school in areas outside academics" appeared to rise in popularity until the age of 14 but then dropped to third place. Students participating in special programs for the gifted were less likely, as they grew older, to mask their true abilities. Other studies have indicated that gifted females appear to be somewhat vulnerable to the pull of cultural expectations that drive them toward seeking peer acceptance rather than leadership and the full development of their abilities.

DEVELOPING LEARNER OUTCOMES FOR GIFTED STUDENTS

Learner outcomes specify student behaviors we want at a particular developmental point. These outcomes provide the basis for creating worthwhile learning experiences, for setting appropriate expectations, and for assessing the extent of learning attained. We may want gifted third-grade students to prepare a science project using a scientific process, selecting a topic of interest, reading a lot about the topic, designing an experiment to test a question of interest, completing the experiment, and communicating the results through a poster and oral presentation. We may want gifted ninth-grade students to conduct a community survey, using basic statistics, on a topic of interest. These are examples of gifted learner outcomes. They each are:

— appropriately challenging for gifted students at the requisite stage of development,

— linked to a specific area of study within the regular school curriculum,

— substantive and worthy of substantial instructional time and student independent time, and

— assessable through authentic approaches.

Need for Learner Outcomes for Gifted Students

First, every learner needs goals for learning and indicators of progress in learning. Without a clear understanding of what is to be learned and how that learning is taking place, the learner loses interest, motivation, and comes to see learning as a process devised by others that is trivial, irrelevant, and a waste of time. Thus, the first reason for stating learner outcomes is to respond to learner needs for making sense of the tasks presented.

Second, gifted learner outcomes provide a clear differentiation of what the students can learn within a given period of time. Since the characteristics of gifted learners imply a capacity to learn basic material much faster than other learners and handle more complex and sophisticated material at an earlier stage of development, appropriate learner outcomes must reflect these distinctions. Current state-developed learner outcomes for all students may be well-informed with respect to the state of the art in the specific disciplines of language arts, mathematics, science, and social studies. However, the characteristics of exceptional learners demand higher expectation levels for performance at every level of schooling. Thus differentiated learner outcomes are necessary in order for gifted students to be appropriately challenged.

Finally, teachers of the gifted need guidance in planning daily curriculum experiences. Random activities that offer short term appeal are poor fare for the capacities of gifted students. Activities must be tied to substantive outcomes; they must have a purpose larger than themselves. To facilitate worthwhile learning, teachers must be able to see and understand the relationship between a classroom activity and its related outcome.

How Learner Outcomes for Gifted Students Differ from Generic Outcomes? Typically, major differences lie in the scope of the outcome, the stage of development at which it is expected, and the implicit proficiencies necessary to achieve it at an exemplary level. Below is a set of ninth-grade English curriculum outcomes for all learners juxtaposed with outcomes that were developed specifically for gifted students at that same grade level.

Generic

— Comprehends a variety of materials.

— Is familiar with the structural elements of literature.

— Develops an understanding of the chronology of American literature.

Gifted

— Evaluates diverse materials according to a set of criteria or standards.

— Creates a literary work in a self-selected form, using appropriate structural elements.

— Analyzes and interprets key social, cultural, and economic ideas as expressed in the literature, art, and music of America at 40-year intervals.

The examples in the gifted set are consistently more challenging, broader in scope, and more focused on specific higher level thinking tasks. They imply that students have mastered the basic underlying skills necessary to undertake required tasks (e.g., that students can basically comprehend what they read), and demand the development of multiple perspectives within and across areas of knowledge. These aspects of differentiation are central in comparing generic and gifted outcome statements.

Assessment

Just as gifted learners need differentiated outcomes, so too, must the assessment approach be consistent with the stated outcome. This is different from the way the more generic outcome for all learners would be measured. The assessment approach should be developed at the same time as the outcome in order to maintain unity of purpose and to ensure that the proposed outcome can in fact be satisfactorily assessed. Incorporating assessment into the teaching-learning process is essential to creating an authentic process. Assessment of outcomes will involve rating student products, whether they are written essays, projects, or original creative work.

How Teachers Can Work with Learner Outcomes

It is important that teachers see learner outcomes as central to their work in the classroom; that they capture the heart of what students need to learn. For this insight to occur, teachers must have the opportunity to engage in the curriculum alignment process. One approach is for teachers to develop activities that underlie each desired learner outcome. These activities can be developed by teams and discussed with other educators at appropriate times. Another approach to alignment is to develop suboutcomes that will lead to satisfactory performance at the end of the academic year. Again, teacher teams are the best way to accomplish this task, which involves a careful analysis of the learner outcome. A third approach to curriculum alignment is to link outcomes to existing classroom materials. Teachers can review basal texts for lessons that support the desired outcome and then explore supplemental resources that contribute directly to student learning.

Alignment with Stated Learner Outcomes

Stated learner outcomes should be the point of departure for creating differentiated gifted learner outcomes. The example used earlier is one model for representing the relationship between the two sets of learner outcomes. Some generic learner outcomes would not need to be altered or adapted for gifted students. Individual districts would decide which outcomes already meet the criteria of acceptability for the gifted and create new ones only where they are needed. This process of curriculum alignment can be effected for an individual learner as well, thus meeting the needs of special populations of gifted learners who require even more tailoring in their curriculum.

Suggestions for Creating Appropriate Learner Outcomes for Gifted Students

— Create a curriculum articulation task force representative of subject areas, grade levels, and a broad cross section of school personnel interested in curriculum.

— Organize subtask forces to examine state/local learner outcomes by subject area and across K-12 levels. (Vertical planning is essential to the success of this task.)

— Review existing state or local learner outcomes, using the stated criteria for judging whether they are challenging for gifted learners at the requisite stage of development.

— Discuss findings with the overall task force. Have each subtask force justify the decisions made regarding adaptations in the generic learner outcomes for gifted students.

— Review gifted program goals/curriculum goals; align with subject area outcomes.

— Create additional learner outcomes for gifted students as needed, using the notes and suggestions of the subgroups.

— Develop analogous assessment protocols for the differentiated outcomes.

— Align the differentiated learner outcomes for gifted students with existing classroom activities and materials; develop new activities and locate supplementary materials as needed.

— Hold a staff development session for all teachers on gifted learner outcomes and the linkages already present in the curriculum that address them. Demonstrate activities and materials that specifically teach to the attainment of gifted learner outcomes.

— Develop an on-going staff development program that assists teachers in facilitating the attainment of the specified learner outcomes.

— Tailor all teacher evaluation instruments to include an emphasis on using activities and materials shared in staff development sessions that contribute to the attainment of specified learner outcomes.

— Use annual assessment data to determine needed changes in key aspects of the teaching learning cycle (e.g., better assessment tools, more activities, more targeted materials, insufficient training?)

— Engage in continued curriculum development tasks such as alignment of activities and materials, creation of curriculum units that fill gaps, and the development of alternative assessment tools and strategies.

HELPING GIFTED CHILD: ROLE OF PARENTS

Most parents greet the discovery that their child is not merely gifted but highly or profoundly gifted with a combination of pride, excitement, and fear. They may set out to find experts or books to help them cope with raising such a child, only to find there are no real experts, only a couple of books, and very little understanding of extreme intellectual potential and how to develop it.

Differences

To understand highly gifted children it is essential to realize that, although they are children with the same basic needs as other children, they are very different. Adults cannot ignore or gloss over their differences without doing serious damage to these children, for the differences will not go away or be outgrown. They affect almost every aspect of these children's intellectual and emotional lives. A microscope analogy is one useful way of understanding extreme intelligence. If we say that all people look at the world through a lens, with some lenses cloudy or distorted, some clear, and some magnified, we might say that gifted individuals view the world through a microscope lens and the highly gifted view it through an electron microscope. They see ordinary things in very different ways and often see what others simply cannot see. Although there are advantages to this heightened perception, there are disadvantages as well.

Since many children eventually become aware of being different, it is important to prepare yourself for your child's reactions. When your child's giftedness has been identified, you might open a discussion using the microscope analogy. If you are concerned that such a discussion will promote arrogance, be sure to let children know that unusual gifts, like hair and eye colour, are not earned. It is neither admirable nor contemptible to be highly gifted. It is what one does with one's abilities that is important.

A United Front

In most other aspects of parenting, it is important for both parents (or the adults who bear primary responsibility for raising the child) to agree on some basic issues regarding the child's potential. Many parents of exceptionally gifted children were themselves gifted or exceptionally gifted children. If they did not learn to accept and understand their own giftedness, they may find it difficult to accept their child's unusual capacities. Raising a highly gifted child may help parents come to terms with many difficult aspects of their own lives, but it helps if they focus first on the needs of the child and come to an agreement about how to meet them.

What the Highly Gifted Need

Exceptionally gifted children have two primary needs. First, they need to feel comfortable with themselves and with the differences that simultaneously open possibilities and create difficulty. Second, they need to develop their astonishing potential. There is a strong internal drive to develop one's abilities. Thwarting that drive may lead to crippling emotional damage. Throughout the parenting years, it is wise to keep in mind that the healthiest long term goal is not necessarily a child who gains fame, fortune, and a Nobel Prize, but one who becomes a comfortable adult and uses gifts productively.

The Early Years

Before your child begins formal schooling, differences can be handled by your willingness to follow the child's lead and meet needs as they arise. It is possible and important to treat an infant's or toddler's precocity with a degree of normalcy. For example, a 2-year-old who prefers and plays appropriately with toys designed for 6-year-olds should be given those toys. The 3-year-old who reads should be given books. The child who speaks very early and with a sophisticated vocabulary should be spoken to in kind.

Public Attitudes

Even when parents can take precocious achievements in stride, friends, family and strangers may not. Unthinking people will comment (often loudly and in front of the child) that a 2- or 3-year-old who sits in the grocery cart reading packages aloud is a phenomenon. It may be surprisingly difficult to avoid letting parental pride lure you into encouraging your children to "perform" in public. Keep in mind the goal of making the child as comfortable as possible with individual differences. The more casually you accept unusual early accomplishments, the more your children will be able to see those accomplishments as normal. Later, when the gifts are no longer quite as noticeable, the child will not feel that what made him or her valuable has somewhat been lost.

Multiple Ages

Highly gifted children are many ages simultaneously. A 5- year-old may read like a 7-year-old, play chess like a 12- year-old, talk like a 13-year-old, and share toys like a 2-year- old. A child may move with lightning speed from a reasoned discussion of the reasons for taking turns on the playground to a full-scale temper tantrum when not allowed to be first on the swing. You can help yourself manoeuvre among the child's ages by reading about developmental norms (Gesell is a good guide) so that you are ready for (and avoid punishing) behaviour that, though it seems childish in a precocious child, is absolutely age appropriate.

School

If your nine month old begins speaking in full sentences, you probably will not tell the child to stop and wait till other nine month olds catch up. You would not limit such a child to using nouns because that is as much speech as most nine month olds can handle. However, in public or private school that may be the approach some educators use. It is important to realize that they are not purposely setting out to keep your child from learning, although that might be the effect. Many educators have never knowingly dealt with a highly gifted child. They do not recognize them, and they do not know how to handle them. Some educators base teaching methods an developmental norms that are inappropriate for highly gifted children.

Although they may be willing to make an effort to accommodate these youngsters, they may lack sufficient information or experience and not know what type of effort to make. When a child enters school already able to do what the teacher intends to teach, there is seldom a variety of mechanisms for teaching that child something else. Even if there were a way to provide time, attention, and an appropriate curriculum, it would be necessary for the teacher to use different teaching methods. Highly gifted children learn not only faster than others, but also differently. Standard teaching methods take complex subjects and break them into small, simple bits presented one at a time. Highly gifted minds can consume large amounts of information in a single gulp, and they thrive on complexity.

Giving these children simple bits of information is like feeding an elephant one blade of grass at a time - he will starve before he even realizes that anyone is trying to feed him. When forced to work with the methods and pace of a typical school, highly gifted children may look not more capable than their peers, but less capable. Many of their normal characteristics add to this problem. Their handwriting might be very messy because their hands do not keep pace with their quick minds. Many spell poorly because they read for comprehension and do not see the words as collections of separate letters. When they try to "sound out" a word, their logical spelling of an illogical language results in errors. Most have difficulty with rote memorization, a standard learning method in the early grades.

Lack of Fit

The difficulty with highly gifted children in school may be summarized in three words: they don't fit. Almost all American schools organize groups of children by age. The highly gifted child is many ages. The child's intellectual needs might be years ahead of same-age peers, although the gulf may be larger in some subject areas than in others. Imagine 6-year old Rachel. She reads on a 12th grade level, although her comprehension is "only" that of a 7th grader. She does multiplication and division, understands fractions and decimals, but counts on her fingers because she has never memorized addition and subtraction facts or multiplication tables. Her favourite interests at home are paleontology and astronomy; at school her favourite interests are lunch and recess. She collects stamps and plays chess.

Although she can concentrate at her telescope for hours at a time, she cannot sit still when she's bored. She cries easily, loses her temper often, bosses other children when they "don't do it right," and can't keep track of her personal belongings. She has a sophisticated sense of humour that disarms adults but is not understood by other children. Putting Rachel into a normal first grade without paying special attention to her differences is a recipe for social, emotional and educational disaster. Even if a gifted program is available (they commonly begin in third or fourth grade), it is unlikely to meet her extreme needs. Educating a highly gifted child in school is like clothing a 6X child in a store where the largest available garment is a 3 (or with a gifted program, a 3X). Parents have to resort to alterations or individual tailoring of whatever kind they can manage.

In dealing with school issues, it's important to remember that you know more about your child than anyone else. Your knowledge, information, and instincts are useful and important, and they should be recognized in designing a school program. Your child genuinely needs individual attention. Anything else may be directly and seriously harmful. There is no ideal school pattern for the highly gifted. However, when normal school patterns lead to difficulty, it is important to obtain real differentiation.

Acceleration

Because highly gifted children may begin school already knowing much of the material covered in early grades and because they learn quickly, some type of acceleration is necessary. For some children and in some situations, grade skipping is the best choice. Placing a child with older children who share interests may be socially and intellectually beneficial and result in a more appropriate curriculum. It is also a simple and economical solution for the school. Some children begin school early; others skip several early grades; others skip whole educational levels, such as junior high or even high school.

Skipping a single year is seldom helpful, because the difference between one grade level and the next is too small. Grade skipping is not without problems, but allowing highly gifted children to stay in a class that meets few if any of their needs may do serious and long-term damage. Another type of acceleration is subject matter acceleration.

A child may take math with a class four grades ahead, reading with a class two grades ahead, physical education with age peers. This type of acceleration considers the varying developmental ages of the highly gifted child. For further flexibility, you might consider evening classes or weekend classes at a high school or college and ask the school to excuse coverage of those subjects in regular classes. A child might go to school with age mates only in the morning or only in the afternoon. This method calls for school and parental flexibility and may lead to logistical problems such as scheduling and transportation, but is often more satisfactory than grade skipping because the child associates at least part of the time with age peers.

When the School Will Not Change

When parents approach teachers and administrators with information and documentation, in a spirit of cooperation instead of confrontation, offering suggestions and help instead of attacking, some positive changes in normal methods usually result. Sometimes, however, schools refuse to make changes for one child. When this happens, parents have few choices. One is to move to a school system that will make changes. Another is home schooling. For many highly gifted children home schooling is a nearly ideal solution to the problem of fit. Instead of laboriously altering ready-made programs, parents can tailor an education precisely to the child's needs. Clubs, sports, scouting, and other activities supply social interaction with other children while parents serve as teachers or facilitators or engage tutors or mentors in various subject areas.

Home schooling is seldom an easy choice. In some districts it is either illegal or beset with regulations that make it almost as rigid as classroom schooling. When both parents or the single resident parent must work, it may be impossible. Some parents and children find the level of togetherness stifling, while others cannot avoid pushing and demanding too much. However, home schooling may be a positive choice for many families. Many children move surprisingly smoothly from home schooling in the early years into high school or college when their intellectual needs outgrow the home environment. One of the major benefits to education at home is the maintenance of self esteem, which is highly problematic in a school environment.

Social/Emotional Needs

In the movie E.T. there was something heartrending in the small alien's attempts to "phone home," in his constant longing for others of his kind despite the loving concern of the family who cared for him. Highly gifted children endure some of that same pain. It is hard for them to find kindred spirits, hard for them to feel they fit into the only world they know. Highly gifted children may have trouble establishing fulfilling friendships with people of their own age when there are few or no other highly gifted children with whom to interact. As a high school student told his mother, "I can be that part of myself that is like my classmates, and we get along fine. But, there's no one I can share the rest of me with, no one who understands what means the most to me." For most highly gifted children, social relationships with age peers necessitate a constant monitoring of thoughts, words, and behaviour.

One of the greatest benefits of the talent searches proliferating in colleges across the country is the chance for highly gifted children to spend time with others like themselves. For 3 weeks in the summer, children who qualify (by scoring high enough on the SAT or ACT in the seventh grade or earlier) attend class on a college campus with other highly gifted children. Rather than feeling like oddballs, they suddenly feel normal. Lifelong friendships may form in a matter of days. Many summer program participants consider the social interaction as valuable as the classes.

What else can you do to help highly gifted children find friends? It helps children to understand that there are different types of friends. They may play baseball, ride bikes, and watch TV with one person, talk about books or movies with another, and play chess or discuss astronomy with another. Some of these friends may be their own age, some may be younger, or more often, older. Only in school is it suggested that people must be within a few months of each other in age to form meaningful relationships.

Techniques For Parents

The following points may be useful for parents to keep in mind as they actively participate in the counselling and guidance role with their gifted child or children. While it can be said that no two gifted children are alike, general principles do seem to apply in this area, particularly, when children are young.

— Be alert to spontaneous expressions of interest in the environment. Provide additional opportunities to acquire knowledge and experience in these areas. Encourage self-initiated exploration of the environment, materials, and activities available while providing sufficient safeguards to prevent injury.

— Talk to your child as you care for him or her; carry the young child about and cuddle him or her. Use your regular vocabulary and talk about what you are doing (e.g., preparing food, bathing, dressing, going for the mail, etc).

— Expose the child to music, art objects, and reading. Provide a variety of materials (e.g., classical music as well as nursery rhymes). Note the child's preferences and involve the child in decisions early by offering a choice between or among acceptable alternatives (e.g., the blue or red shirt; a cracker or toast; a bath before or after dinner).

— Talk about the properties or attributes of objects - colour, size, shape, utility, texture, etc - and encourage the child to note similarities and differences.

— Be sensitive to the child's moods, degree of well-being (e.g., fatigue, illness, overstimulation, etc.) and allow for lapses in performance levels without being critical.

— Encourage your child's sense of playfulness and the ridiculous as well as interest in innovation and inventiveness. Select toys that lend themselves to multiple uses but don't underestimate your child's ability for adapting common toys or objects to uncommon application.

— Broaden the child's personal, social, physical and learning environment through activities which take into account physical, social, and intellectual development. Don't underestimate his or her ability to profit from activities which might not normally be associated with chronological age. Let the child set the pace. First experiences may need to be largely observational with the degree of active participation increasing as the child's confidence and interest are aroused. As a rule, parental involvement in the form of encouragement, equipment, and special lessons should be geared to the degree of interest the child demonstrates. Encouragement and support of the child's demonstrated interest will nurture the development of self-initiated activities, confidence, and self-reliance.

— Encourage the development of self-help skills, acceptance of responsibility, and the ability to follow through on activities. The child should quickly be involved with and become responsible for putting away any toys and clothing, for dressing and toilet activities, and for assisting other family members in the routines of daily living.

— Be attentive to the development of good listening and communication skills. Actively listen to your child and encourage expression of thoughts and feelings both verbally and non-verbally. The tiny toddler with limited language can still graphically relate the experience of watching daddy's plane land at the airport or the duck feeding in a pond or even the sad tale of a bird flying into a picture window - complete with appropriate facial expressions and sound effects.

— Encourage your child's sensitivity to and sympathy for the needs of others. Gifted children tend to be unusually aware of the feelings of others and often seem to share the intensity of the pain or joy the other is experiencing. Since this can be a traumatic event, it is important that the child be encouraged to cope with empathetic feelings in a constructive way.

— Assist and encourage your child's special interests to the degree that the family is compatible in doing so, including such sacrifices as are willingly made. Do not feel however, that the gifted child's interests and wishes should take precedence over all other family members and their needs.

— Encourage your child to be self-reliant and resourceful. The gifted child can readily become his or her own best advocate in the community. Help the child early to become acquainted with community resources such as libraries, museums and other educational and vocational resources, transportation and communication networks. Provide opportunities for mastering the skills which facilitate access to and use of such resources. Also assist your child in becoming aware of human resources and encourage him or her to seek out others who can share special interests and/or who have the expertise to further the child's development.

— Encourage the development of the child's natural bent for moral, ethical behaviour and for community service. Gifted children usually display an intense interest in fair play and resent the unequal treatment of their peers or themselves. They also show an interest in learning which extends to the learning of others. Thus, they often make natural tutors and derive enjoyment from activities which offer little challenge to them as individuals but provide the opportunity for them to assist children younger or less able then themselves. They also readily understand philanthropic activities at an early age and get much satisfaction out of participation in community projects.

DUAL EXCEPTIONALITIES

Identification of giftedness in students who are disabled is problematic. The customary identification methods - standardized tests and observational checklists- are inadequate, without major modification. Standard lists of characteristics of gifted students may be inadequate for unmasking hidden potential in children who have disabilities.

Children whose hearing is impaired, for example, cannot respond to oral directions, and they may also lack the vocabulary which reflects the complexity of their thoughts. Children whose speech or language is impaired cannot respond to tests requiring verbal responses. Children whose vision is impaired may be unable to respond to certain performance measures, and although their vocabulary may be quite advanced, they may not understand the full meaning of the words they use (e.g., colour words). Children with learning disabilities may use high-level vocabulary in speaking but be unable to express themselves in writing, or vice versa.

In addition, limited life experiences due to impaired mobility may artificially lower scores. Since the population of gifted/disabled students is difficult to locate, they seldom are included in standardized test norming groups, adding to the problems of comparison. In addition, gifted children with disabilities often use their intelligence to try to circumvent the disability. This may cause both exceptionalities to appear less extreme: the disability may appear less severe because the child is using the intellect to cope, while the efforts expended in that area may hinder other expressions of giftedness.

The following lists are intended to assist parents and teachers in recognizing intellectual giftedness in the presence of a disability.

Characteristics of Gifted Students with Specific Disabilities

Gifted Students with Visual Impairment

— Fast rate of learning

— Superior memory

— Superior verbal communication skills and vocabulary

— advanced problem-solving skills

— Creative production or thought that may progress more slowly than sighted students in some academic areas

— Ease in learning Braille

— Great persistence

— Motivation to know

— Sometimes slower rate of cognitive development than sighted students

— excellent ability to concentrate

Gifted Students with Physical Disabilities

— Development of compensatory skills

— Creativity in finding alternate ways of communicating and accomplishing tasks

— Impressive store of knowledge

— Advanced academic skills

— Superior memory

— Exceptional problem-solving skills

— Rapid grasp of ideas
— Ability to set and strive for long-term goals
— Greater maturity than age mates
— Good sense of humour
— Persistence, patience
— Motivation to achieve
— Curiosity, insight
— Self-criticism and perfectionism
— Cognitive development that may not be based on direct experience
— Possible difficulty with abstractions
— Possible limited achievement due to pace of work

Gifted Students with Hearing Impairments

— Development of speech-reading skills without instruction
— Early reading ability
— Excellent memory
— Ability to function in the regular school setting
— Rapid grasp of ideas
— High reasoning ability
— Superior performance in school
— Wide range of interests
— Nontraditional ways of getting information
— Use of problem-solving skills in everyday situations
— Possibly on grade level
— Delays in concept attainment
— Self starters

— Good sense of humour
— Enjoyment of manipulating environment
— Intuition
— Ingenuity in solving problems
— Symbolic language abilities (different symbol system)

Gifted Students with Learning Disabilities

— High abstract reasoning ability
— Good mathematical reasoning ability
— Keen visual memory, spatial skills
— Advanced vocabulary
— Sophisticated sense of humour
— Imaginative and creative
— Insightful
— Exceptional ability in geometry, science, arts, music
— Good problem-finding and -solving skills
— Difficulty with memorization, computation, phonics, and/or spelling
— Distractibility and/or disorganization
— Supersensitivity
— Perfectionism
— Grasp of metaphors, analogies, satire
— Comprehension of complex systems
— Unreasonable self expectations
— Often, failure to complete assignments
— Difficulties with sequential tasks
— Wide variety of interests

Research indicates that in many cases, a child is diagnosed with ADHD when in fact the child is gifted and reacting to an inappropriate curriculum. The key to distinguishing between the two is the pervasiveness of the "acting out" behaviours. If the acting out is specific to certain situations, the child's behaviour is more likely related to giftedness; whereas, if the behaviour is consistent across all situations, the child's behaviour is more likely related to ADHD. It is also possible for a child to be BOTH gifted and ADHD. The following lists highlight the similarities between giftedness and ADHD.

Characteristics of Gifted Students Who Are Bored

— Poor attention and daydreaming when bored

— Low tolerance for persistence on tasks that seem irrelevant

— Begin many projects, see few to completion

— Development of judgment lags behind intellectual growth

— Intensity may lead to power struggles with authorities

— High activity level; may need less sleep

— Difficulty restraining desire to talk; may be disruptive

— Question rules, customs, and traditions

— Lose work, forget homework, are disorganized

— May appear careless

— Highly sensitive to criticism

— Do not exhibit problem behaviours in all situations

— More consistent levels of performance at a fairly consistent pace

Characteristics of Students with ADHD

— Poorly sustained attention

— Diminished persistence on tasks not having immediate consequences
— Often shift from one uncompleted activity to another
— Impulsivity, poor delay of gratification
— Impaired adherence to commands to regulate or inhibit behaviour in social contexts
— More active, restless than other children
— Often talk excessively
— Often interrupt or intrude on others (e.g., butt into games)
— Difficulty adhering to rules and regulations
— Often lose things necessary for tasks or activities at home or school
— May appear inattentive to details
— Highly sensitive to criticism
— Problem behaviours exist in all settings, but in some are more severe
— Variability in task performance and time used to accomplish tasks.

Questions to Ask in Differentiating between Giftedness and ADHD

— Could the behaviours be responses to inappropriate placement, insufficient challenge, or lack of intellectual peers?
— Is the child able to concentrate when interested in the activity?
— Have any curricular modifications been made in an attempt to change inappropriate behaviours?
— Has the child been interviewed? What are his/her feelings about the behaviours?

— Does the child feel out of control? Do the parents perceive the child as being out of control?

— Do the behaviours occur at certain times of the day, during certain activities, with certain teachers or in certain environments?

Implications for Students with Dual Exceptionalities

Commitment to identifying and nurturing the gifts of students with disabilities implies specific changes in the way educators approach identification, instruction, and classroom dynamics.

Identification

— Include students with disabilities in initial screening phase.

— Be willing to accept nonconventional indicators of intellectual talent.

— Look beyond test scores.

— When applying cutoffs, bear in mind the depression of scores that may occur due to the disability.

— DO NOT aggregate subtest scores into a composite score.

— Compare with others who have similar disabilities.

— Weight more heavily characteristics that enable the child to effectively compensate for the disability.

— Weight more heavily areas of performance unaffected by the disability.

— Allow the child to participate in gifted programs on a trial basis.

Instruction

— Be aware of the powerful role of language; reduce communication limitations and develop alternative modes for thinking and communicating.

— Emphasize high-level abstract thinking, creativity, and a problem-solving approach.

— Have great expectations: these children often become successful as adults in fields requiring advanced education.

— Provide for individual pacing in areas of giftedness and disability.

— Provide challenging activities at an advanced level.

— Promote active inquiry, experimentation, and discussion.

— Promote self-direction.

— Offer options that enable students to use strengths and preferred ways of learning.

— Use intellectual strengths to develop coping strategies.

— Assist in strengthening the student's self concept.

Classroom Dynamics

— Discuss disabilities/capabilities and their implications with the class.

— Expect participation in all activities; strive for normal peer interactions.

— Facilitate acceptance; model and demand respect for all.

— Candidly answer peers' questions.

— Treat a child with a disability the same way a child without a disability is treated.

— Model celebration of individual differences.

Gifted students with disabilities must be provided with appropriate challenges. The personal and societal costs of not developing their potential cannot be overstated.

3

Role of Guidance and Counselling

Guidance is an act of showing the way for some people, like adolescents, who cannot find the right path. It is directing, pointing, leading and accompanying. Guidance is saying "Yes" to someone who is asking for help. It is saying "Yes" to an invitation of someone who wants a temporary companion along life's way. Guidance is giving directions to the lonely, confused, unloved, the suffering, the sick and the lost. It is pointing to some possibilities of thinking, feeling and acting. It is leading the person psychologically, emotionally and even spiritually to some newer ways of meaningful living. It is accompanying those who are fearful and uncertain, those who need someone along the rugged path of life's journey.

From an objective point of view, guidance is part and parcel of the counseling profession. It is called directive counseling. High school and even college students need guidance when they are unsure of what choices to make or what directions to take. The guidance counselor "opens up" a world of choices for these persons for them to choose from. It is like presenting the universe when all that a person sees is the lonely planet earth. The guidance counselor enlarges and widens the horizon of people who sees only a narrow path or a concealed view of that path. Thus, the focus is on possibilities and choices.

Usually, guidance occurs in schools. High school and college students avail of guidance and counseling services in their school. More often, young people are unsure of what to do, how to react or respond, and how to act in certain choices. When this occurs, they need someone older, wiser and more experienced to show them the way, to guide them. This is the role of the guidance counselor—to extend assistance when necessary to those who are confused, uncertain, and needing advice. However, some adults may need guidance too. There are certain moments in one's life when some unresolved complexes get in the way and the person may want advice or direction. Thus, although guidance occurs more often in schools, it could also be found among friends or circles of friends in the adult world and even formally, in the counselor's or therapist's office.

Counseling is guiding and more. It is a way of healing hurts. It is both a science and an art. It is a science because to offer counsel, advice or assistance, the counselor must have the knowledge of the basic principles and techniques of counseling. The counselor must be able to use any of these basic principles and techniques as paradigms in order for him to counsel well. However, it is not enough to use know these basic principles and techniques. The other important aspect is for the counselor to know how to counsel—the art of counseling. This aspect considers counseling as a relationship, as a sharing of life, in the hope that the person who is hurting will be healed. As a relationship, counseling involves the physical, emotional, and psychical or spiritual dimensions.

The counselor must have the ability to relate to the counselee in an appropriate physical manner without being too intimate or too close for comfort or being too distant or aloof. The emotional dimension in counseling includes empathy, sensitivity and the ability to interpret non-verbal clues of the counselee in order to understand unresolved complexes or pent-up feelings. The psychical or spiritual dimension embraces the counselee's "soul content" what lies inside. This is what is called the interiority of the person. The counselor must have the gift or grace of catching a glimpse of the interior world of the person, particularly his spiritual condition, for this is very important in healing the person's hurts. .

Counseling is a relatively short-term relationship, characterized by an interpersonal relationship between the counselor and the counselee. It is theory-based, handled professionally by trained people, guided by ethical and legal standards that focus on helping or giving care to people who need to resolve developmental and situational problems. Counseling focuses on making important changes in one's thinking, feeling and behaving. It is a more than guiding because it aggressively promotes making changes in the counselee's life-style. It may even entail a "paradigm-shift" when warranted. It is generally short-term and the main goal is the resolution of problems. It deals with normal people having normal problems.

Counseling is an active listening. Although considered as a noble yet thankless profession, it deals with making important changes in the intellectual, emotional, physical and spiritual aspects of the counselee through a process philosophy. As a process, it encompasses exploration, goal setting and action to facilitate new ways of behaving, thinking and feeling. Counselors believe that clients are not sick, just stuck.

OBJECTIVES OF SCHOOL GUIDANCE AND COUNSELING PROGRAMMES

Students are challenged daily to make decisions in an environment fraught with tension and uncertainty. Faced with social, economic, and cultural issues to a degree not experienced by previous generations, students must have proactive choices to nurture the potential they each have to become successful learners. Guidance and Counseling Programmes are educational programme which create options for students to develop and emphasize strategies which enhance this potential. Every student deserves to be surrounded by a culture of high expectations and a rich array of options for the future. They deserve rich educational and career guidance in order to define the choices to the options he or she chooses. They deserve rich curriculum, instruction, and services to be able to realize the options developed through the guidance process.

Guidance and Counseling is a process of helping people by assisting them in making decisions and changing behavior. The purpose of a guidance and counseling program is to impart specific skills and learning opportunities in a proactive and preventive manner which ensures that all students can achieve school success through academic, career, and personal/social development. As students achieve developmental competencies, their perceptions of themselves and their opportunities should become better defined. Guidance counselors should be actively involved in school improvement, curriculum, instruction, and assessment. Hopefully, this will result in a re-examination of individual guidance and counseling programs. As the need for accountability increases, guidance counselors should review their programs on a continuous basis. This is the rationale for a guidance curriculum person: the need for improved student achievement for all students.

The Guidance and Counseling Program is an integral part of each school's total educational program. It is developmental by design and includes sequential activities organized and implemented by certified school counselors with the support of teachers, administrators, students, and parents. The Guidance and Counseling Program includes:

— Guidance curriculum (activities that all students, in the same ways, master the skills and knowledge of the educational objectives).

— Individual planning (activities that enable students in different ways to master skills and knowledge).

— Responsive services (activities done with some students to help them overcome social and emotional problems).

— System support (management and support tasks that make the educational system work).

Vewing guidance and counseling from a statewide perspective, several challenges emerge that reflect a need to refocus the energy of guidance and counseling efforts:

1. *There is a strong misconception about the role of guidance and counseling*: Guidance and counseling cannot be seen as the exception rather than the rule. A better job must be done in communicating the added value of guidance and counseling to the entire educational community of parents, business, and community leaders.

2. *The ability to work with the whole spectrum of integrated student services.* Too often, the Guidance and Counseling Program is viewed as a reactive, almost punitive function for some students. The development of a program with various components with specific content, goals, and prevention steps is needed to reach the identified needs of all students.

3. *Results accountability*: The Guidance and Counseling Program places emphasis on individual development. Because self-development is primarily intangible in nature, many activities within the programs are difficult to measure. Guidance personnel should create and implement a process to demonstrate that the guidance and counseling program does affect growth and development, and results in life-long learning.

4. *Asset building*: All individuals possess, within themselves, a level of commitment, motivation, values, and skills. The specialized training and unique skills of counselors should be manifested in a program that is designed and delivered to address and build upon these internal assets in a positive and proactive manner. This will lay the foundation for developing the competencies and self-efficacy youth need to make healthy and productive choices throughout their lives.

Local school systems should work to transform these challenges into opportunities for the Guidance and Counseling Program. The Framework for Building a Comprehensive Guidance and Counseling Program" model focuses on two major areas that contain the following components:

Structural components

— Mission and Principles

— Functions of Guidance and Counseling

— Resources

— Budget

Programmatic components

— Curriculum (Learner Competencies)

— Individual Planning

— Responsive Services

— System Support

— Mission Development

It is important that the Guidance and Counseling Program operates as a planned and structured program with specific content. Having a mission that describes what the guidance and counseling program does and how it gets done clarifies the role of the program and guidance personnel.

Philosophy

Of all of the educational programs, the Guidance and Counseling Program clearly speaks to the inner growth and development of learners. Principles that govern the operation and delivery of the program should convey the essence of asset building and development, both emotionally and academically, in all learners.

Principles

The School Guidance and Counseling Program should:

— Promote respect for individuality and diversity.

— Be available to all learners at each educational level.

— Be developmental and career-oriented in meeting all learners' needs to facilitate academic success.

— Be integrated with the total educational/career process.

— Be evaluated for success.

— Utilize technological and community resources effectively.

— Be delivered equitably.

Benefits of a Comprehensive Guidance and Counseling Program

— Prepares students to be productive, contributing citizens with a strong work ethic.

— Provides continuity for smooth and effective levels of transition from kindergarten through post-secondary.

— Facilitates a school/home/community network.

— Enhances and encourages a model for life-long learning with emphasis on appropriate decision making and communication skills in a diverse and technological society.

— Encourages students to learn positive human relationships as a means of managing conflicts.

Functions of Guidance and Counseling

Guidance and counseling programs consist of four primary functions:

— Program Design and Planning/Leadership

— Establishes and promotes a school guidance and counseling program.

— Develops a written school-based guidance plan based on learners. needs.

— Implements an individual plan of action.

Counseling

Facilitates and implements delivery of counseling services in areas of self-knowledge, educational and occupational exploration, and career planning to facilitate academic achievement. Adheres to established system policies and procedures in scheduling appointments and obtaining parental permission.

— Schedules time to provide opportunities for counseling.

— Counsels learners individually by actively listening, identifying and defining issues, discussing alternative solutions, and formulating a plan of action.

— Leads counseling or support groups for learners experiencing similar issues.

— Evaluates effectiveness of group counseling and makes revisions as necessary.

Guidance/collaboration

Coordinates with school staff to provide supportive instructional guidance activities that relate to students: self-knowledge, educational and occupational exploration, and career planning to facilitate academic achievement.

— Collaborates with school staff in planning and scheduling guidance activities.

— Conducts classroom guidance activities related to identified goals and objectives.

— Gathers and evaluates data to determine effectiveness of classroom guidance and student comprehension, making revisions where necessary.

— Provides direct/indirect assistance to learners preparing for test taking.

— Provides information to students, parents, and teachers on student test scores.

— Provides information to students and parents on career planning.

— Assists students in their transitions to the next educational/career level.

— Leads skill-building groups in student self-knowledge.

Consultation/coordination

— Consults, as needed or requested, with system/staff, parents, and community about issues and concerns.

— Exchanges relevant information about situations with school/system staff and parents.

— Collaborates with school staff in developing a strategy or plan for improving school climate.

— Follows up on counseling and consultative referrals.

— Consults with school system in making referral to community agencies.

UNDERSTANDING THE PSYCHOSOCIAL DEVELOPMENT OF CHILDREN'S

Erikson's Stages of Psychosocial Development

Erik Erikson translated Fraud's theory of psychosocial development into "a more relevant format to meat the needs of American culture of mid-twentieth century". Freud's theory of development is primarily based an emotions; to Freud, mental health and healthy development leads to the ability to work and to love. Erikson's Eight stages of psychosocial development focus on the idea that defined task or crises of each stage must be achieved for full potential in the next stage. Erikson's view is optimistic, focusing on strengths which develop within each stage. With successful resolution the individual will develop the "basic virtue" suggested in the stage. With no resolution or only partial resolution, the opposite counterpart may be the overwhelming outcome, with resulting delays in development.

Erikson's theory of psychosocial development of the individual is a preset developmental plan, where personality develops according to determined steps. Society encourages challenges that arise at predetermined times (Erikson's tasks or crisis). Each stage presents a task which must be completed for a positive outcome. The resolution of one task lays the foundation for growth in the next Stage. Erikson stresses socialization, culture and history; the resolution of each task depends on an individual's interaction with their culture. Erikson's theory emphasizes continuing development throughout life — a life span approach which is open to inclusion of theories of cognitive and physiological growth and development.

Stage: Infancy

Task: Development of Basic Trust

Negative Counterpart: Mistrust

Outcome of Successful Resolution: Hope

The task at this stage is to resolve a "crisis of basic trust in the world through consistent parenting, versus developing a sense of basic mistrust of the world due to inconsistent parenting or absence of parenting. If the parenting is consistent and of a positive, nurturing quality then, according to Erikson, a sense of hope can develop, sustaining the development of ego Identity or self-concept. According to Erikson , development of a sense of hope "does not depend on absolute quantities of food or demonstrations of love, but rather an the quality of the maternal relationship". In other words, it's not the skill with which a child is bathed, dressed or held, but the manner in which love and warmth is expressed our society's emphasis is on the nuclear two parent, independent family.

This cultural norm may not be the only, or best, way to raise children. Margaret Mead, in her studies of other cultures, questioned the "one mother" caretaker and described cultures in which several "mothers" (aunts, grandmothers, neighbors) all take part in child rearing, giving a child greater opportunity to receive nurturing. The child/mother relationship is important to psychosocial development, but more important may be receiving loving attention and care from not only one but many sources. Fathering is an important factor in psychosocial development. In our culture the accepted norm is a father who is not as involved with parenting as the mother. More modern, androgenous couples may divide caretakinq equally, allowing the child to receive care and comfort from both parents. When a disability is present, a father may be excluded even more than usual.

If the mothering an infant receives is inconsistent, inadequate to their needs or rejecting in nature, the child develops attitudes of mistrust, suspicion, fear toward self and others in the world. Says Erikman "A sense of mistrust will prevent or delay cognitive development and achievement of other stages of psychosocial development". An infant, during the first six months, takes in the external world. Tao much stimulation and the infant "tunes out" as a defence, and the integration of experiences for cognitive and affective growth may become impossible, or delayed. There is more control over the environment, at least in terms of responding and signals the child can send indicating need for care.

The child begins to touch, grasp, and co-ordinates their responses to the environment. The infant becomes a social being, and, according to Erikson: "The infant's first social achievement, then, is his willingness to let the mother out of sight without undue anxiety or rage because she has become an inner certainty as well as an outer predictability". The child needs to feel that the world is safe, that there is some protection from harm when they begin to explore, needs to trust their own feelings. The child needs experience to master skills (albeit small skills in this stage), and through experience find stimulation far further exploration. An unsafe or unresponsive environment will not stimulate future exploration, nor will an inconsistent environment in which the child has no way of knowing whether or not it is safe or unsafe to explore.

Feeding

In early infancy, a major factor in the interaction between child and parent is the success or failure of feeding. Feeding is meant to be a source of gratification — sometimes a disability means this may be a painful procedure. If the child is difficult or unresponsive during feeding, the parent feels either successful in the task or not successful. If feelings of success are the result, the parent will feel relaxed and confident; if feelings of failure are the result of the feeding interaction, the parent will be overly concerned and stiff. The infant will reflect the parent's worry with stiff responses or feeding difficulty. The infant's stiff response, in turn, effects the parent's ability to relax. Feeding, rather than having a time of joy and intimacy, becomes a time for worry and consternation.

The interaction is not rewarding for either parent or child and negatively effects the building of trust which, according to Erilson's Stages, is mast important at this stage. Kleinberg says that "without the developmental framework of basic trust the child may grow up to view the world and his or her place in it as fragmented and threatening". The child needs consistent care to relieve distress of hunger, and pain. Haphazard care that does not co-ordinate with the child's needs does not allow the infant to begin to develop a basic sense of trust. This, according to Erikson, is more than just psychological; "The first demonstration of social trust in the baby is the ease of his feeding, the depth of his sleep, the relaxation of her bowels".

Physical Interaction

The infant who cannot relax, cannot give over to the caregivers his/her body for care and comfort, does not begin to develop a sense of trust, of hope for future comfort. Along with feeding, the child needs tactile stimulation, with cuddling and stroking. When being changed or dressed, the child can be cuddled and touched lovingly, or, if the caregiver is distant and stiff, the child can be dressed and changed and bathed in a mechanical, distant fashion. It is not the amount of stimulation received but the quality which is most important.

Attachment and Rejection

Parents may also be overwhelmed by and fearful of holding or touching the child with a disability. They may fear losing the child through death, and be reluctant to become attached; they may even act as if the child has died, and begin mourning. When such children survive and become strong enough to come home, the process of attachment — or maybe reattachment - may not happen. There may even he a subtle process of rejection. Reactions of grief and mourning are normal under the circumstances and should not be denied or ignored.

Actual rejection by birth parents may necessitate fostering, with a progression of many caregivers. All these factors may combine to create a sense of mistrust in an infant, interfering with future attempts to relate and trust in the future. If the parent is distant, or anxious, and limits the amount of stimulation and interaction, the infant may become anxious and stiff, which, in turn, does not encourage relaxed interaction. If a child is neglected or abused in the first six months, there is a lessening of attempts to communicate, and motor development is retarded, along with cognitive delays. During the second six months, an infant can become withdrawn, apathetic and depressed, as well as whiny and clingy, if parent/child interaction is insufficient. A situation such as hospitalization, due to illness or disability, can cause anxiety through lack of consistent care, or lack of warmth and comfort.

Effects of Disability

Disability can be present at birth or at any time thereafter. The stress for the family is great and often the family needs outside support. Mothers and fathers have had a vision or have imagined an ideal child, and suddenly have to deal with the reality of a child with a disability. This reality may effect parental attachment or rejection. Hospitalization and prolonged treatments may physically separate the parents and child at crucial times, when maternal bonding is taking place. The physical condition and appearance of the child may actually cause rejection by the parents, and require the necessity of fostering or acute hospitalization, resulting in numerous, inconsistent caregivers.

Pain

Infants with a physical disability may undergo a series of painful surgery and other treatments. An infant is completely vulnerable to pain, and cannot distinguish from internal or external pain. Many infants born with disabilities of bone growth may be immobilized in casts or same other restraints.

Interventions

Consistent caregiving might be impossible for the new born child with a physical disability, due to complications of the disability and hospitalization. At each contact, no matter how brief, the parents and other caregivers should make every effort to "connect" with the infant, stroke and physically touch and cuddle the child. The infant with a disability may well need extra stimulation, eye contact when possible, talking and caresses. Parents and caregivers need accurate information about the specific disability to be able to cope, become comfortable with the infant and to have hope for the future. Especially, they need to understand, in some cases, that the infant's reactions to the parent may be effected by the disability.

Physical disabilities from birth may have lifelong psychological consequences. The world may seem threatening and fragmented — no one, from the infant's view, can be trusted.

Stage: Toddler

Task: Basic Autonomy

Negative Counterpart: Shame and Doubt

Successful Resolution: Self Will

If an unsafe or inconsistent environment discourages autonomy and exploration of the environment, the child may feel frustration, shame and doubt about their own self identity. "The establishment of independence is the major theme of toddlerhood". As the child grows to toddlerhood, contacts with other children increase as does the need for independence from parents. The child begins to learn the cultural rights and wrongs of dealing with others — sharing, no hitting. The child is beginning to acquire, according to Erikson's stages, a sense of autonomy. They also are beginning to understand that events can be predicted; differentiation of self physically and emotionally comes about through increased cognitive skills.

Two processes related to self awareness come into use - individual actions and feelings and the recognition of others as separate. The child is mastering skills as well as reacting to what others do. The toddler must explore and try new things. Parents need to allow safe activities so that the child can explore. A safe environment is critical to the sense of developing autonomy. The actual mobility of the child — whether they can move independently or not — is critical to developing a sense of autonomy as well. The child is beginning to experience their own will, and their struggle is between the need for help and a safe environment and their inner urge for independence of action.

Erikson describes it as a toddler gaining a "sense of self-control without loss of self-esteem" from which experience comes "a lasting sense of good will and pride; from a sense of loss of self control and ... overcontrol comes a lasting propensity for doubt and shame". The toddler needs emotional and physical safety at this point, balanced against the need to explore and exert self will. According to Erikson, lack of autonomy at this stage creates a lasting sense of doubt about others. The child first moves toward autonomy from the mother, learning to choose and guide their own personal actions. In this fashion, a child learns socially acceptable ways of handling frustration, learning control of behaviour and cooperation with others in play.

Effects of Disability

Physical impairment at this stage will limit the child's interaction with their environment, and in turn, as previously discussed, may adversely effect normal cognitive development. A child with a physical disability may be overprotected by frightened parents who cannot stand to ME the child struggle or are concerned that the toddler may hurt themselves. More negatively, the parents may have decided that the child cannot accomplish anything in a normal fashion and ignore or show a lack of support and confidence. Such a child will not be encouraged to reach their potential. The toddler who is not challenged and encouraged to interact with the environment, who is overprotected, or who has seen no confidence expressed in them will doubt their ability and cease to initiate any action: they become passive, demanding and even depressed.

Energy

A normal toddler has unbounded energy and curiosity. A toddler with a physical disability may have low energy levels or may have pain when they move. They may have no control over their body, bowel, bladder, or limbs. Their limited movement may not allow them to develop the simplest of skills such as feeding themselves, moving from one spot to another, reaching a desired toy.

Separation

A toddler separated from family through repeated and prolonged hospitalization is often in strange surroundings. They may feel abandoned and regress to infantile actions. Hospitalization and treatments may physically restrict the active toddler, and they lose any sense of control over their own actions.

Interventions

Early childhood stimulation programs at special preschools equipped and staffed to handle various disabilities are essential. The parents and caregivers need information about specific disabilities and the toddler needs a stimulating and accessible environment with which to interact. At this stage, if the child cannot move into the environment, then a special, stimulating environment should be moved to where the child is. A balance of encouragement to autonomy in a safe and stimulating environment is necessary to allow the toddler to begin to reach full potential. Support for the parents and family is also essential, where questions can he honestly answered, and fears lessened.

Stage: Preschool

Task: Initiative

Negative Counterpart: Guilt

Successful Resolution: Purpose and Direction

The environment may be impossible to control or to approach, and choice may be unavailable to the child with a disability. Limitations due to disability may cause frustration and guilt feelings about forced dependence. The child may have lowered self esteem and lack of initiative. At this stage, the child begins to recognize him/herself as a separate person. They fluctuate between dependence and independence, needing loving guidance one day and refusing adult supervision or instruction the next. Cognitive and physical mastery is slowly attained and skills are developed.

Children are always "daring things", and a healthy child will take initiative in many ways: they begin to assume responsibility for self and attain mare self control rather than needing constant supervision. At this stage role models begin to be important, and play is the focus of their daily activities. According to Erickson, "initiative is a necessary part of every act and man needs initiative for whatever he learns".

Effects of Disability

The limitations of disability often isolate the child from the immediate environment and from normal daily interaction with peers. Continuing medical and surgical interventions may mean long and painful separation from family during hospitalizations, and this in turn may lead to overprotectiveness and guilt on the part of the parents. Rough and tumble play may be prohibited, and peers begin to ask embarrassing or hard to answer questions. The lack of ability to easily interact with toys and people and the adult attention a child at this stage may receive due to a disability may make the preschooler demanding — and one who may not have learned acceptable social skills for group play.

Pain

Physical disability interferes with the preschooler's increasing need to explore, play and interact. The disability may not allow the child to obtain control over their own body — their basic care in toiletting may be their parent's responsibillty. They may need help with tasks of daily living. Parents may need to perform intrusive and painful medical treatments; they may be able to attain self care if parents are able to let go of these interventions as the individual matures. One effect may be infantalizing the preschooler, postponing the mastery of physical independence. Conflict between parents and the child may begin in this stage, when the preschooler wants to be able to make their own choices.

Preschool age children have a primitive sense of cause and effect. They may have a sense that their disability, and the related medical treatments, are punishment. This punishment may be for real or imaged crimes. Parents may feed into this idea, consciously or unconsciously, by restraining activity with admonitions of "Be careful or you'll hurt yourself" or with threats of "Be good or you'll go back to the hospital". Medical treatments, hospitalization may he seen as Punishment. X-ray machines, operating rooms, etc. may be seen as monsters. The child's imagination builds these monsters into a frightening fantasy which parents must approach with gentleness and love.

Play and Illness

Play can be a tool to help children master anxiety. Play can normalize otherwise frightening situations. Play, especially when hospitalized, reminds the child of outside situations, home and family. Therapeutic play can be of great use to the counsellor dealing with physically limited children. Desires, frustrations, fears and angers can be acted out with toys of manipulative size, and the meanings and reasons discussed with the child or student who may otherwise be unable to explain their feelings.

Interventions

Preschool children, as do toddlers, need stimulation and the ability to explore their environment. Special preschool, or mainstreamed preschools where children with disabilities interact with their able bodied peers, are a necessity so that the preschooler begins to learn social rules. The family will need mare and more support from the community and special needs groups as the child grows, as well as possible peer counselling from families who have had the same experience.

Stage: School Age

Task: Industry

Negative Counterpart: Inferiority

Successful Resolution: Competence

At. this stage the child's identity comes largely through the mastery of skills. Disability may prevent goals being obtained, generates frustration and a feeling of being cheated out of experience may prevail. The child may simply feel helpless and "give up" feelings of helplessness and depression are common, as are feelings of inferiority. Research into the helplessness syndrome shows that "The feelings of helplessness can become a self perpetuating phenomenon ... sabotages the desire to respond to environmental demands, retards the ability to perceive success ... results in a sense of hopelessness". The child at this stage has a desire to accomplish and master new skills, and to make meaningful effort. The focus is on mastering tasks which are essential for success in adulthood — reading, writing, numeracy as well as interpersonal communication skills and physical skills. The focus is on education and competition.

Effects of Disability

According to Erikson, "Many a child's development is disrupted when family life has failed to prepare him for school life, or when school life fails to sustain the promises of earlier stages". Disability can certainly be the "disruption" in the family or the school which prevents the child from being prepared. The inability to compete with peers on all levels elicits feelings of incompetence, worthlessness and helplessness; not only competition but individual mastery of skills is important Kleirlherg says, Being normal, able to be competent in academic pursuits, social interactions and physical sports is very important to the school age child. Equally important is the desire to be physically independent and chronic illness (and disability) can drastically interfere with these developmental tasks.

Disability may make individual mastery of skills difficult or impossible. Success in these areas leads to an increased eagerness to learn, failure to master skills may lead to apathy. The child begins to have a perception of him/herself as a total person with rising emphasis on physical development and body image. The disabled child may now be experiencing rejection from peers due to the disability along with the inability to master physical skills.

Peers

According to Erikson, this stage of development deals with mastery, competency and the founding of peer relationships. The goal is tied up with developing a sense of self worth. Individuals need to have success academically, socially and physically. School-aged children look outwardly to peers and adults outside the family to measure and establish their self worth. Negative attitudes and outright rejection results in anger and self-hatred, and lower self-concept and self-esteem.

Uniqueness

Children with physical disabilities come in contact, perhaps for the first time, with the stares and comments of peers. Some physical disabilities result in malformations of the physical body, spasms and obvious differences. Being different, being labeled as weird or abnormal can be devastating to the child who has come from the relative supportive atmosphere of the family and perhaps a special school. Many physically disabled children may cope by focusing on academic achievement, compensating for the lack in some way by being good in school. They may also learn much about their own condition and seem very sophisticated about their needs and specialized treatment.

Hospitalization

On the other hand, many children with physical disabilities may have had their schooling interrupted by illness, hospitalization and lack of transportation and may be lacking academic skills. Their attendance may be inconsistent and combined with their feeling of differentness, often leads to a sense of failure and a resulting fear or dislike of the school setting. Enforced absences due to hospitalization or illness removes the student with a disability from the flow and rhythm of the school — missing work and being outside of the cliques formed over time. A child with a disability may have learned that it is easier to fake a symptom and return home, where they are safe and accepted. Reintegration into the classroom after long periods away becomes more and more difficult.

Fear of Death and Mutilation

School age children develop an understanding of their own mortality. They begin to understand that they may never be a 'normal' adult and may come to fear the possibility of death. Because of this fear of both death and possible 'mutilation' the child may become overly dependent on parents, avoid risks involved in taking part in daily life, become overly fearful of medical treatment, unmanageable in school, home or hospital. Such children may retreat into themselves dwelling on the fear of physical pain and mutilation. They may react with denial, rebellion, immaturity, overdependence depression, anxiety, helplessness or mature acceptance. Many factors influence the rejection or acceptance of a disability and the alert teacher or counsellor will identify and acknowledge these indicators.

Interventions

The school takes a bigger role in possible interventions at this point; though parents are still the main caregivers in most cases Legislation for integration, in some cases, ensures that able bodied children and children with disabilities are able to interact as much as possible. School based curriculum should include awareness programs so that negative attitudes to disability can be dealt with in the classroom. Family intervention may include counselling with the family members about the child's need for as much freedom as possible; community support for the family on many fronts is a necessity.

Success is important for the child in all grades, and special education teachers may be necessary to design appropriate curriculum. Technology may be the greatest asset a child with a disability has, so that the most severely disabled person can learn to communicate their thoughts to others — and financial support of schools and individuals is an area of great concern.

Stage: Adolescence

Task: Identity Achievement

Negative Counterpart: Role Confusion

Successful Resolution: Affiliation

Disability may cause tasks of daily living to be very difficult — an individual may be fully dependent on physical help which effects the self-view as an independent, autonomous person. Physical isolation and constant dependency on others for tasks of daily living may have robbed the young adult of the ability to establish their identity. Roles of student, worker, wife or husband may seem to be impossible to obtain; the attitude that society holds may have a greater effect on the individual at this point than the actual disability. The individual may have a loss of will to try to accomplish any new task, and may be resigned unhappily to not having what others have.

During the adolescent years, career choices and marriage may be the overwhelming focus. Of great importance is the learning of good social skills, so that the adolescent can fit in with their peers, as well as be able to search for a job. There is also the task of transition from school to work. This can he a period of uncertainty and fear, and on the part of the individual with a disability and on the part of their families, who may want to protect them from disappointment and harm. Who and what one is comes through the ways in which we participate in our society — disability may intrude on each of these areas.

The sexual identity of the adolescent is tied up in the image they held of their bodies — this is especially difficult for the person with a disability to come to terms with when their body may be distorted by the disability. The physical changes of adolescence constitute a major developmental crisis for the individual , and their concern is body image and peer acceptance. When tasks which have come before have not been successfully completed or short circuited by disability, the individual may feel a sense of isolation from society, a sense of incompleteness, and a sense of loss.

Effects of Disability

All positive aspects of the stages before this must be established to give the individual a feeling of wholeness. Lack of identity, lack of a sense of trust and hope, a feeling of inferiority may result in isolation and an inability to take part in society. Erikson says about the adolescent, "In their search for a new sense of continuity and sameness, adolescents have to refight many of the battles of earlier years ...". The disabled individual may have complication of lack of education and poor social skills, and many unresolved psychosocial crises.

Transitions

For the person with a disability, the normal transition periods are the worst times — when peers are getting their first jobs, having relationships marrying, having children. The lack of these involvements for the individual with a disability may cause depression and grief.

Lack of Support

Many of the tasks for the individual with a disability may he caused more through a lack of resources rather than an individual lack of skills or will. Disability or the community's attitude to the disability may he a reason for the adolescent to withdraw from interaction with peers and cease trying to be independent; the individual becomes a "patient" or "client" of some social agency

Body Image

The stress and complications of daily living increase as an individual moves into the adolescent stage. The task of adolescence is to find and establish an identity. They must also strive for emotional, if not physical independence, from parents and family. In the search for an identity an individual with a physical disability has heard, seen and felt many negative perceptions about body image, abilities and personal worth. The negative reactions by others coming together at adolescence strengthens the normal adolescent feelings of difference. The adolescent is involved in forming their identity deciding who they are and focusing planning what their future may be. The added stress of a disability enters many dimensions of the adolescent personality; disability has effects on self image, on how an individual relates to the world and on future plans for career, education, and marriage.

The adolescent years are often full of times of great self doubt; the adolescent's body changes quickly, they are very self conscious. Every change or event brings with it a new trauma — acne, unruly hair, appearance is very important as is the approval of peers. To be different is a problem — belonging to a group is important. Physical disability can affect the body growth; a disability such as Cerebral Palsy causes evident and major differences, short stature due to tone deformities makes one obviously different. Having to use a wheelchair, braces or crutches makes an individual stand out as different. There may he obvious body differences for a student with a disability, as well as other events which mark the individual as different — drugs, daily injections, medical treatments.

Sexuality

For adolescents, body image is tied into a growing sexual awareness. The real or perceived lack of attractiveness (in normal ways) to the opposite sex begins to effect their social life. A disabled adolescent may be able to maintain normal social relationships to some sex peers but at the onset of puberty may be socially isolated from opposite sex relationships often, social restrictions are more the product of an inability to actually get to functions due to lack of transportation, or to enter the building due to inadequate physical access. The adolescent with a physical disability may exhibit inappropriate sexual behaviour for many reasons — loneliness, attention seeking, self gratification. The individual may not have been taught other social skills and so may use sexual activity as a way to draw attention to their need.

Interventions

There are many types of interventions which would be suitable during the adolescent and young adult stage, hut the suitability depends on the needs of the individual. As people mature, their needs change and vary, and no one program or design will provide the necessary needs. Housing, transportation, work, and career choices all play a role in the decisions an individual must make. Any planned interventions or programs must take into account that the individual with a disability has the right to make their own choices — and has the right to choose wrongly.

Too often, programs are offered by well meaning services which have little to do with what the individuals want the individual with a disability is often not consulted by parents, educators of medical personnel, who are used to making decisions for the child, but forget that the adult needs to make their own choices. Programming and interventions often fall by the wayside due to lack of funds, and the financial situation of the society as a whale has effect on the individual when it comes to many aspects of housing, transportation and employment. As a young person or adult with a physical disability, the individual must become aware that they have choices and may make more headway with fulfilling their needs through self help groups and consumer advocacy groups than depending on the traditional structures of school and home.

Piaget's Theory of Cognitive Development

Piaget's theory of cognitive development is age-dependent and is not a theory of emotions but of cognition. Piaget's theory suggests that the ability to reason develops through specific age-stage periods future skills depending on the mastery of those before. It is mentioned briefly here because running throughout Piaget's theory is the need for an individual to move, explore, master, construct through play and movement and the use of language to recall or categorize what has been learned. Coupled with Erikson's theory, we can have a more complete picture of the individual's need to interact with the environment. If the environment is safe — that is if caregivers have provided safety, nurturance, encouragement — then normal cognitive development can take place along with normal psychosocial development viewed in this manner, it is easy to see how physical disability can effect the psychosocial development, which, in turn, can greatly effect the cognitive growth of the individual at every stage.

Impact of Environment

Some aspects of maturation may depend solely on hormonal control —growth (size) and sexual maturation may be two sets of such strongly programmed and hormonally controlled developing systems. Severely and profoundly handicapped persons still reach sexual maturation. Among the most damaged of person, one does not find 30-year-old infants but 30-year-old cognitively or socially retarded adults. Some experiences, such as highly attentive mothers interacting with their children, help children acquire vocabulary. The environment provides opportunities for learning, or conversely, due to the physical limitations of a disability, the inability to access the environment denies opportunities for learning. Research with humans and animals show that the organism which is able to act within an environment has the opportunity to develop normal brain functioning. Experience is needed for normal functioning, and experience is provided by the environment surrounding the individual. Since all things are interrelated, the individual, — in this case we are discussing the child with a physical disability, — has effect on the caregivers and the caregiver shapes the child's environment positively or negatively.

Effect of Disability

The child with a physical disability may need assistance in gaining access to a stimulating environment. The child with a disability may need assisted exercise for muscle tone, which would otherwise be achieved through interaction with the environment for a normal child. The child's social environment may also need special enrichment and it may require extra encouragement for the child with a disability to take part in social activities and achieve mastery of skills through participation. The child with a disability needs special encouragement to explore, and perhaps special equipment. All of this certainly requires special effort on the part of the caregivers.

Emotions and Disability

When caregivers do not respond to a child's emotional displays (which may be quite different than normal in a child with a disability) distortion of emotions may develop. Studies have shown that children with handicaps may be slower to develop emotions and that the emotions may be weaker in expression than normal. The child with cerebral palsy may jerk or stiffen when touched. This may he interpreted as rejection by the caregiver; in turn the child feels rejected.

Attachment and Disability

The process of the mother/child relationship is called attachment. Bowlby, refers to this as the emotional tie between mother and child. It is often referred to as "bonding" of mother and child. The success of bonding is the source of a person's identity, the beginning of security. The attachment process, if successful, becomes the basis for the child to be able to eventually separate successfully when the time comes. Attachment, or bonding, is necessary for all children and parents. Parents of disabled children may need to be taught more about specific disabilities so that they may react more normally to their children's reactions, which parents may interpret as rejection. Parents also may need to understand more about the specific disability so that they are not fearful of touching the child, which the infant may interpret as rejection.

Self Concept

As an individual gains mastery and skills, their sense of self enlarges. The child develops a social self, a cognitive self, a physical self and a personal self. Disability may effect development in any or all of these areas through lack of interaction with the environment or rejection by caregivers or Peers. Teachers and Parents must provide support in all areas to facilitate total potential development.

Relationship of Disability to Developmental Tasks

Disabling conditions interfere with normal growth and development, psychologically, cognitively and physically. The burden of disability may cause the child much anxiety and contributes to the feeling of a lack of control over life's events. This "learned helplessness" may lead to a lack of motivation to do or try any new thing. Since exploration of the environment is linked to cognitive development, physical disability can negatively effect normal cognitive development even when the disability has no direct affect on mental development.

Kleinberg says, "The child faces a variety of developmental tasks. These are determined by such factors as physical maturation, increasing cognitive and communicative capacities and changing social and affective needs". According to Erikson's stages of development, tasks which must be mastered at each stage may be short circuited by the intrusion of a disability; lack of mastery of certain tasks at particular stages leads to non-mastery or the negative counterpart of each stage. The disabled child may suffer more from the lack of mastery of certain tasks than from the disability itself.

COUNSELLING CONSIDERATIONS

School counsellors, regular classroom teachers, school support personnel as well as community therapists and counsellors may all eventually deal with individuals who have a disability. With the focus on mainstreaming physically and mentally disabled students into the regular classroom whenever appropriate and possible, classroom teachers and school counsellors who have had no special education training are brought face to face with individuals with disabilities. This encounter may challenge some attitudes which the teacher, counsellor and support staff may never had to give thought to until it happens.

An individual with a disability may have learned to cope well with the problems caused by the disability if help is needed it may be due to other problems from other sources. As mentioned above, it is often not the disability itself which causes the greatest problems but the environment, the attitudes of others toward the disability, or the lack of appropriate support services available, such as housing or transportation.

A disability can be defined as an inability to perform a certain task. Some individuals cannot walk, some cannot talk, some cannot see—and there are tasks associated with each ability that those individuals cannot perform. A handicap is not so easily defined; poverty can be handicap, lack of education can be a handicap. Handicaps have more to do with the environment than the individual. In an adjusted environment a person with a disability has no handicap. These definitions are somewhat interchangeable, and for the sake of not repeating the same word over and over again, one is often used in place of the other. Yet, there is much truth to the two definitions which help define our attitude toward disability.

Attitudes and Psychological Behaviour

Attitude and the use of language which reflects our attitudes may be a bigger burden than the individual's physical disability. This section will discuss some of the negative attitudes held by individuals towards people with disabilities, much of which is formed by misconceptions and misinformation about specific disabilities and their effects on the human body and mind. Anyone who will be dealing with an individual with a disability must first come to understand what their own attitude towards disability is, where it came from and how to deal with the attitude in a more positive manner. Language reflects how we think, and the use of language has effect on attitude. The phrase "person with a disability" focuses on the person, first, who has a disability second. Phrases like "confined to a wheelchair" seem negative beside "uses a wheelchair for mobility", and the wholesale term "the disabled" is much less personal and individual than "people who have disabilities". The use of the more positive and personal description reflects our concern with the person.

Composition of Attitude

Attitudes may be thought of as positive or negative emotional reactions to an object, accompanied by specific beliefs. People hold many attitudes toward a wide range of topics, in varying intensities. The strength of the attitude often depends on early learning experiences, available factual information, influence of significant others and the beliefs of the larger community. Less than a decade ago, researchers were concluding "that more than 504 of the people surveyed express slightly positive attitudes toward disabled people" and "research demonstrates generally negative and stereotypical attitudes from the general public toward the disabled".

Since then, individuals like Terry Fox and Rick Hansen have positively affected the world view of what persons with disabilities can accomplish. As well, the media and government have paid attention, generally, to language used to describe the person with a disability. Such changes have come about through the efforts of the disabled themselves; legislation concerning education and employment also has effect on the behaviour of the system. The general view of the person with a disability is less intelligent, less happy, less likable than a "normal" person. Such negative attitudes are usually based on myth, false assumptions and stereotypes. Stereotypical views of people with disabilities are that the person is different, which contributes to social isolation.

Effect of Attitude on Self Concept

Self concept is created largely through our interaction with others. The feedback we receive from those with whom we interact give us a picture of ourselves as cheerful, shy, friendly, etc. Some of this feedback comes from the non-verbal messages we receive, such as facial expression, and body language. Society' expectations of us shape our behaviour. Many individuals with disabilities learn early in life that they have a negative role in this society. They have received negative feedback about their worth, both verbally and non-verbally. Their response is often passivity, rigid thinking, and failure to take part in life — because the expectations placed on the individual with a disability are negative.

Negative attitude can be more debilitating and damaging to a person than the physical disability itself. School aged youth, who are involved in the development of self identity, learning social skills as well as academic growth are most susceptible to devaluation by their peers and adults around them. When a child's interaction is limited to their family that experience may be supportive and non-threatening. Because the environment has been supportive; they may not perceive themselves as disabled; as the child's world grows larger, the generally negative attitude that society holds towards disability has its effect on the individual. Rejection by peers has a profound negative effect on self confidence and self esteem. Avoidance by peers and teachers, coupled with lowered expectations by adults about them all hamper motivation to achieve and participate.

Peer Attitude

The first and major influence on the child is the family, the next most important environment is school. When the child with a disability enters the regular classroom, it may be their first non-family contact, as well as their first experience in a non-special classroom filled with able bodied peers. The initial response, on both sides, may be apprehension due to an unfamiliar situation. Students with disabilities may be isolated or rejection by their peers, and in general, the more visible the handicap, the more rejection and isolation. Because children are generally concerned with physical skills and activities, perhaps being unable to take part means, to the student's pears, that the child is incapable of any activity.

Educator Attitude

The effect of teacher attitude has been well studied, but the effect of counsellor attitude has received less attention. We know from research that teacher attitude has considerable impact on students; eye contact and conscious or unconscious positive reinforcement all effect how students respond. The expectation of the teacher has positive or negative effect on the student; the child with a disability is no different in their responses to their teacher. If a teacher has fears, holds stereotypes about disability, or has lowered expectations of a student who has a disability, these are conveyed to the student, who responds with apathy, lowered self-expectations and a feeling of helplessness.

Thirty years ago, handicapped individuals in a regular school system were viewed as different and unable to meet regular goals in school. Rules, then, were changed for the person with a disability. The advent of the '60s and '70s saw less emphasis on special education, especially separate education, and the beginning of legislation regarding mainstreaming physically disabled children into regular school.

Simply legislating the rights of handicapped individuals to receive education alongside their able bodied peers does not take care of the problems which plague regular classroom teachers. Lack of preparation time, overcrowded classes and inadequate time schedules are problems for all teachers, but the addition of a student with a disability into the classroom intensifies the problems with time and discipline all teachers have.

Regular classroom teachers, unlike special education teachers, rarely have exposure to students with disabilities. Any introduction to disabilities may have been through texts which present stereotypical views of disabilities as "problems". The text may focus on low intellect, low achievement and disruptive behaviour of special students with disabilities; such labeling and stereotyping may lead regular teachers to believe that students with disabilities will be difficult to teach. This may result in lowered expectations in many areas, including social skills. If a student has been previously labelled, reduced expectations may be the result.

When a teacher is faced with a student with a disability, that teacher must have a willingness to accept such a student into their classroom. Teacher's educational backgrounds and knowledge about disabilities is a factor in development of positive attitudes. In-service training to develop teacher skills are seen by regular classroom teachers as useful, and in-service training has a positive impact on attitude change.

Counsellor attitudes to Disability

We can assume that counsellors and teachers, like other humans, have both negative and positive attitudes towards disability, and have had both negative and positive experiences. A counsellor or teacher who will be dealing with students with disabilities must examine their attitudes closely prior to contact. Honorable intentions to help will be useless if the unspoken attitude is negative, or one of pity or dismay. The unspoken attitude is more likely to be conveyed clearly through body language, actions and non-verbal communication.

The job of teaching positive attitude to a student's peers cannot leave the counsellor or teacher unaffected. If a teacher or counsellor is gathering together accurate information about specific disabilities, they come to know more and more about how negative attitude affects the person with the disability. In fact, any school personnel who deals with a student with a disability can be perceived as a role model for all students and the task of a role model is a serious one. Attitude is a major factor in dealing successfully with a student with a disability.

Not only must the counsellor or teacher come to terms with their personal attitude toward disability, but they must also foster a positive environment which would allow change in negative attitude. This may be done by direct intervention through programming, workshops and in-servicing of fellow professionals. Such programs and in-services would focus on overcoming negative attitudes and may be presented to the student's peers, teachers, counsellors, administrators and school support staff.

Making Attitude Changes

Two general means of changing negative attitudes according to Lomhana are contact with persons with disabilities and the dissemination of accurate information about specific disabilities.

Contact

Interaction between persons who have disabilities and non-disabled people is vital to reverse the strongly entrenched social stereotypes. The differences are minimized when disabled and able bodied people interact; anxiety and fears on both sides lessen. Exposure through such organized events as panel discussion with panelists who are disabled but active and independent can do much to educate the able bodied about the day to day barriers faced by persons with disabilities.

Contact is most effective when prolonged and on a personal, interactive level. A creative counsellor or teacher can find many well designed programs available through the school system to foster positive contact, or can approach individuals and associations in the community to help them do so.

Information

Accurate, clear information about specific disabilities can decrease anxiety and increase awareness. Teachers and counsellors may become less fearful of dealing with disabilities when supported by access to accurate information. Myths and misinformation can be dispelled and confidence can be fostered. Personal information about the experience of the person with a disability can also point out that human problems are all the same and that people with disabilities and able bodied people are more alike than different. Adolescent and adult literature written about or by persons with disability can be used as a resource to educate and change attitude.

Contact Plus Information

To foster the most positive environment for changing negative attitude to positive, a combination of contact and information is best. A program or in-service which includes information plus personal contact with persons with disability, such as a speaker or a visit by a person with a disability, makes for a lasting change of attitude.

Counsellor Role in Attitude Change

It is often the school counsellor's job to provide in-service training and information about disability attitudes and resources for the classroom teacher. If the classroom teachers feel competent and well supported, they may be more willing to accept students with disabilities and have a more positive attitude toward disability in general. Attitudes are complex because of the influence that attitudes have on the individual, counsellors as well as teachers need to be ready to foster positive attitudes toward persons with disabilities.

In an ideal society, all would accept one another despite differences; but we are not yet in an ideal society. Negative attitudes exist, and are often thoughtlessly promoted and expressed. They have a profound effect on the individual. Some attitudes which are negative are often not overly expressed, but are evident in negative behaviour. It is often the action rather than the word which carries the message. Counsellors, teachers, and other educational support personnel need to understand and come to terms with their own attitudes regarding disability.

To be able to deal effectively with persons with disabilities, the counsellor and teacher needs to realize that their attitudes will come through to the student with a disability in both verbal and non-verbal ways. Teachers and counsellors need to have a clear understanding of various disabilities, what the effect of the disability may have on the person, and at the same time know that individuals with disabilities have common human needs and are more alike than different. As well as understanding and coming to terms with their own personal attitude, the effective counsellor and teacher must have an understanding of how individuals with disabilities, and their families, cope with life with a handicap.

All humans have basic needs of security, affection, belonging and achievement. There are two myths surrounding disability that most counsellors, teachers and the general public have come to believe. The first myth is that the existence of a disability makes the person with the disability different from able bodied people. The second myth is that having a disability makes all persons with disabilities the same. Neither is true, though there are certain differences in how people cope with the environment when a disability is present, and there are certainty common experiences among people who have similar disabilities. To counsel persons with disabilities and be helpful, teachers and school counsellors will have to identify the true counselling needs of students with disabilities.

Counselling Needs of Disabled Children

Many persons with disabilities successfully come to terms with the disability, particularly those with conditions which began at birth. Their counselling needs will centre around normal developmental concerns which students in their age group may normally have. Other students with disabilities may have issues which are generated because of the presence of a disability, such as issues about body image, self concept and attitudes of others towards them. They may have family problems due to the disability which are more 'debilitating' than the physical handicap.

Personal Adjustment to Disability

Personal adjustment to disability is closely linked to the reactions of the student's parents, family members and society at large.

Adjustment and acceptance to disability is affected by the way society adjusts and accepts the person who has a disability.

Part - Not the Whole

The person with a disability needs to see the disability as a part of them, not the whole. Handicapping conditions can overwhelm the entire self concept; when this happens, the person often develops unnecessary psychological dependence on others, feelings of depression, loss of motivation, and a feeling of powerlessness. The disability becomes the focus of the individual's life, their whole identity. The disability becomes the reason they cannot achieve, are not loved, do not belong. The focus of counselling may be, in this case, to help the individual identify all the other things they are, their strengths, and take the emphasis off the disability.

Ignoring the Disability

At the other end of the Spectrum from the disability being the total focus of the person's life, the individual may deny the existence of the disability. They desire to he "just like everyone else". Plans and dreams are made without taking into account the effect of the disability. No coping strategies can be developed if the disability is denied, and constant failures to accomplish what has been planned lead to frustration, anger and unnecessary problems and delays. The individual who denies the existence of a disability, or denies the severity of it often places themselves in situations which are destined for failure. The focus of counselling in this case may be to help the individual find their true limitations and match their interests and skills with ability.

Coping

When does the counsellor know that an individual is coping well with a disability? There are some positive signs that tell a counsellor whether or not an individual is coping positively with life, according to Roesseler and Bolton, in their text "Psychosocial Adjustment to Disability".

Signs of Coping:

1. The individual's values enlarge to encompass more than their personal disability and its effect on them.
2. The effects of the disability are contained and the individual is open to learning new skills to help overcome their limitations.
3. The disability is seen as an inconvenience, and is not seen as devaluing the person's worth.
4. Other values are more important than physical perfection; kindness, wisdom, effort are seen as important.
5. The individual realizes that not all life is determined by disability.
6. Individuals stop comparing themselves with outside sources and look to inward assets and begin to develop them

Counsellors and teachers who deal with individuals with disabilities should also be sensitive to signs that a person is not coping positively with their disability. Any individual with a disability, considering all that they may have to deal with on a daily basis, may on occasion succumb to feeling of being overwhelmed and cannot cope for a short period of time. Some individuals may be completely overcome by the feeling of not being able to cope, and there are some signals which suggest that the individual is not coping well.

Signs of Not Coping:

1. Individuals act as if the disability did not exist, and no effort is made to accommodate for the disability.
2. Normal standards are idolized.
3. What an individual can accomplish, what they physically can do, is ignored. New skills are not accepted as valuable.

4. Deficiencies are compensated for by exaggerated striving. This puts extra stress on the individual to overachieve in some specific area — and this is often encouraged and praised by adults as being good.

Personality of disability

The results of numerous studies reviewed by Roessler and Boltonsuggest that there is no "personality of disability". Vash, a psychologist who herself is severely disabled, agrees. The teacher or counsellor cannot expect all persons with disabilities to be similar, nor can they expect people with certain disabilities to exhibit certain personality traits. Labeling and stereotyping of persons with disabilities by the medical profession and other professionals for the sake of convenience has generally led to the acceptance of the belief that certain disabilities go along with certain personality types. Rather, Roessler id Bolton suggest that the following has shown to be true:

1. Specific disabilities are not associated with certain personality types.
2. The degree or severity of a disability does not relate to the degree of psychological adjustment -an individual with a minor disability may be less able to cope with its effects than a severely disabled person.
3. There are a wide range of individual reactions — two persons with very similar disabilities may react altogether differently.

Counsellor Role in Personal Adjustment

Counsellors and teachers can he supportive to the individual as the person with a disability evaluates themselves. Counsellors can challenge the student at the appropriate developmental level and teachers can provide success oriented training. The most important thing to remember is that the person is an individual and that needs are individual. Buscaglia stresses that the professional needs to keep constantly in mind that each person is unique, that persons with disabilities are people first and disabled second. One of the most difficult thoughts to keep in mind is that the person with a disability has human needs and has a right to choose wrongly, a right to fail and a right to suffer.

Right to Choose

Like all human beings, people with disabilities have the right to decide what is right for them, and when the environment is supportive they also may have their own manner of doing things. This idea may cause friction between the individual and the helpers when the non-disabled feels the need to impose their ways of functioning on the person with the disability. Counsellors and teachers must be ready to broaden their view of how things are done and be ready to accept the individual's way of accomplishing the task.

Counsellors, teachers and parents are more effective when they remember that the individual with a disability also has the right to honest information about their condition, about their ability to do and achieve. False praise, false hope and false dreams may do more damage than good. Honesty about the disability and its effects does more than pretense about what the disability is and what its limitations may be. Implicit in all counselling is the belief that the individual has the right and ability to determine the course of their life. The counsellor or teacher must have respect for the individual's feelings and allow them responsibility for their own actions. Fostering independence rather than dependence is the key to the individual's success as they take part in living their life.

Factors Affected by Disability

There is a lack of evidence that there is a personality type related to disability, but disability does have an impact on the personality. These differences may separate students with disabilities from their able bodied peers.

Maturity

Students with physical handicaps may be generally less mature than non-handicapped students. This may be due to social isolation and opportunity to interact with peers of the same age.

Relationships

Persons with disabilities may have more problems establishing social relationships. This may be due to social isolation as well, but may also be affected by society's view of what qualities a person should have.

Emotions

Children with disabilities experience greater anxiety, conflict and defensiveness, and may he more inhibited than non-handicapped children. This, in part, may be due to their experience with negative attitudes of peers and significant others. Knowing about specific disabilities is important for the counsellor or teacher since characteristics of specific disabilities can limit a person's physical or academic ability, and directly effect the individual's self concept and body image. Some general assumptions may be made about specific disabilities, which can serve as a starting point to counselling. Identifying such things as methods of positive or negative coping skills may help the counsellor, but it is best to keep in mind that it is the existence of the disability which has the greater impact than the type or severity of the physical involvement.

Learned Helplessness

A problem which counsellors and teachers should be alerted to is the possibility that the individual with a disability is overcome with a feeling of helplessness. This syndrome is a theory of Martin Seligman. Seligman's basic theory is that the experience of not being able to control the environment, or learning that events are uncontrollable, leads to a psychological state of helplessness, which may not be related to the real ability of the individual. If a person comes to believe that his or her actions will not affect the environment, the likelihood that they will even attempt a response decreases, and the attitude will become "Why bother? It won't make any difference what I do." If actions have no effect, the next logical step is to cease all action.

If a child learns early in life that outcomes are independent of their response or request, they stop responding and it is difficult in later life to attempt to control situations. The syndrome of learned helplessness has effect on cognitive growth and may cause effective disturbances — the child may seem non-responsive, uninterested in life around them and dull. The feeling of helplessness is self perpetuating. Anxiety, frustration or fear is the result. If the feelings of no control persist, depression may be the end result. Learned helplessness undermines motivation and retards the ability to perceive success.

Seligman believes that motivation and emotion are influenced by environment. A child whose environment does not respond to their needs comes to believe in their own helplessness. Being helpless in one situation leads to the feeling of helplessness in another situation — feelings of learned helplessness are frequently transferred to other settings.

This learned helplessness has behaviours which a counsellor or teacher may observe. Individuals, and their families, may have been in countless situations in which they have no choices, in which their desires have no effect on the outcome. As a result, they have learned to react with helplessness and this may transfer to situations in which decisions must be made or action must be taken.

Symptoms of Learned Helplessness.

1. Few voluntary responses, only answers to direct inquiries.
2. Negative thinking and difficulty learning how to act to effect the outcome.
3. Passivity in all situations.
4. Increase of all of the above over time.
5. Depressed appetite, sexual interest, less socialization, lack of self care, nó desire to put out any energy.
6. Physiological changes such as weight loss or gain.

Seligman feels that learned helplessness has its roots in infant development for the child with a disability. When an infant's environment responds, the child has a sense of mastery The helplessness syndrome can result from separation from mother, from stimulus deprivation due to isolation, or from a combination of these things. Individuals experiencing reactions to grief and loss may also exhibit symptoms of the helplessness syndrome.

To overcome the feelings of helplessness, children need warning clues about coming events, such as physically painful treatments, or parent's departure. The child needs to predict events; children can deal with unpleasant events and cope better if they are given a warning and an honest explanation. What a counsellor or teacher may interpret as apathy on the part of the student with a disability may be more attributed to the helplessness syndrome; what may seem like an inability to learn may be the effect of this syndrome as well.

Adolescent Issues

Though development is effected by disability at each age, adolescents and their families have some special additional problems. Adolescence is the time when individuals are attempting to gain their independence from family and establish their future identity.

Disability as an Excuse

An adolescent may come to use their disability as an excuse to avoid social contact and school. They may become ashamed of their disability, ashamed of being different. They may retreat into a world of home, hospital, or other safe institutions. They may even refuse medication or treatment to bring about a health crisis, so they may regain their safe haven through hospitalization. Physiotherapy may be refused as well, because of its focus on the disability. This is often done to avoid the critical stares of peers, the questions or comments about the disability.

Attitudes of Others

The opinion of others is important to adolescents. They form their view of self through comments and attitudes of others. The differences of having a disability, using a wheelchair, having problems of muscle control, often stigmatizes the individual, giving rise to feelings of shame. The move from a neighbourhood school into a less personal selling of high school can be a devastating experience. Teachers, counsellors, school support staff and parents can help the young adolescent make the transition with support, encouragement and care. Older adolescents may need special attention, helping them find out about themselves, their disability and what they can rather than can't do.

Defence Mechanisms

An adolescent will develop various and personally individual methods of coping with the attitudes of others and their own acceptance or nonacceptance of their disability. Defence mechanisms, methods of making reality more bearable, may include:

— Denial

— Testing Limits

— Challenging Behaviour

— Anger

— Regression

— Withdrawal

— Depression

Denial : Adolescents who are physically disabled may use denial as a protection against the devastating emotional effects of disability. Spinal cord injured individuals may refuse to believe that their condition is permanent and refuse to deal with the reality of the paralysis. At this stage, they may refuse to do daily self care, refuse physical treatments.

Denial can be a mechanism of escape — escaping the fear of death or disfigurement. Denial may be, at times, an effective and necessary coping strategy. Care should be taken when asking an individual to face reality. Too soon or too blunt an approach may leave an individual unable to cope with reality "all at once". Rather, strategies which introduce the reality of situation gently may allow for adjustment and gradual acceptance.

Testing Limits: The Stage of adolescence is the time of testing of the limit of abilities, as well as limits set by parent and schools.

Challenging Behaviour: The adolescent with a disability may carry this time of testing to the extreme. The individual may attempt things which are impossible and even put themselves in danger. They may refuse medications or supportive medical treatments and actively challenge decisions made by parents.

Anger: Adolescents with a disability may have unexpressed anger and rage at their situation and may act out physically or verbally to teachers, parents, peers or siblings. They may resort to sarcasm and name calling; their rage at their own helplessness and their embarrassment at being disabled and different may be expressed in verbal or physical abuse of others.

Regression: Pain due to disability, dependency on others for daily living tasks, and the obvious physical differences due to disability may combine to make an adolescent with a disability use regression as a coping strategy. It may he easier to retreat to an earlier age than struggle with interdependence. The individual with a disability may lack social skills, and not be used to risk taking; they may seek to be cared for and accept many parents' attempts to keep them dependent and "secure".

The normal adolescent at this stage is achieving more physical and emotional independence from parents; the physically disabled adolescent may be struggling to achieve emotional independence while needing physical dependence. Parents play an immeasurably important role in helping the physically disabled adolescent achieve a realistic, healthy balance between physical dependency and emotional independence.

Withdrawal: Choosing to drop out of school or enter into a very restricted but secure environment, such as a special school or sheltered workshop, may allow an individual a way of withdrawing which is acceptable. They may have little interest in anything, little energy to do even simple, daily routines. Parents and teachers may accept or even encourage this to protect the individual from stigmatization, feeling that it would be cruel to allow the individual to be faced with a challenge they may fail.

Depression: Times of mild depression may not be uncommon during adolescence. An individual with a disability may have bouts of severe depression. While focusing on the plans for the future, adolescents may suffer from feelings of loss, and need a time to grieve for a loss of a 'normal future'. Long term depression, including resignation and apathy, may require professional intervention. The individual may speak of suicide. Such threats should be taken seriously. Pat responses such as "you'll get over it", "it's not so bad", "you're not as bad off as some" are not helpful or realistic. The truth is that the disability exists, and it causes problems for the individual, it won't go away. Rather than platitudes, adolescents need alternate coping strategies. The opposite of challenging behaviour, depressive behaviour, may occur. Adolescents with a severe disability may feel hopeless and refuse all outside help. The loneliness, boredom and isolation associated with disability may lead to substance abuse, to help them escape a seemingly hopeless reality. Drug abuse may be easy, as the availability of pain medication or anxiety-lessening drugs may be high through prescription misuse. The stage of adolescent is the stage when planning for future in career, education and life is a focus. Choices may be limited by the extent of the disability.

The personality, interests and abilities of the individual affect choices, as well as the disability. The reality of the world of work is that those with disabilities face many barriers - actual physical barriers as well as attitudinal barriers. The individuals with disabilities — even those with mild disabilities — face discrimination on the job market. There is a need for realistic goal selling and vocational guidance for individuals with disabilities. As an adolescent reaches young adulthood, issues of career, marriage and independent living become important. Some individuals may never achieve total physical independence but should be encouraged to look to emotional independence and realistic goals — and to make their own decisions as to the course of their lives.

Adolescent Sexuality

Infancy and early childhood are less of a problem in terms of sexuality identity than the advent of puberty and adolescence. The development of secondary sexual characteristics in puberty draws attention to the fact that an individual is no longer a child. Puberty is the beginning of the time when the individual becomes very interested in bodily changes and their body image. For the most part, sexual maturation comes about for both the individual who is disabled and the individual who is able bodied.

Problems arise when adults delay sexual education, out of a tendency to treat their maturing child as the dependent infant they once were. The individual with a physical disability may be more closely supervised than an able bodied individual. This constant observation may delay or prevent the experience of self and other body exploration. An even greater problem may be the lack of peer interaction -a most important method of sexual exploration during adolescence. Erikson identifies adolescence as a time of experimentation. Adolescents withphysical handicaps are limited in opportunities for experimentation, and may have lower self esteem about sex and sexuality.

Parents often over-protect their child with a physical disability especially about sexual concerns. These needs may be unrecognized or even denied by parents who focus more on physical daily care.

Frank and open discussion of sexuality is difficult in our society, but especially so for individuals with a disability. There are many stereotypes about disability and many myths about the sexuality of persons with disability. There is an unspoken cultural belief that "the right to be sexual is reserved for young, physically flawless people". The myth that an individual who is disabled is not sexual makes it comfortable for others to deal with that individual. The adolescent with a physical disability has the same sexual needs as an able bodied person — and the same rights. Teachers, parents and support personnel are among those who may help the individual achieve a sexual identity or squelch this powerful source of human interaction through active disapproval or passive unwillingness to discuss sexual matters openly.

In the school setting, counsellors or teachers will probably be working with either one individual or with a group receiving sexuality education. The "problem" which brings an individual to counselling may not initially seem to be related to an issue of sexuality. The identified problem may range from severe acting out and inappropriate sexual behaviour to quiet withdrawal or depression.

The empathetic and open minded counsellor will allow and encourage the individual student to find a way to uncover the root of their problem. The counsellor may see such behaviour by the individual student as:

— inappropriate sexual talk or jokes
— aggressive sexual behaviour
— excessive shyness
— inability to function normally around persons of
— the opposite sex
— obsessive sexual thoughts
— fear of male teachers on the part of female
— adolescents
— fear of sexual molestation

Parents may express these fears as well, especially for females, and develop a desire to overprotect their children from all sexual or perceived sexual contact or conduct.

Issues of Sexuality

In the text Treating Families with Special Needs, it is suggested that sex counselling may be categorized into the following areas:

— Developmental problems arising from ignorance of sexual norms for adolescence.
— Health Related Problems arising from sexual self image affected by physical impairment.
— Gender Role Related Problems arising from gender

— Role stereotyping (men are aggressive, women passive).

— Life Style Problems arising from expectations not being met.

— Reproduction Problems related to birth control use.

— Sexual Trauma Problems arising from traumatic sexual experiences such as sexual assault or sexual harassment.

— Sexual Orientation Problems involving confusion about sexual orientation.

— Sexual Obsessions which are repetitive and problematic for the individual.

— An individual may have one or several problem areas. The counsellor who deals with the individual's sexuality concerns needs to be well versed, open minded and flexible.

— Techniques which work for able bodied students work for persons with a disability, with consideration for the individual frustrations caused by the handicap.

It is important that counsellors, teachers and parents recognize the right of the person with a disability to the sexual expression. It is of utmost importance that the counsellor/teacher/parent come to terms with their personal understanding of what being physically disabled, impaired or handicapped, means in issues of sexuality. It is also important that caregivers recognize that adolescents with disabilities, like all adolescents, need information about sexuality that is clear and accurate, presented to the individual in a manner appropriate to their developmental level. Truthfully, sex education should begin early in life and include social skills as well as sexual information.

Parents

Since the individual with a disability, child, adolescent or adult, usually lives with a family atmosphere, counsellors and teachers need to have some empathy with the experience of the parents. Parents are the single most important influence on the development of a child. There are many problems facing parents who give birth to a child with a disability, or whose child becomes disabled at any age. Lombara suggests that the following may be a common experience for families with individuals who have a disability:

1. Lack of professional services in many geographic areas.
2. Difficulty obtaining accurate information on disability and often difficulty obtaining an accurate diagnosis on the handicapping condition.
3. Distrust of various conflicting professional opinions as to the eventual future of their child.
4. Discouragement from over-involvement or under-involvement in their child's education or treatment.

Parents of children with disabilities share common needs with all parents. Counsellors and teachers should remember that parents know their child best, know how the child copes with life and are ultimately responsible for the implementation of treatment or suggestions from professionals. They are, in most other ways, no different than parents of non-disabled children. Parents of children born with or acquiring a disability do have some specific needs. They may need help adjusting to the disability, help to understand what the condition is and the probable outcome. They may feel a greater need to be involved in the child's life and the decision making about their child's treatments and education.

Emotional Aspects

In some cases, the emotional difficulties of the parents may be a greater problem than the child's disability. The attitude of parents significantly influences the child's development and the child's own attitude toward their disability. Parents of children with disabilities have considerable emotional stress not only because of the disability but as a result of expectations which seem to have been dashed. They may mourn the loss of their imagined child while having to deal with the severe realities of having a child with a disability. Parents need help in many ways. They may feel uncertain of their own parenting abilities and hand over the care of the child to others. Insecure parents need more moral support and concrete suggestions about the care of their child at any stage, not just directly after birth.

Counsellor Role With Parents

Parents, teachers and counsellors are part of a team concerned about the child's development. Counsellors are often asked to conduct a wide variety of services and often wind up coordinating a larger team of professionals. Parents may need help understanding and coming to terms with their own attitude towards the child and the disability they may need help exploring their own feelings as well as needing support and services from the community in times of crisis and on an ongoing supportive basis. Counselling for grief issues is important - grief may cause ongoing depression. Each transition the child makes or misses may make issues of mourning resurface.

Counsellors may often act as a consultant for educational and social needs and may be asked to provide information to help parents cope with their feelings. The counsellor or teacher of a student with a disability must be willing to accept their own limitations and be willing to create an accepting environment for the child and the parents.

Siblings

A school counsellor who may deal with persons with disabilities may eventually have to deal with the whole family, including the siblings of the person with the disability. Individual able bodied students may have problems which have their root in the fact that they are siblings of persons with disabilities. There is some research regarding siblings of persons with disabilities;

the majority of it comes from research on persons with mental handicaps. Seligman and Grassman found that the following points are relevant to brothers and sisters of persons with disabilities.

1. Some siblings benefit from the experiences of having a brother or sister who is handicapped. They are more tolerant, more aware of existing prejudice and may be more certain about their own future goals.
2. Some normal siblings were harmed from the experience; they were bitter about the family situation, felt guilt over their feelings towards parents and the handicapped child, and felt fear about the possibility of being "defective".
3. Some were often exempt from the care for the disabled sibling, whereas daughters were more active in daily care.
4. Parental acceptance of the individual with the disability was a major factor affecting acceptance of the disabled person by their siblings.
5. Upper income families had more opportunity for outside care and support but there was also guilt over this.
6. Lower income families had to care more for the disabled member themselves — larger families fared better because they shared the responsibility.

Brothers and sisters were found to respond differently to having a disabled sibling, and lower income families had other day to day concerns about survival issues as well as issues surrounding the disability of one member.

Feelings of Able Bodied Siblings

Siblings hold many irrational fears surrounding disability, such as fear of catching it. They may also develop similar symptoms in order to gain attention from parents. Older children may harbour feelings of anger toward the situation, and guilt about their feelings of anger. They may feel ignored and unappreciated, and may feel or actually be isolated because of their sibling's disability. Parents insensitivity contributes to the anger and resentment felt by an able bodied sibling. Parents sometimes embrace the myth that their handicapped child is the only needy one.

Aims of Counselling With Siblings

The feelings of able bodied siblings may be ignored and negated, or punished by parents. The counsellor who works with siblings of children with disabilities should keep in mind that the able bodied child may have unexpressed anger and that they need to come to terms with their feelings, learning that feelings of anger and guilt are normal, and that expression of this anger is necessary.

The family needs encouragement to communicate — open communication about the nature of the handicap is essential; the non-disabled members of the family need to know such things as the cause of the disability, the outcome, how society perceives the disabled member. The able bodied family members need reassurance that they are loved for themselves, just as the disabled member needs to know they are loved for themselves. Seligman suggests that counselling with able bodied siblings of children with disabilities has four major aims:

1. Siblings should come to a deeper and broader understanding of their personal feelings towards the disabled family member.
2. Able bodied siblings should develop skills and attitudes which enable them to handle problems and feelings constructively and be able to plan how to solve such future
3. The counsellor may help the able bodied siblings make future career and life plans which are realistic and take into account the needs and desires of the individual
4. The counsellor can assist the family in strengthening the relationship between the able bodied sibling and other family members.

4

EVALUATION

Evaluation describes the process of examining information about an evaluand (thing being evaluated). Evaluation is often used in an educational context, but applies to many other areas, such as computer science, business, and engineering. Often evaluation is confused with assessment. However, evaluation is broader than assessment and involves making a judgement as to the effectivness of an assessment. A successful evluation should be transferable and confirmable (varifiable).

NATURE OF EVALUATION

The discipline of evaluation is devoted to the systematic determination of merit, worth, or significance. It is divided into fields according to the type of entity evaluated for example, program evaluation, or personnel evaluation and there are more than twenty of these recognized fields of evaluation. Some specific aspects of evaluation methodology have been developed to solve problems of evaluation in only one or a few of these fields (e.g., bias control in panel selection, systematic side-effect identification in program evaluation, road-testing techniques in product evaluation).However, the underlying logic of the process of evaluation for example, the difference between merit and worth, or between grading and ranking and a substantial portion of its general methodology (e.g., techniques of measurement, causality determination, applying the requirement of informed consent) are shared across all or many of these fields.

Many of these general techniques (the 'general methodology') come from the applied social sciences, and are learnt by students in the normal course of education in those fields. But the logic of evaluation has been developed for and applies only to evaluation; and the field-specific methodologies of evaluation must also be mastered in order to deal with evaluation in the fields to which they apply. Teaching evaluation therefore focuses on these evaluation-specific topics, the general logic and the special methodologies.

Evaluation in applied psychology

Just as it was previously found that a good grasp of probability and statistics had become an essential tool for a great deal of work in applied psychology, so we now find that a knowledge of the logic of evaluation and of some of its specialized methodologies are increasingly crucial for much investigation in applied social science. Funding agencies letting evaluation contracts or assigning staff to evaluation increasingly want to know not only what is happening when an intervention is supported, and exactly what causes the results familiar questions for applied social science but also

(i) whether the intervention is worth what it cost,

(ii) whether there are unintended bad results as well as planned good ones,

(iii) whether the methods used in the intervention were proper by current professional and ethical standards, and

(iv) whether there are better ways to do the same thing. This is the domain of evaluation, and none of those questions can be answered reliably without some use of its special logic and its special methodologies.

In order to reach evaluative conclusions it is usually necessary to establish or identify two kinds of premises: factual premises (e.g., about nature, performance or impact) and value premises (e.g.,about the relevant legal or scientific principles).There are usually many of these premises in the evaluation of complex entities (or entities with complex functions),and there may be several hundred of them. To obtain the required kind of overall evaluative conclusion, it is typically necessary to combine all of them by means of what is called 'the internal synthesis process.'This synthesis step is one of the key logical processes in evaluation and is a long way from the simple deduction and statistical inference that are more common elements in scientific inference.

Factual premises in a field like program evaluation are commonly established using the standard procedures of social science, sometimes with the assistance of other disciplines such as history and jurisprudence. Value premises usually come from one or more of eight sources:

— legal principles;

— scientific and mathematical standards of truth (especially relevant when the program disseminates information or is based on scientific theories or common assumptions);

— professional, cultural, or organizational standards of proper conduct (e.g., the APA testing standards);

— needs assessments;

— definitions (which provide linguistic standards of propriety);

— market research;

— logic; and

— ethics.

Again, the social sciences are a common source for several of these types of values e.g., the scientific standards of truth used in judging the quality of the assertions or assumptions built into or propagated by the program. From psychology, we frequently encounter premises about maturational rates, cognitive processes, or leadership research. The logic of evaluation comes in with the frequent need to balance these value considerations when they conflict: that logic originates in jurisprudence and moral reasoning, but has been expanded to cover other fields of evaluation besides these, e.g., evaluation of alternatives in high-stakes decision-making.

Evaluation Field

The better-known fields of applied evaluation vary considerably in quality as well as in their relevance to and dependence on the social sciences. While most of program and personnel evaluation is heavily dependent on the social sciences and capable of a high degree of objectivity and utility, others vary independently on these dimensions. Some come close to being pseudo-evaluative (e.g., wine tasting, art criticism), some are partially valid (architectural criticism, portfolio management, literary criticism), and some support highly valid evaluations but are not dependent on the social sciences (e.g., the reviews done by appellate courts, the evaluations of claimed proofs of Fermat's Theorem in mathematical journals).Eight of these applied fields are of particular importance, for practical or logical reasons: they fall into two groups. The 'Big Six' are the fields of program, personnel, performance, policy, proposal, and product evaluation (the latter including technology assessment).The 'Super Two' are:

1. intradisciplinary evaluation the evaluation of the entities that are the currency of a discipline's economy such as theories, hypotheses, classifications, data, research designs and results, practitioners, contributions, and journals and of the discipline itself: and
2. meta-evaluation, the evaluation of evaluations themselves, a practice that demonstrates the reflexive nature of evaluation and the reflective integrity of its practitioners. The first is the backbone of all disciplines it is what makes

them disciplines. The second is the backbone of evaluation it is what makes it consistent by making it practice what it preaches.

Of the Big Six fields the conventional fields of evaluation program evaluation is the one with the largest associated job market at the moment, with personnel evaluation (an Human Resources staple) and performance evaluation (especially in the educational area, where its academic fountain is often referred to as 'tests and measurement') coming next

TYPES OF EVALUATION

There are three main types of evaluation: formative, summative, diagnostic, criterion and normative.

— *Formative evaluation*: It is an ongoing classroom process that keeps the students and educators informed of students' progress. The main purpose of formative evaluation is to improve instruction. This type of evaluation helps the teachers understand the degree to which students are learning the course material and the extent to which their knowledge, understanding, skills, and attitudes are developing. Students are provided direction for future learning and are encouraged to take responsibility for their own progress.

— *Summative evaluation*: It is a type of evaluation used at the end of a term, course, or program for purposes of grading, certification, evaluation of progress, or research on the effectiveness of a curriculum, course of study, or educational plan. The essential characteristic of summative evaluation is that a judgment is made about the student, teacher, or curriculum with regard to the effectiveness of learning or instruction, after the learning or instruction has taken place. In fifth-grade arithmetic, for example, summative evaluation would have as its major purpose to determine the degree to which a student can translate word problems into quantitative solutions or his accuracy and rapidity in handling division. Further purposes would be to grade pupils and the report to parents or administrators.

— *Criterion-based evaluation*: Evaluation is criterion-based when it seeks to assess a learner's performance level based on success criteria implicitly or explicitly defined according to the objectives. It does not involve comparing a learner's performance level with other learners' performance levels. It seeks to determine the extent to which goals and objectives targeted by a particular course have been reached.

— *Diagnostic-based evaluation*: Evaluation is diagnostic when it aims at assessing the individual features of learners in relation to the requirements of courses or curricula. Therefore, the goal of diagnostic evaluation is to identify the distinguishing features of the subject targeted by the evaluation as such features may determine the expected results. Diagnostic evaluation may be conducted at the beginning of any new course or curriculum. In such cases, its aim is to ascertain whether the learner has the skills required to enrol for the course. Diagnostic evaluation may also be implemented during or at the end of a particular course.

— *Normative evaluation*: An evaluation is normative when it compares the performances of a particular learner to the performances of the other learners of the same level or class taken as the reference group. The merit-based listing of learners relates to such a normative evaluation. It is important to remember that different assessment techniques are selected or devised to gather information related to how well students are achieving the learning objectives or the curriculum and to the type of learning outcome (knowledge, understanding, skill, attitude, value, or process), the subject area content, the instructional strategies used, the students' levels of development, and the specific purpose of evaluation. It is also important when evaluating student progress to relate it to the Common Essential Learning's, Gender Equity, Resource Based Learning and

Aboriginal Perspectives. These program considerations aid in a full understanding of the course presented to them. They should be able to differentiate between bias and non-bias information or information that is leading or not equitable in gender or race. These are important qualities they can be further assessed on.

PHASES OF THE EVALUATION PROCESS

Evaluation can be viewed as cyclical process: preparation, assessment, evaluation, and reflection. The evaluation process involves the teacher as a decision maker throughout the four phases.

Preparation Phase

Decisions are made which identify what is to be evaluated, the type of evaluation (formative, summative, or diagnostic) to be used, the criteria against which student learning outcomes will be judged, and the most appropriate assessment techniques with which to gather information on student progress. The teacher's and student's decisions in this phase form the basis for the remaining phases.

Assessment Phase

The teacher identifies information-gathering techniques, constructs or selects instruments, administers them to the student, and collects the information on student learning progress. The teacher continues to make decisions in this phase. The identification and elimination of bias (such as gender and cultural) from the assessment techniques and instruments, and the determination of where, when, and how assessments will be conducted are examples of important considerations for the teacher.

Evaluation Phase

The teacher interprets the assessment information and makes judgements about student progress. Based on the judgements or evaluations, teachers make decisions about student learning programs and report on progress to students, parents, and appropriate school personnel.

Reflection Phase

This phase allows the teacher to consider the extent to which the previous phases in the evaluation process have been successful. Specifically, the teacher evaluates the utility and appropriateness of the assessment techniques used. Such reflection assists the teacher in making decisions concerning improvements or modifications to subsequent teaching and evaluation.

All four phases of the evaluation process are included in formative, diagnostic, and summative evaluation.

FORMATIVE EVALUATION

Formative evaluation is particularly useful for evaluating long-term conflict resolution work in intractable conflicts. In these conflicts, interconnected disputes, with multiple causes and systemic impact, the dynamics, participants, and even issues may change over time, and thus conflict resolution activities need to refocus on the new realities as they emerge. In fact, it may be useful to conduct repeated formative evaluations periodically throughout the life-cycle of a long-term conflict resolution process. At its most basic, *formative evaluation* is an assessment of efforts prior to their completion for the purpose of improving the efforts. It is a technique that has become well developed in the education and training evaluation literature.

For conflict resolution efforts addressing intractable conflicts, appropriate formative evaluation can be a powerful part of an intervention strategy. By assessing efforts, and adjusting strategies in response to the assessment, conflict resolution practitioners can better respond to the changes in conflict dynamics that occur in intractable conflicts. Conflict resolution practitioners can thus recalibrate their efforts to better respond to current conflict dynamics, and make other mid-course corrections as necessary. In addition, by monitoring implementation through a formative evaluation, conflict resolution practitioners can also recognize opportunities to fine tune or even redefine their strategies. Finally, by involving the parties in the formative evaluation effort, conflict resolution practitioners can develop additional commitment on the part of participants and funders to conflict resolution.

For conflict resolution work, formative evaluation offers an opportunity to keep everyone on board, and either keep on track or determine when it is necessary to switch tracks. Robert Stakes is quoted as saying, "When the cook tastes the soup, that's formative. When the guests taste the soup, that's summative." Formative evaluation can take many forms. It is most often conducted by the conflict resolution practitioner (the cook in Stakes' metaphor), but many involve all the stakeholders.

Key Roles for formative evaluation

Formative evaluation encourages a process of reflective practice. More specifically, formative evaluation can strengthen conflict management systems in many ways. These include:

— *Rapid feedback*: Primarily, formative evaluation provides *rapid feedback* on the efficacy of conflict management and resolution work. While a project in is progress, a formative evaluation process provides feedback on how the work is going.

— *Documentation*: A formative evaluation process can *document* how conflict management and resolution work is proceeding, what techniques are used, what problems encountered, and what impacts are made in early and middle stages of work. Such documentation may be useful

— *Planning*: Formative evaluations assist with *planning* and allows for revision of or recommitment to plans. Formative evaluation involves a comparison of program implementation with program plans. It also allows for a reconsideration of program goals and plans. When a formative evaluation reveals that a program has diverged from previous plans, those involved in the work can choose to revise plans to take advantage of new opportunities or return to previous plans in order to respond to current realities. Information from formative evaluation can provide input to future planning and implementation, thus forming the project's future.

The rapid feedback, documentation, and planning roles of formative evaluation make formative evaluation a useful component of reflective conflict resolution practice.

Types of formative evaluation

There are many evaluation tools — observation, in-depth interviews, surveys, focus groups, analysis, reports, and dialogue with participants, each of which can be part of formative evaluation. Depending on the goals of the formative evaluation, it may emphasize one or more of these tools. Within the range of formative evaluation approaches, there are four main goals for formative evaluation, each of which may be more or less emphasized depending on the program needs. Each of these approaches to formative evaluation are briefly summarized below, with a focus on their applicability to formative evaluation of conflict resolution work in intractable conflicts.

— *Planning evaluation*: Planning evaluation clarifies and assesses a project's plans. Are the goals and timelines appropriate? Are the methods utilized to reach the goals appropriate? In addition, a planning evaluation can lay the groundwork for future formative and summative evaluations by developing indicators and benchmarks. In conflict resolution work, it is often useful to include a planning evaluation component in order to ensure that all stakeholders share common enough visions of the project plans. A planning evaluation can be a form of consensus building amongst those involved in conflict resolution.

— *Implementation evaluation*: An implementation evaluation focuses on the extent to which a program is proceeding according to plan. Information about ways in which a program is not proceeding according to plan can be used to either revise plans or to revise programming. In conflict resolution assessment, implementation evaluation can be a useful component to feed into a planning-focused evaluation. Where work is not proceeding according to plan, participants and facilitators can use an implementation evaluation with a planning focus to ask themselves why things are not going according to plan, and adjust plans or strategies accordingly.

— *Monitoring evaluation*: A monitoring evaluation is usually conducted by an outside evaluator during the course of a program. A funder may choose to monitor implementation of a conflict resolution project by visiting a workshop, checking in with participants, or talking with project personnel. For long-term conflict resolution work, a monitoring evaluation can provide a funder useful reassurance that money is being well spent.

— *Progress evaluation*: A progress evaluation assesses a program's progress. The project's unique goals should serve as a benchmark for measuring progress. Information from a progress evaluation can later be used in a summative evaluation. In conflict resolution work, a progress evaluation might assess attitude change part-way through a multi-year program, providing both feedback on what's working, and evidence of impact early on in a program.

Limitations of formative evaluation

Formative evaluation by itself does not meet the needs of most conflict resolution initiatives. Formative evaluation's focus is on improving work in progress. It should be employed to the extent that it improves work. Formative evaluation is not an end in itself. Funding limitations often limit the intensity of formative evaluations. Where possible, formative evaluations should form part of funding proposals so that appropriate attention can be given to mid-course assessment and mid-course corrections in long-term conflict resolution work.

Finally, it should be acknowledged that, like all evaluations, formative evaluations may yield results that identify fundamental problems with a conflict management or resolution process. For example, when conflict management techniques are used to address a seemingly tractable dispute that is inherently part of an intractable conflict, a formative evaluation of the conflict management initiative might uncover the potential negative impacts of "successful" dispute management. In other words, where one initiative seems successful based on its own goals, formative evaluation could consider even the relevance of the goals themselves, and raise the long-term questions about dynamics which are perpetuating intractability by addressing some issues part-term.

How to conduct formative evaluations

Formative evaluations can be conducted according to varied evaluation methodologies, but should usually incorporate the following considerations:

— Involve multiple stakeholders

— Involve multiple evaluation tools

— Consider plans, implementation, monitoring, and progress.

The particular shape of a formative evaluation will depend on the context, including the program being evaluated and the resources available. A well-developed form of formative evaluation is described in the Action-Evaluation essay. Other forms of formative evaluation may be more appropriate where it is not possible to involve all stakeholders as consistently as is preferable in a full action-evaluation approach. For example, a training team might discuss amongst themselves the progress in their week-long training every evening, but involve the participants in an explicit formative evaluation for a short session in the middle of the training.

Formative evaluation does not need to take over a project and infuse itself into every aspect of the work, but should be incorporated to the extent that it can improve work. Like all types of evaluation, implementing a formative evaluation in a conflict resolution program requires resources. However, these resources can be well-spent when a formative evaluation supports the reflective practice of conflict resolution, particularly in the long-term efforts that so often focus on seemingly intractable conflicts.

SUMMATIVE EVALUATION

Summative Evaluation typically involves the preparation of a formal report outlining the impact of a program. For instance, an evaluation report will typically detail who participated in a program, what activities affected them, and what gains or improvements resulted from their participation. Often this report will include details regarding what prerequisites or conditions are essential or helpful to the replication of the program, program costs and benefits, and disaggregated results showing findings for specific subgroups of participants.

There is no crisp dividing line between formative evaluation and summative evaluation. Much of the information gathered during formative evaluation activities may be reported in formal summative reports, particularly during the early development of new programs, in order to show how the program is responding to challenges and reaching benchmarks and milestones along the way toward intended outcomes. Usually, a compelling case that your program has had a positive impact requires measurement of program targets before, during, and after implementation of the program. This requires careful program planning and early adoption of appropriate data collection methods and a management information database.

Your summative evaluation report is a showcase for outcomes associated with your program, produced independently by a respected research and development institution. NWREL's Evaluation Program maintains a large, expert staff and state of the art facilities for statistical and qualitative analysis, technical writing, and graphic display of findings. In addition to written reports, we can produce a variety of multimedia presentations of your data, suitable for use in slide shows, publication on the world wide web, etc.

Summative Evaluation and Formative Feedback

Summative evaluation is a judgment about teaching that is used to make a decision a decision about promotion, tenure, or, even, teaching awards. A summative evaluation of teaching attempts to summarize the complex phenomena of teaching. It typically consists of global ratings of teaching, thus, reducing teaching to generalities.

An example of summative evaluation is end-of-course student ratings. Student ratings instruments prompt students to rate six to ten aspects of teaching (e.g., organization, clarity, enthusiasm, etc.), and they ask students to make an over-all, summarizing judgment of the instruction. Students' ratings are then averaged and given to faculty as summaries of their teaching. The overall summary rating of instruction may even be shared with students and other faculty members. Such ratings are easily compared and then used for making decisions and answering questions of accountability.

Individual faculty members have little control in the traditional summative evaluation process. They usually do not choose the instrument by which they are evaluated; they do not choose the time of the semester at which they are evaluated; nor do they choose the groups of people (e.g., students, department chairs, administrators, or fellow faculty members) to whom the results are distributed.

Formative feedback differs from summative evaluation in several ways. In their sourcebook on formative assessment of teaching, Rando and Lenze describe formative feedback as information gathered for the purpose of improving and developing teaching. This information is meant to inform change. The feedback itself must be specific and concrete enough to suggest actions for improvement. It is typically requested well before the end of a semester of teaching, so that the faculty member may use the information to improve teaching in the current course.

For example, consider the professor who asks her students, halfway through the semester, to write a few sentences about how the current instruction has promoted or hindered learning. This faculty member has gathered information that she may now use to make teaching and learning more effective. The formative feedback process entails requesting information, making sense of the information, and implementing changes based on the information collected. This process belongs to faculty members.

They are responsible for making all decisions along the way. They may gather, analyze, and react to the information on their own; or they may decide to invite an instructional consultant to assist in this process. In the case of the professor whose students responded in writing to the current instruction, the faculty member chose the method of collecting data and, after reading students' responses, determined which of the issues would be addressed.

Several other examples of formative feedback exist. Faculty may opt to conduct classroom assessment for the purpose of improving teaching. They may ask an instructional consultant to videotape their teaching in order to reflect on teaching development. They may even invite trained facilitators to conduct small group "quality control" interviews with students. In all of these examples, only the faculty member who has initiated the formative feedback process need see the results.

Issues involved in their co-existence

The distinctions just drawn between these two concepts exist at the definitional level; but in practice, the two are intertwined. For example, how can faculty's teaching be judged fairly unless they are provided opportunities to improve and develop their teaching? A system that judges teaching without any effort to support the development of good teaching ultimately fails. Before successfully negotiating the co-existence of summative evaluation and formative feedback, at least two issues must be considered.

First, the two must reside in separate offices. If faculty are to trust formative feedback, formative feedback activities must be separated from summative evaluation activities. Consider the junior faculty member who is contemplating a midsemester review of his teaching. Not sure of the value he places on students' feedback, he wants to request that a peer visit his classroom. In order to be trusted, formative feedback must be provided by someone other than his department chair or faculty members who are responsible for his tenure review. Feedback provided by these folks, no matter how helpful and well-intended at the time, could be subconsciously held against the faculty member as examples of "inadequacies" when making summative decisions. Thus, administrators must see to it that the formative activities are in some way shielded from summative evaluation.

Second, summative evaluation must evolve. If a college truly advocates formative feedback, its summative evaluation procedures must not hamper formative efforts. That is, universities cannot uphold two climates at the same time: the punitive climate often associated with summative evaluation precludes the supportive climate necessary for formative feedback. Thus, summative evaluation systems must become more humane.

Two universities have navigated the waters between formative feedback and summative evaluation. Duquesne University added a formative feedback program to an already existing summative evaluation process. The University of Massachusetts added a new summative evaluation system to an already existing formative feedback program. These two cases offer powerful insights about the co-existence of formative feedback and summative evaluation.

Case of Duquesne University

Since 1986, Duquesne University has used end-of-semester student rating instruments for its summative evaluation of teaching. In 1989, faculty asked why there was no formal support system to assist faculty in their development as teachers. Furthermore, faculty wanted to know about alternate methods for reviewing teaching. Subsequently, the University Teaching Committee was formed to 1) create a faculty development center, 2) develop alternate means for reviewing teaching, and 3) revise old student evaluation instruments. Committee members immediately began working on plans for the "Center for Teaching Excellence." They decided its mission would be to develop and improve faculty members' teaching. The Center would offer a variety of services to faculty members, including individual consultations, classroom visitations, instructional videotaping, or midsemester formative assessment. The director of the Center was to report directly to the provost, thereby increasing the importance and visibility of the Center. While the University Teaching Committee made plans for the Center for Teaching Excellence, committee members also created new student evaluation forms and developed a Peer Review program to supplement its traditional summative evaluation procedures.

The addition of a peer review program lessened the defensiveness that had previously surrounded summative review. As the committee designed it, the peer review system consisted of three reviews. The first occurs in the first year of employment in order to acquaint faculty with the process and identify for faculty strong and weak aspects of their teaching. The next review takes place in the third year in time for third year contract renewals. The last review occurs in conjunction with the tenure decision.

In each review year, a team of two peers visits the assigned faculty member's classroom at one scheduled time and at one unannounced time. The committee developed their own observation instruments and their own evaluation process, beginning with an initial meeting look at teaching materials and objectives and ending with a feedback report to the faculty member. The summative evaluation process became more fair with the addition of the Peer Review program. Faculty realized that there were many differences between teaching in traditional classrooms and teaching in the clinical setting. Thus, the Committee developed two sets of guidelines for peer review, one for classroom settings and the other set of guidelines to accommodate clinical teaching.

Even though the Center for Teaching Excellence and the Peer Review program were connected in University legislation, the Center does not have a role in the peer review process. Faculty perceive the Center as sufficiently separate from Duquesne's summative evaluation process; thus, they trust its staff to assist them in improving teaching. Of the faculty who responded to the yearly evaluation of the Center, just under 100 percent said, "Yes, I have benefited from the existence and programming of the Center for Teaching Excellence."

Duquesne stands as a good example of how administrators and faculty can work together to create a formative feedback program for a school that once had only summative evaluation. Duquesne's experience also suggests that with sincere efforts to improve and develop teaching, existing summative evaluation systems will ultimately change to be more fair and, consequently, better accepted.

Case of The University of Massachusetts at Amherst

At the University of Massachusetts at Amherst, a thriving Center for Teaching has for seven years offered instructional consultations, videotaping services, and other resources to develop faculty as teachers. The teaching culture at this university is notably supportive. With the recent addition of several new programs for newly hired faculty members, new faculty now count on the Center's voluntary, mid-semester, formative evaluation service.

At the same time, there is increasing pressure from the legislature and board of directors to assess student learning and quality of teaching. One way the University has proposed to address these concerns is through end-of-course, summative evaluations. The University's recently hired Associate Director for Assessment was asked to create a new student rating instrument to assess both student learning and quality of teaching. Staff in both the Center for Teaching and the Office of Planning and Assessment were concerned about how a new summative evaluation process might affect the existing supportive climate for teaching.

Although the mission of the Center for Teaching concerns only formative assessment, Center staff acknowledged that formative assessment ultimately prepares faculty for summative evaluation, and that an unfair summative evaluation system would undermine the formative feedback process. Thus, the two offices crossed the formative-summative line in order to consult in the creation of a new, reliable and valid student rating form and a humane evaluation process. The Office of Planning and Assessment was ultimately responsible for the creation and implementation of its new rating instrument, but the director of the Center for Teaching acted as a consultant to the assessment office. Staff in both offices agreed that careful planning and development of the summative evaluation system was crucial to ensuring continued emphasis on development and support for teaching.

Currently, the new evaluation system has been piloted and well-received in several departments. Although the rating instrument has not yet been finalized, word about its clarity and its facility has spread on campus. Other department continue to ask to be on the pilot list. It seems that this University is carefully and successfully incorporating a new summative evaluation system while preserving the existing formative feed-back process.

Action items

At most universities, committees, rules, standards, and guidelines already exist to guide the summative evaluation process. For exam ple, tenure reviews follow preset procedures that ultimately assist department chairs and senior faculty in making decisions about junior faculty. If summative evaluation and formative feedback are to co-exist, universities must provide an infrastructure for formative feedback as well. This infrastructure includes a commitment to developing faculty as teachers, rewards for good teaching, a process by which all faculty are given the opportunity to develop as teachers, and a support system for developing teachers. Without the infrastructure to cultivate formative feedback, efforts to foster both will fail.

Hand in hand with this first recommendation, faculty and administrators must commit to making summative evaluation systems more humane. This means standards must be outlined clearly, faculty must receive feedback along the way to the tenure decision, faculty must receive some sort of formal mentoring, and tenure decisions must not come as a surprise.

The following list suggests specific items for action.

- Employ faculty development offices to develop and improve teaching.
  - Offer services to faculty on a voluntary basis.
  - Emphasize the development of teaching, not the repair of teachers.
  - Keep faculty development activities separate from summative evaluation.
- Place value on faculty members' efforts to conduct formative assessment.
  - Reward faculty for commitment to teaching improvement.
  - Encourage teaching portfolios to showcase development as teachers.
  - Publish (in college newspaper) innovative efforts to improve teaching.
- Create fair summative review procedures.
  - Outline the steps taken to get tenure.
  - List clearly the criteria for gaining tenure.
  - Provide checkpoints along the way to tenure.
- Create fair summative review instruments.
  - Review the literature on student ratings.
  - Consider alternate means for evaluating teaching summatively.
  - Consult with those responsible for providing formative feed-back.

NORM-REFERENCED EVALUATION

Norm-referenced evaluation is used for large-scale system evaluation, provincial rankings for scholarship and psychoeducational testing for special needs. Norm-referenced evaluation:

— compares one student's achievement to that of other students;

— requires a large reference group for comparison; and

— is based on a normal distribution, which shows how achievement in a particular area is distributed over an entire population.

Norm-referenced evaluation is not meant for classroom evaluation because a classroom does not provide a large enough reference group. Practices that are congruent with a norm-referenced evaluation system such as using a bell curve, natural breaks, or computer programs that rank students, provide percentages, stanines and corresponding letter grades are not compatible with a criterion-referenced evaluation system.

CRITERION-REFERENCED EVALUATION

Criterion-referenced evaluation is expected for classroom evaluation. From the information collected through assessment activities, teachers evaluate student performance. They use their insight, knowledge about learning and experience with students, along with the specific criteria, to make judgments about student performance in relation to specific learning outcomes. Criterion-referenced letter grades in Grades 4 to 12 indicate students' levels of performance as they relate to the learning outcomes set out in Integrated Resource Packages for each subject, course or grade. Criterion-referenced evaluation:

— compares student achievement and performance to established criteria; and

— provides information that helps students and teachers redirect efforts, practice learning and establish future learning goals. The steps for criterion-referenced evaluation are following:

Planning

— Identify the learning outcomes from the IRPs, IEPs and other specific goals, objectives or purpose for the learning that will be reflected in the unit or lessons.

— Consider what it might look like when the student has met the learning outcomes.

— Identify and analyze the key features, understandings, attributes or qualities that will be demonstrated.

— Establish a preliminary set of criteria and consider ways the students might demonstrate their learning.

Instruction

— Involve the students in the process of refining the criteria. Provide models or examples in order that the students have a clear picture and understanding of the expectations.

— Provide learning opportunities that allow the students to practice and refine their knowledge.

Assessment

— Build a performance scale from the criteria to assist in the collection of assessment information.

— Use the criteria and performance scale to monitor learning and make necessary adjustments to instruction.

— Provide formative feedback to the students.

Evaluation

— Use the criteria for evaluation of the students' performance by comparing the students' performance or demonstration to the criteria and the performance scale.

— Involve the students in self-evaluation and, when appropriate, peer evaluation.

Reporting

- Conference with the students and provide meaningful feedback to support the students' learning.
- Communicate the students' progress to parents.

CRITERION- VERSUS NORM- REFERENCED TESTING

Many educators and members of the public fail to grasp the distinctions between criterion-referenced and norm-referenced testing. It is common to hear the two types of testing referred to as if they serve the same purposes, or shared the same characteristics. Much confusion can be eliminated if the basic differences are understood.

A student's score is usually expressed as a percentage. Student achievement is reported for individual skills. Each individual is compared with other examinees and assigned a score—usually expressed as a percentile, a grade equivalent score, or a stanine.

Student achievement is reported for broad skill areas, although some norm-referenced tests do report student achievement for individual skills.

The differences outlined are discussed in many texts on testing. The teacher or administrator who wishes to acquire a more technical knowledge of criterion-referenced test or its norm-referenced counterpart, may find the text from which this material was adapted particularly helpful.

DIAGNOSTIC EVALUATION AND TREATMENT

The first step to getting appropriate treatment for depression is a physical examination by a physician. Certain medications as well as some medical conditions such as a viral infection can cause the same symptoms as depression, and the physician should rule out these possibilities through examination, interview, and lab tests. If a physical cause for the depression is ruled out, a psychological evaluation should be done, by the physician or by referral to a psychiatrist or psychologist.

A good diagnostic evaluation will include a complete history of symptoms, i.e., when they started, how long they have lasted, how severe they are, whether the patient had them before and, if so, whether the symptoms were treated and what treatment was given. The doctor should ask about alcohol and drug use, and if the patient has thoughts about death or suicide. Further, a history should include questions about whether other family members have had a depressive illness and, if treated, what treatments they may have received and which were effective.

Last, a diagnostic evaluation should include a mental status examination to determine if speech or thought patterns or memory have been affected, as sometimes happens in the case of a depressive or manic-depressive illness. Treatment choice will depend on the outcome of the evaluation. There are a variety of antidepressant medications and psychotherapies that can be used to treat depressive disorders. Some people with milder forms may do well with psychotherapy alone. People with moderate to severe depression most often benefit from antidepressants. Most do best with combined treatment: medication to gain relatively quick symptom relief and psychotherapy to learn more effective ways to deal with life's problems, including depression.

Depending on the patient's diagnosis and severity of symptoms, the therapist may prescribe medication and/or one of the several forms of psychotherapy that have proven effective for depression. Electroconvulsive therapy (ECT) is useful, particularly for individuals whose depression is severe or life threatening or who cannot take antidepressant medication. ECT often is effective in cases where antidepressant medications do not provide sufficient relief of symptoms. In recent years, ECT has been much improved. A muscle relaxant is given before treatment, which is done under brief anesthesia. Electrodes are placed at precise locations on the head to deliver electrical impulses. The stimulation causes a brief (about 30 seconds) seizure within the brain. The person receiving ECT does not consciously experience the electrical stimulus. For full therapeutic benefit, at least several sessions of ECT, typically given at the rate of three per week, are required.

EVALUATION DESIGN APPROACHES

After you determine your evaluation questions, you will then choose evaluation design features or approaches that are most appropriate given each question and situation. This module presents some guidelines, along with the strengths and weaknesses of various approaches, but it is important to keep in mind that every situation is unique. There is no "one and only" way to meet every evaluation situation.

To answer any question, you need to carefully plan and execute each step of the process in order to get good answers. All evaluations pose their own special challenges in terms of gathering and analyzing data. When answering descriptive questions, we need to figure out whether the information we need is best gathered through the use of structured or unstructured interviews, focus groups, document analysis, observation, surveys, the use of existing data, or some combination of these and other strategies. Then we need to specify a plan for the data collection and analysis, reporting, and getting the results used. In total, this is the evaluation design.

In general, open-ended evaluation approaches (e.g., those that use unstructured interviews, focus groups, or observation) work best when we are evaluating a relatively untried intervention, or when the context is very different from other places it has been implemented. An open-ended evaluation design allows for the possibility of gathering information we hadn't anticipated (such as unexpected ripple effects).

When the intervention is something we understand fairly well and have seen implemented in a similar context, we are more likely to have a clear idea of what descriptive data we need. In this case, it makes sense to devise a more structured evaluation approach (e.g., using structured interviews or surveys) that is focused on obtaining very specific information. The reality is that most descriptive evaluation questions fall somewhere between these two extremes - we may have a fairly good idea of what we need to know, but we have learned to expect the unexpected. In such cases, a mix of evaluation approaches (some focused, some open-ended) is best.

Choices about evaluation approaches for normative questions, which compare "what is" with "what should be," follow a similar logic to those for descriptive questions. The added layer of complexity is determining the "what should be" part of the equation. In the simplest cases, there may be a clearly specified goal or target, or some appropriate standards for implementation. In other cases, a needs assessment may be required to identify "what should be." A needs assessment looks at where "dysfunction" (or unsatisfactory functioning) is occurring in the target population or area, as it relates to the intervention. For a farming advisory intervention, you might investigate in what areas and why certain farmers are getting less-than-optimal yields or market prices, and identify the skills, knowledge, and resources that prevent them from achieving better results. In this case, "what should be" might be the level of farming yield and income that could reasonably be achieved, given the right advice and know-how about how to access needed resources.

Impact questions pose the greatest challenge; this is where we need a well thought out design (as opposed to a particular approach to answering a relatively straightforward descriptive question). In any evaluation with questions involving impact, the evaluation design must be able to rule out other feasible explanations for the observed results in order to conclude that the invention had an impact. In other words, we need to be sure that any observed changes were due to the intervention, rather than to something else.

To reduce the possibility of being fooled into thinking we know something as true which really is not, there is much that we can borrow from social science methods. Using experimentation, it is possible to control the implementation of a program, policy, or project, who receives it, and the environment in which it is delivered. When you can control everything but the intervention, you can then be fairly certain that any differences you observe are the result of that intervention.

Supposing you have a fertilizer that is intended to increase the crop yield of corn. Let's say you have a greenhouse where you control the temperature, water, and soil conditions. You create two separate growing areas within the greenhouse and randomly plant the seeds in the testing area and the control area. Both areas receive the same temperature, sunlight, and water and are planted in the exact same soil mixture. The test area receives the fertilizer and the control area does not. At harvest, the yields are measured. If the test area has a higher yield than the control area, you will conclude the fertilizer made a difference.

Now let's think about what happens when you're working in the field instead of the controllable environment of the greenhouse. It is possible that your two areas are close together and the fertilizer can run off into the non-test area, thus giving you an imperfect measure of the impact of the fertilizer. You might move the non-test area to a different part of your field but the soil, light, temperature or rain may be slightly different. The two fields may also receive different amounts of attention While you can still measure impact, you may be less certain about concluding that the fertilizer alone caused those results.

In the complex world in which development interventions take place, it becomes difficult to identify impact in the midst of other factors. In the agricultural case, let's suppose an irrigation intervention was implemented during a time of ideal weather and strong demand for the crops. The income in the area where the irrigation intervention was implemented increased over prior years. But is the higher income a result of the intervention? Or is it caused by other factors, such as general economic good times or an unusual period of political stability.

Multi-site and cluster evaluations present special challenges as well as unique opportunities for looking at impact questions. The context at each site and the nature of the intervention often vary considerably across different locations. This can help identify some of the situational and implementation factors that enhance or hinder impact - but the analysis can be considerably more complex. This complexity may limit the extent to which the data collection and analysis phases can be conducted in a highly participatory mode, and it may also limit the viability of rapid assessments as an option. Evaluation designs can help us determine the impact of a program to the extent that they give us control over the implementation and measurement of the program. The intent is to eliminate other possible explanations for what we observe.

Elements of Impact Evaluation Design and Data Collection Strategies

Evaluators doing traditional experimental evaluation will focus on these major elements of design:

— Before and after measures

— Comparison groups

— Random assignment to the comparison groups

For some of the newer approaches (such as cluster and multi-site evaluation and rapid assessment), we may draw on other tools, including:

— Use of control variables

— Use of natural variations.

— Causal tracing strategies

When we talk about eliminating other possible explanations, we are talking about internal validity. Internal validity refers to the design's ability to rule out other explanations for the observed results. An evaluation design with strong internal validity enables you to be much more confident that the intervention caused the observed results. A design with weak internal validity makes it harder to convince others that the intervention caused the observed results. Yet it is important to keep in mind that these threats are just possible rival explanations; they might not actually exist. It is very context related. Common threats to internal validity are:

— History (events occurring at the same time);
— Maturation of subjects (just getting older changes the results);
— Testing (learning how to take the test);
— Instrumentation (changes in data collection instruments or procedures);
— Regression to the mean (averaging out of scores over time);
— Selection bias (participants may be different to begin with); and
— Attrition (a specific group of people may drop out).

Elements of Impact Evaluation Design

Before and After Measures To answer whether an intervention made a difference, the evaluation has to show that the key measures changed as a result of the intervention. Before and after measurement is one way to measure change. Change is measured by comparing key measures after the intervention began against the measures taken before the intervention began. The "before" measure might be called a baseline. However, a design with just before and after measures is insufficient to demonstrate that the intervention alone caused the change. Maybe the people changed their behavior because they were being observed or maybe something else occurred at the same time as the intervention that really caused the changes we observed.

It is also important to remember that in a situation where there is little change in the measures, you should be hesitant to conclude that the intervention did not work. An intervention to reduce poverty was implemented in a country. Everyone was eligible to receive the intervention so there was no comparison group. At the end of ten years, the proportion of people in poverty did not change. Can you conclude that the poverty reduction intervention did not work? Without a comparison group, you cannot tell if poverty would have been worse if the poverty reduction intervention was not in place. The intervention may have been effective in holding the line on poverty in spite of declining economic conditions. To strengthen this design, you would want to compare your intervention group to a group who did not receive the intervention.

Comparison Groups If an intervention causes change, then those who participate in the intervention will show more change than those who did not. Returning to the irrigation intervention, we would need to compare a similar agricultural area that did not receive the irrigation program with the one that did. If the income in the area that received the irrigation program increased while the income of the comparison group did not, then we would have stronger evidence that the irrigation program caused a positive outcome. However, not all the other factors have been ruled out. What if the community that receives the irrigation intervention is different in some important ways from the comparison community that did not? Maybe other industries moved into the intervention area, thus increasing income. Or maybe the comparison community grew different crops and their crops did not command as high a price as the crops grown in the irrigation community. In some interventions, there will be those who receive it and those who don't. This design can be used in evaluation, as might be done in the evaluation of a job training program for laid off workers were more motivated or had more job experience, so it was easier for them to find new employment. To strengthen this design, it is necessary to randomly assign people to participate or not to participate in the program.

Random Assignment

In the ideal world of science, we would be able to randomly assign people (or things, farms, roads, cases, whatever) to receive the intervention or not. Random assignment makes the groups comparable. For example, if we randomly assign communities to receive the irrigation intervention or not, we make the groups relatively equal in terms of a variety of factors we cannot control. Given the equality of the groups in terms of a host of factors, we would feel more confident in concluding the intervention had an impact if the intervention group had higher income than the control groups. However, random assignment is not always an option. Sometimes all eligible people are supposed to receive the intervention, and/or it would be unethical to withhold it from some of them. Sometimes you cannot make people participate in an intervention. In this instance, it may be more practical to provide an intervention in a selection of sites rather than provide interventions in multiple sites and then randomly assign participants.

It is possible, however, to be in a situation where the intervention is not large enough to accommodate all those who apply. A manager might want to assign those with the best chance of benefiting from the intervention to participate. This may be a way to get the most benefit from limited program dollars. For example, the training program is likely to show the best results if it chooses highly motivated people to participate. However, from an evaluation perspective, if the best people are assigned to the program, there is likely to be a bias in the results. Actually, in this type of situation, random assignment may not only enable the use of a strong design to measure impact, it may also be more equitable; no bias and favoritism is in play when assignment is based on chance.

Use of Control Variables

As noted above, sometimes it is not possible to randomly assign people to groups for comparison purposes. However, it might be possible to find a group of people (or a village, etc) who will not be receiving the intervention yet, and who could be used to compare results with. But without random assignment, there is still a good chance that the comparison group differs in important ways from the group receiving the intervention. If that's true, the intervention might look effective (or ineffective) simply because of pre-existing differences between recipients and non-recipients.

In such cases, one option is to collect data about factors that might be different between the two groups, and that seem likely to impact outcomes. These variables are then built into the data analysis as "control variables." This allows us to rule out some alternative explanations even when random assignment is not possible.

Use of Natural Variation

Sometimes it is not possible to find a meaningful comparison group of any description, especially if the intervention has been implemented across a wide area, as is the case with multi-site and cluster evaluations. Does this mean that there is no hope of figuring out whether any changes observed are due to the intervention or not? Not at all; and the answer lies in natural variations in the intervention.

Suppose a prenatal care program has been implemented in all the villages in a particular geographical area, and you have been asked to conduct a multi-site evaluation. As with any large intervention, more often than not there is some variation in the extent to which the program actually reaches its target population, and also in the quality of the services delivered. Now, suppose you find better newborn health and lower infant and mother mortality in those villages where more mothers received more frequent and better quality service. Such evidence adds to the confidence with which you can attribute health outcomes to the intervention, especially compared to just looking at overall outcomes across all participants.

Causal Tracing Strategies

Many of the strategies described above for determining whether observed changes are due to the intervention (as opposed to some other cause) require a fairly structured and heavily quantitative data collection strategy, and relatively complex statistical analysis. For the evaluator conducting a rapid assessment, or one evaluating a very small or new and untried intervention, such strategies may be neither practical nor advisable. What options are available when the sample size is small, the data collection strategies are largely open-ended, and/ or when sophisticated statistical analysis is not feasible? Thankfully, there are some useful resources available on how to use "causal tracing" strategies, which are particularly suitable for qualitative and mixed method (qualitative and quantitative) studies, and especially when the target population is small.

Broadly speaking, the principle is the same - systematically rule out alternative explanations until you are as sure as you need to be that the changes you observed are indeed (or are not) caused primarily (or at least substantially) by the intervention. The following is a list of nine possible sources of evidence you might gather when using causal tracing:

1. Causal list inference (we know that this particular outcome is almost always caused by one of the following: A, B, C, or D; on this occasion neither B, C, or D occurred, so we can be pretty sure the cause was A.)

2. Modus operandi (MO) inference - use this if more than one possible cause occurred (we know that this outcome is almost always caused by one of the following: A, B, C, or D; on this occasion, neither C nor D

   occurred, which narrows the cause down to A or B; in addition, only the characteristic causal chain/MO/telltale pattern of events for A was present; this inference is strengthened if the MO for A is highly distinctive/very different from that for B.)
3. Temporal precedence (the observed effect only happened after the intervention had begun, not before)
4. Constant conjunction (the effect was observed everywhere the intervention was implemented)
5. Contiguity of influence (a plausible mechanism links the intervention with the observed effect; inference strengthened if we can find evidence of the mechanism in action)
6. Strength of association (the observed change was much stronger where the program was implemented than it was where other possible causes were present)
7. Biological gradient (the more of the intervention someone/ a village received, the larger the observed change)
8. Coherence (the relationship we see between the intervention and the observed change fits logically with other things we know about the intervention and this particular outcome)
9. Analogy (the pattern we see between the intervention and the observed changes resemble the well-established pattern we know about between a related intervention and its effects)

When designing your data collection strategy, you should consider which of the above pieces of evidence it is feasible and necessary to gather, and plan ahead how you will obtain them. You certainly do not need all of these to be able to make causal attributions; just gather the pieces that make the most sense, and that together will give you sufficient certainty about your findings, given the decisions that will be based on your evaluation.

Types of Impact Evaluation Design

Experimental design

The classic experimental design, sometimes called the true experiment, is considered the strongest design for impact questions because it rules out most other possible explanations. Random assignment, its essential component, assures that the comparison groups are comparable. It contains before and after measures for the comparison groups. However, it is often difficult to generalize to a larger population, since experimental studies are usually small. While this is rarely used because of its lack of feasibility, it is possible. The evaluation of the impact of textbooks in a developing country is an example of an experimental design, with random assignment.

Quasi-experimental Designs

"Quasi" means they are similar to true experiments except that the comparison groups have not been formed by random assignment. Sometimes you can create a comparison group by matching on key characteristics. Other times you will find a comparison that is not exactly the same as the group that received the intervention but is similar enough to provide some comparison For example, you might be able to compare a village that received an economic development intervention with one in the same geographic area that did not.

In these designs, you may have to collect more information to make a case that the intervention outcomes cannot be explained by factors other than the intervention. Common examples of quasi-experimental designs are non-equivalent comparison design, interrupted time series design, and correlational design using statistical controls. An example of a quasi-experimental design is the evaluation of El Salvador's EDUCO Program.

Correlational Design

Correlational designs are often used when we are seeking to answer questions about relationships. Correlational designs can be used with data already available, or with new data. For example, if you wanted to find out if having women in political offices results in a more honest government, a correlational design could be used. Data about the proportion of women in political office in the different areas within a country and the amount of reported corruption could be correlated with each other.

Correlational evidence alone cannot establish causality - even if governments with more women in office were less corrupt, it would still be necessary to rule out any plausible alternative explanations for the relationship before concluding that women were the cause of honesty!

Non-Experimental (or Pre-Experimental) Design (for Descriptive and Narrative Questions)

These are weaker designs for determining impact because they are missing several design elements. Sometimes they have a before and after measure but no comparison group. Sometimes they have a comparison but no measures before the intervention. Sometimes they lack both a comparison and a measure before the intervention; this is called a one-shot design because it is like taking a photograph of a situation at one point after an intervention was implemented. Non-experimental designs work perfectly fine for descriptive and normative questions but are weak for impact questions unless they are supplemented with serious qualitative causal analysis.

Sometimes the evaluation question focuses on whether citizens or intervention beneficiaries are satisfied with services they received, or why they do not use services. Sometimes the question may be to find out the current status of people who participated in an intervention a few years ago. To answer these kinds of questions, a survey using a cross-sectional design might be used. A cross-sectional survey selects a representative sample of citizens, intervention beneficiaries, or former intervention participants at one in time. It would then gather data from them and report what they said.

For instance, in evaluating a program designed to economically empower women to launch their own small businesses, the evaluators may want to find out the views of women who have been through the program. Their views can shed light on whether what they learned in the economic empowerment program helped them launch a viable business, the kind of business they went into, and whether what they learned in program was useful for running the business. With limited resources, they may opt to conduct a short survey of recent program graduates (a one-shot design). Or they may survey both women who recent graduated from the program and women who had been through a traditional business skills program, or who had simply received seed money but no training or support aimed at economic empowerment (a static group comparison). These are non-experimental designs.

A longitudinal study is one in which repeated measures of the same variable are taken from the same people (or from sample groups in the same population). A panel design is a special type of longitudinal design in which a smaller group of people is tracked at multiple points in time, and their experiences are recorded in considerable detail. Panel designs almost always use qualitative (e.g., open-ended survey questions, in-depth interviews, and observation) as well as quantitative data. Panel designs can give a more in-depth perspective on any changes people may be experiencing as a result of an intervention. For example, a study looking at

Poland's family allowance used panel data gathered from the same people between 1993-1996 to find out how the allocation of social benefits affected families' transition into and out of poverty.

A time series design might be used to track key performance indicators over time before and after an intervention. Tracking agricultural production over time might yield a good picture of the overall trend. An intervention intended to produce more trained primary school teachers lends itself to a time series design that tracks the number and percent of primary school teachers with advanced education. A performance audit seeking to compare the performance of intervention against standards (a normative question) is likely to use a non-experimental design. For instance, if the donors expect students to meet specified scores on standardized tests, then the evaluators will gather that data and compare it against the standard.

An evaluation seeking to answer a descriptive or normative question can be just as valuable as one seeking to answer a question of impact, depending on what needs to be known. Descriptive designs can provide important insights. There is much to be learned, for example, by answering a descriptive question about how parents and teachers feel about efforts to decentralize schools.

Case Study

A case study is frequently used when the researcher wants to gain an in-depth understanding of a process, event or situation. It is useful when the question deals with how something works or why something happens, and is especially useful when the intervention is relatively innovative or experimental or not well understood. Case studies are frequently used in evaluating development interventions.

Case studies can use qualitative and/or quantitative methods to collect data. They can consist of a single case (a one-shot, before and after or single time-series design) or they can consist of multiple cases (comparative designs). They can focus on in-depth understandings of individuals, an organizations, communities, programs, cities, and/or nations. If we were interested in monitoring public transportation in a country, we might simply track key indicators against the baseline and targets. We might do a national study if the indicators are the number of miles covered by public transportation, capacity, ridership, and revenues received.

However, if we wanted to answer other kinds of questions that require more in-depth data collection, we would opt for case study. We might choose a single case study or we might choose a few different locations to gain a wide-range of experiences.

For instance, if we wanted to learn more about people's choices about using public transportation, we will have to gather the data from them. This will require more resources to collect this data if done on a national scale. It is more manageable to gather that data in a more narrowly defined geographic area-a single case. Alternatively, researchers might opt for a multiple case study, where several cities might be selected. The cases might be selected in several ways:

- Randomly
- Convenience (easy for the researchers to access)
- Judgmentally or purposively selected based on some specific criteria
    - Best case, typical case, worst case, or a mix
    - Only large cities or cities of varying sizes.

The same data collection strategies used in the single case study can be used in multiple case studies. Case studies make sense in development where the intention is about understanding a specific situation in order to make or adjust policy or practice. But not only are case studies more practical than trying to do large national studies, they also provide in-depth information that is often appropriate to the decision-maker's focus. A comparative case study of the use of free immunization clinics would provide greater understanding about why one is more successful.

Key Points About Design

— There is no perfect design.

— Each design has strengths and weaknesses.

— There are always trade-offs in terms of time, cost, and practicality.

— Acknowledge trade-offs and potential weaknesses.

— Provide some assessment of their likely impact on your results and conclusions.

5

Tools of Evaluation

INTERVIEWS

Oral examinations, also called viva voce, involve a verbal exchange between the student and the assessor.

Advantages

— Interaction between assessor and assessed is possible.

— Video- or audio-recordings enable post interview analysis or record keeping.

— Test qualities not assessed by written tests (verbal fluency, self confidence, ability to argue a point in a discussion).

Disadvantages

— Special skills are required of the examiners, and some training, as for professional interviewers, should be available.

— Reliability is generally low.

— Can be very subjective.

— Create stress which is counter-productive, though this stress can be reduced by letting the student have some say in the questions asked, or by revealing key questions (not follow-up or probe questions) before the examination.

Reasons for the use of an oral examination

By the fifth semester of the sequence students have had considerable experience in thinking about literature and in articulating their responses to it. An oral examination at this stage does not make demands upon them which they feel incapable of meeting.

By this stage some students have developed particular areas of interest and are beginning to become independent thinkers about literature. The oral examination gives them an opportunity to take up points and pursue them in a way not always appropriate in a response to a set examination or essay question. (It is always possible to say to a student, in an oral examination: "That is an interesting idea. Would you like to develop it further.")

The oral examination is more demanding because it allows the examiner to probe understanding. Students cannot hide behind a learned opinion or borrowed position. (It is always possible to ask: "Just what exactly do you mean by that? Why do you think that critic says that? What about the position taken by X?")

The oral examination requires students to think on their feet, i.e. to adapt their knowledge and insights to a variety of demands and defend their position. Students in the final semesters of their sequence should be able to perform in this way. At the beginning of their course of study, on the other hand, it is probably sufficient to expect that students will arrive at some understanding and be able to express it.

Form of the oral examination

Each student has a session which lasts approximately twenty minutes. Students have selected a general topic on which they wish to be examined. e.g. King Lear. Every student who has selected that topic will be asked the same set of questions.

The prepared questions demand a hierarchy of responses. Some are designed simply to establish that the student has a basic, literal knowledge of the topic (e.g. of the events in King Lear). Some are designed to see whether the student has thought about the significance of that knowledge (e.g. "In the source play for King Lear Cordelia does not die. Why do you think Shakespeare modified the story to include her death? How do you see her death in relation to the 'meanings' of the play as you understand them?). Some are designed to encourage students to pursue any particular interests or insights they may have had ("Do you agree with...?" "If you were producing a performance of the play would you...?") and there is always a final question: "Is there anything else you would like to say about this play/topic that we haven't covered?" Some questions are designed to see whether students have related their thoughts about the topic to wider issues (e.g. "King Lear was one of the least often performed of Shakespeare's plays during the nineteenth century. Since World War II it has been one of the most frequently performed and discussed plays. Have you any thoughts about why this might be so?").

If students have difficulty in answering questions some prompt questions are asked. But if the difficulty persists, such that it is apparent that the student does not have sufficient knowledge or understanding to answer the question, we pass on to the next question. It is important, in that situation, to move on without undermining the student's confidence by making it apparent that they have 'failed' a section of the examination.

The examiners

Ideally two or three staff members conduct the exam, sharing the asking of questions, and discussing the student's responses at the conclusion of the examination. In recent years staffing constraints have made this difficult, and sometimes it has not been possible to use additional staff. For this reason the oral examination is never worth more than 40% of the total. Notes are made on the student's responses as the examination proceeds, and a grade is decided before the next student is dealt with.

Assessment

Broad grades rather than precise marks are awarded, but perhaps with a plus or minus modification, which may be taken into account when determining the final, overall result for the subject.

For a pass grade a student needs to demonstrate a basic knowledge of the topic and some considered, but not necessarily subtle or original, views about its significance. For a credit grade a student would need to demonstrate, as well as the above, some understanding of the range of possible views about the topic and be able to defend the personal position which (s)he has adopted. For a distinction grade a student would need to display some understanding of the more subtle issues involved in the topic, and demonstrate some critical thinking about these issues. For a high distinction grade a student would need to demonstrate a superior understanding of the issues involved and some original thinking about them.

Comments

The oral examination is an excellent discriminator. It is readily apparent if students do not have a sound basic understanding of their topic; prepared answers are no defence. Students who have real interest and genuine insights are able to develop these effectively in this context, because the range of questions does not limit them to exploring only one issue or set of related issues.

The oral examination is an opportunity for students to use their oral communication skills in a formal but flexible context.

Although the examination takes a long time to administer there is, of course, minimal 'marking' time required. The size of the group involved has never exceeded thirty students; it would be very difficult, with limited staff, to use this method with large groups. Surveys of student opinion have elicited favourable comments on the oral examination as a method of assessment. Most students say they found the experience much less threatening than they anticipated, and felt that it gave them an opportunity to demonstrate what they had learned during the semester.

OBSERVATION OF STUDENT PERFORMACE

Observation and recording of students' are important activities in the special education classroom. Accurate behavior observation is essential in identifying students' needs and developing effective instruction. One of the ways in which special education programs provide more intensive services to students with learning difficulties is by more carefully monitoring and adjusting the learning/teaching process. The teacher can play an important role in gathering and organizing information about student progress. This information is particularly important when the teacher is providing all or part of the instruction during a tutoring or small group format. The systematic collection of data allows the teacher to continue to make instructional decisions without being physically present during the learning activity. Data collection and systematic behavior observation provide an objective basis for making decisions and documenting student behaviors and performance. It can make teacher judgment more accurate and reliable. When carried out systematically, it also provides more frequent information on student progress.

Teachers gather information about student performance in order to determine where to begin instruction, in order to determine which instructional approaches might be the most effective, and to assess student mastery of skills. This information is most helpful when it is collected as early as possible. This avoids students making repeated errors and missing vital basic information or skills. It allows the teacher to employ additional resources or to fine-tune educational strategies for students. To maximize the benefits to students it is important to find out what is working and what is not working as quickly and efficiently as possible.

Data on student performance can also give the teacher clues about how to adjust the classroom environment. This may include deciding on grouping strategies, adjusting the number and type of practice activities, changing locations in the room and a variety of other variables in the classroom. When student progress is monitored the effect of these changes is easier to determine. For example when a student with a learning difficulty is participating in a regular classroom activity, the special education teacher may ask the teacher to observe and record the amount of time that the student spends on assigned tasks. This may lead to recommendations or changes in the way assignments or procedures are adjusted in the classroom. After the changes have been made, an observation can be used to determine if the amount of time the student spends working on the assigned tasks increases. This allows the special education teacher and the teacher to provide support to the regular classroom teacher.

Data on student performance is also critical to providing information to students themselves. This information may be gathered from scoring practice activities and worksheets but also may involve observation of behavior or performance by the teacher. These alternatives allow a greater range of immediate feedback and provide additional opportunities to identify areas in which students are successful. Observation techniques may sometimes provide a more accurate reflection of what a student has learned than more traditional methods. As an example, the teacher has developed a plan to encourage a student to remain in their seat during silent reading time. A part of the plan is a daily discussion with the student about their improvement in in-seat time. The teacher creates a chart which displays the percentage of time the student is in their seat for each day of the week. During a daily conference the teacher shares the chart with the student and puts a copy in their folder. This procedure provides a record of the student's progress which can be used by the teacher and also can be used to share and reward successes with the student.

Data collection and behavior observation is also an important part of reporting student progress. In the previous example of charting in-seat behavior, the teacher could use information collected by the teacher to keep the student's parents informed of their progress and classroom behavior. Charts and data summaries can become important elements of a students portfolio.

Collection of data regarding a student's performance is an important part of the process of verifying a student's eligibility for special education programs. One criteria was that a student's observed performance in the classroom must be consistent with test results. Information about a student's actual performance in the classroom is important because it provides information about how a child performs in a real classroom situation with real teachers, curriculum and materials. It helps to substantiate that a problem exists. The observation process is also used to collect information about the classroom and the performance of the students peers so that the MDT can make judgments about the classroom and learning environment of the student. With some disabilities, information about the frequency and seriousness of behavior problems may be one of the primary criteria used to determine whether they are identified as having a disability.

Concerns about data collection and observation

Accuracy

It is important that the information collected be as accurate as possible. In order to be accurate, the procedure must minimize the chance for errors and observer bias.

Consistency: Behavior observation techniques involve taking a sample of student behavior. The observation method should be one which can to carried out reliably from one time to the next. The teacher and para should be confident that the results of the observation reflect the actual behavior of the student being observed. In other words, if you repeated the observation at a different time would the results remain similar.

Ease of measurement: The accuracy of an observation is often affected by the how easy it is to determine exactly whether a behavior has occurred. If the observer is required to provide insight, interpretation and/or judgment it is probably too difficult to accurately record what occurs. The following provide some example of observations which might lend themselves to accurate measurement:

— counting the number of times a particular behavior occurs

— timing how long a behavior lasts

— scoring an item as correct using a key

The following are observations which are more difficult to make because they require more judgment on the observers part.

— grading the quality of a speech

— judging art projects

— sportsmanship

Ease of recording: Accuracy also requires that the observer have a systematic way to record and report information. The system for recording the results of the observation must contain enough information so that the observation is useful but must not be so complicated that it interferes with the observation.

Techniques to improve accuracy: Techniques which have been used to improve the accuracy of data collection and behavior observation include:

— Clear description of observation procedure,

— Clear specification of behaviors to be observed,

— An established scoring and recording system, and

— Opportunity for the observer to learn and practice the observation technique.

Meaningfulness of observations

The second major concern with data collection and behavio observation is that the behaviors being observed and the techniques used must provide teachers with information that is relevant and useful.

Relationship to true activities/objectives/outcomes: Care must be taken to select behaviors which are relevant to the instructional process. Often the usefulness of the performance or behavior data is determined by how relevant the observed behaviors are to the objectives of the instructional program.

Sensitivity: The observation method utilized must be sensitive to changes in the frequency or the amount of behavior. The time allotted for the observation must be sufficient to observe the behavior occur.

Observation under appropriate conditions

Student performance and behavior can vary markedly depending on the setting. Behaviors on the playground may be much different than during a classroom activity. An important element in obtaining a meaningful observation is choosing the appropriate setting for the observation and describing the conditions under which the observation occurred. This description of conditions is often necessary to interpret information correctly.

Measurement of performance not disability or other factors

The teacher must carefully select the performance criteria or behavior to be observed to reflect student knowledge or skills. Performance should not be affected by some extraneous variable or condition which is not of immediate interest. For example, choosing number of words written correctly during a timed spelling test might be a poor way to measure spelling performance in a student with motor coordination problems. It would be difficult to determine whether the student did not know the spelling or whether they were unable to correctly write the words in the time provided.

Comparisons of performance

Tests, particularly achievement tests, are often used to compare a students performance with other students. This can be done because all students have done the same activities under the same conditions. Data collection and behavior observation in the classroom often occur under a wide variety of conditions with a limited number of students.

The information collected is often used to verify whether a student is meeting a specified criteria rather than to make comparisons with other students. Data may also be collected a number of times on the same student as a means of measuring progress. When comparisons are important in order to make data more meaningful, observations may also be made on a number of other students in the same setting.

Interference/integration with the instructional process

The last concern with data collection and behavior observation is that it coexists gracefully with the instructional process in the classroom. Often teachers include data collection and behavior observation as an integral part of the instructional process itself. Teachers and students themselves are involved in gathering data about their performance as part of the instructional process. Consider the following when collecting behavior and/or performance data.

— Observation procedures should not be a distraction from instruction,

— Observation should not take undo time away from instruction,

— Data collection should provide a learning experience for students,

— Results should lead to frequent changes and improvements in instructional process,

— The process should not create undo anxiety for students,

— The process should encourage cooperation rather than competition among students, and

— The process should respect the privacy and dignity of students.

Observable behaviors

One of the problems associated with observing and evaluating student behavior is the accuracy of the results. In order to be accurate the observation procedure must be established so that it remains consistent from from one observation time to another and from one observer to another. A key element in making the observations consistent is the definition of the exact behaviors being observed. The accuracy of the observation is improved if the behaviors being observed are defined so that they are observable and measurable. This allows the observer to accurately count the number of times a behavior occurs or determine when a behavior begins and ends. Without specifying exactly the behavior being observed it is difficult to be consistent and the meaning of the observation may vary.

Observable behavior: A behavior which can be noted through one of the senses. Observable behaviors are usually described by action words such as touching, walking, saying. or writing. These do not include feelings or intentions which are inferred from other behaviors.

Measurable behavior: In order to be measurable a behavior must first be observable. In addition, an observer must be able to clearly determine whether the behavior is occurring, count the occurrences of the behavior and/or time the duration of the behavior. Behaviors which have a discrete beginning and ending are the easiest to measure. Even though the teacher may be interested in complex behavior problems or in students' feelings or attitudes, such as anger or sadness, these concepts are difficult to define and measure. By identifying specific observable and measurable behaviors associated with feelings, the teacher can more easily and accurately measure and record progress.

Observation techniques

There are several observation techniques that are used within the schools to record student performance or behavior. This lesson will describe six such observation techniques, ways to report the information and the role that the teacher can play in the observation and recording of students' performance and behavior. These techniques include:

— Frequency

— Rate

— Duration

— Interval Recording

— Time Sampling

— Anecdotal Records

All of these techniques rely on precisely identifying the behaviors in observable and measurable performance terms to make the results meaningful and reliable.

Teachers' role in observations

As long as the planning for obaservation has been done by a teacher, anyone that is able to make accurate observations can perform the actual observation of the behavior.

When developing an observation period, the teacher will take the following considerations into account.

Defining observable behaviors: The target behavior will need to be defined in a way that it is observable an measurable to anyone that may be observing that student. It is possible that both the teacher could observe the same student at the same time and note different behaviors. Clearly identifying specific behaviors being observed makes communicating and interpreting the results of the observation more accurate. The teacher should be the one to identify and define the behavior.

Where the observation is to take place: Certain behaviors occur in specific locations thoughout the day. It is up to the teacher to determine where behaviors are occurring so that the time observations take place will coincide with the behavior. If a student is kicking other students on the playground, then observing them in the classroom will not provide an accurate observation. However, if a student is talking out in class, the classroom would be an appropriate location. The teacher needs to establish the location in order for the observer to collect accurate information.

When the observation is to take place: The target behavior will also determine the time of the observation. The teacher should schedule the observation during a time in which the behavior is likely to occur and for a length of time that will allow opportunity for the behavior to occur.

*What observation technique is to be used:*In determining the observation technique to use, the teacher will take into consideation the specific behavior and the information that they will want to gather from the observation. A teacher will need to have an understanding of these techniques and practice them before they can use them in an observation.

Frequency: Frequency counts are a record of the number of times a specific behavior occurs within a specific time period. Frequency counts are useful for recording behaviors which have a clear beginning and ending, are of relatively short duration, and tend to occur a number of times during the specified time period. In order to perform a frequency count, the following are required:

— a specific time period,

— a specific behavior, and

— a method for tallying the number of events.

A tally sheet is usually used to identify the behavior being observed and to record the the frequency or the number of times which the behavior occurs. Below is an example of a tally sheet and how the frequency of a behavior might be recorded.

Rate: Rate is very similar to frequency. Recording rates of behavior included gather information on both the frequency of the observed behavior and the length of the observation time. Rate is the ratio of the number of times a behavior occurs within a specific time period AND the length of the time period. The ratio is computed by dividing the number of events by the number minutes, hours, or days that the observation occurred. The frequency or number of times a student leaves their seat during math class may be reported as a rate if the length of the class or the length of the observation period is known.

The rate of a behavior can. also be averaged across a number of observation period to report an average rate. From a series of observations it may be determined that a student's average rate of "out of seat" behavior may be twelve times per hour. For example, if the list contains 20 words and the student requires five minutes to write the list, the rate would be four words per minute.

Duration: Recording the duration of a behavior is done by recording the starting and ending time of a behavior and computing the length of time that the behavior occurs. This technique is usually used to observe behavior which occur less frequently and continue for a period of time. An example of duration recording could be for a student who has crying episodes in class. Everytime the student cries in class, you would record the beginning and ending times, and then calculate the duration of the crying episode. A few other examples of when duration recording could be used include how long it takes a student to finish a math assignment, the length of time a student takes cleaning up, or how long a student spends continuously tapping their pencil on the desk.

Interval recording

Interval recording is a technique that measures whether or not a behavior occurs within a specific time interval. The total observation time is divided into smaller intervals, and the observer records whether or not the behavior occurrs within that interval. By using the interval recording technique, the teacher can get an estimate of both the frequency and duration of the the behavior. The observer marks only once whether the behavior occurred at anytime within that interval. Interval recording requires the observer's undivided attention, since the observation is continuous for a set period of time. An example of interval recording could be for a child who throws their toys during free-time. If the free-time lasts for 15 minutes, then that time could be broken into 1 minute intervals. If in the first minute, the child throws the toy the the interval is marked. If in the next minute, they don't throw a toy then the interval is not marked. However, if in the third minute, the child throws three different toys, the interval is only marked once again.

Other examples of when interval recording may be used include, a student who talks to other students around them during work time, the amount of socializing that a student does at recess, or if a student is attending to a book during personal reading time. Interval recording will work for any behaviors that can be observed, however there is a strong time demand upon the observer which may make this technique inappropriate or undesirable to use.

Time sampling

Time sampling is similar to interval recording in that the observation time is divided into intervals, however in time sampling, the behavior is recorded only if it occurs at the end of the time period. When the specified amount of time has expired, the observer looks at the student and determines whether or not the behavior is occurring. In general, this technique is used for behaviors which are longer in duration. For example, if the behavior is identified as "being out of seat", the observation time might be 15 minutes with intervals of 1 minute. The teacher would mark at one minute intervals whether the student being observed was out of his or her seat.

SELF ASSESSMENT

Self assessment is the process of gathering information about yourself in order to make an informed career decision. It is the first step of the Career Planning Process and is often conducted with the help of a career development professional.

What should a self assessment look at? A self assessment should include a look at your values, interests, personality, and skills. Here is an overview of the tools you can use to accomplish this.

— *Value Inventories*: Value inventories measure how important different values are to you. Examples of these values, which play an important role in one's job satisfaction, include autonomy, prestige, security, interpersonal relations, helping others, flexible work schedule, outdoor work, leisure time, and high salary.

— *Interest Inventories* : The questions in an interest inventory ask about your likes and dislikes regarding various activities. The premise of this self assessment tool is that people who share similar interests will also enjoy the same type of work. Examples of interests are reading, running, playing golf, and knitting.

— *Personality Inventories*: A personality inventory looks at one's individual traits, motivational drives, needs, and attitudes. The most frequently used personality inventory is the Myers-Briggs Type Indicator(MBTI).

— *Skills Assessment*: In addition to determining what you're good at, a skills assessment also helps you figure out what you enjoy doing. The skills you use in your career should combine both characteristics. You can use the results ot the skills assessment to make some changes by acquiring the skills you need for a particular career.

Assessing Your Collaboration A Self Evaluation Tool

Many individuals and groups recommend working together to form strong problem-solving collaborative relationships to improve the present status and future well-being of children, families, and the communities in which they live. Moreover, many local, state, and federal children, youth, and family initiatives now require collaboration among multiple sectors.

Presently, Extension professionals and community groups are working collaboratively to develop innovative solutions to promote positive development in children, youth and families. Effective collaborations are able to generate positive outcomes for the audiences they serve. Collaboration is defined as "a process through which parties who see different aspects of a problem [or issue] can constructively explore their differences and search for solutions that go beyond their own limited vision of what is possible".

Many scholars have suggested that there are key features involved in the collaborative process. For instance, Ash emphasize the idea of specific factors underlying characteristics of inter-organizational relations; other scholars focus on central features or salient themes of partnership arrangements. Still others outline strategies that can assist collaborators when facing challenges and difficulties.

Recently, other scholars have identified common factors and characteristics influencing the collaborative process. For example in their comprehensive review of collaborative factors, Hogue, Parkins, Clark, Bergstrum, and Slinski from the National Network for Collaboration identified specific factors, such as leadership, communication, community development, and sustainability. In an empirical study, Keith et al. identified five major characteristics: leadership, unity, communication, participation by citizens, and informal organizations, and successful accomplishments. Borden has identified four factors: internal communication, external communication, membership and goal setting.

Given the importance of these factors, a self-evaluation tool was developed to assist existing and forming groups. The tool is a self-assessment exercise allowing groups to rate their collaboration on key factors. Key factors examined here include goals, communication, sustainability, evaluation, political climate, resources, catalysts, policies/laws/regulations, history, connectedness, leadership, community development, and understanding community.

With this tool, collaborative groups identified strong factors and challenging factors, that is, factors that need to be worked on. The identification of the challenge factors facing the group can assist in the development of strategies to address these issues, thus allowing the group to move forward and accomplish their goals. In all cases, the self-evaluation tool can be used to strengthen the collaborative group. The following is a descriptior. of the Collaboration Check-list.

A Collaboration Checklist

Each of the following factors influences the collaborative process. After reading a brief description for each of the areas place an X in the box that best reflects your opinion of how your collaboration is functioning in each of the areas using the following scale: 1 = Strongly Disagree, 2 Disagree, 3 = Neither Agree or Disagree, 4 = Agree, and 5 = Strongly Agree.

Each of the factors are identified and defined:

— *Communication* - the collaboration has open and clear communication. There is an established process for communication between meetings;

— *Sustainability* - the collaboration has a plan for sustaining membership and resources. This involves membership guidelines relating to terms of office and replacement of members;

— *Research and Evaluation* - the collaboration has conducted a needs assessment or has obtained information to establish its goals and the collaboration continues to collect data to measure goal achievement;

— *Political Climate* - the history and environment surrounding power and decision making is positive. Political climate may be within the community as a whole, systems within the community or networks of people;

— *Resources* - the collaboration has access to needed resources. Resources refer to four types of capital: environmental, in-kind, financial, and human;

— *Catalysts* - the collaboration was started because of existing problem(s) or the reason(s) for collaboration to exist required a comprehensive approach;

— *Policies/Laws/Regulations* - the collaboration has changed policies, laws, and/or regulations that allow the collaboration to function effectively;

— *History* - the community has a history of working cooperatively and solving problems;

— *Connectedness* - members of this collaboration are connected and have established informal and formal communication networks at all levels;

— *Leadership* - the leadership facilitates and supports team building, and capitalizes upon diversity and individual, group and organizational strengths;

— *Community Development* - this community was mobilized to address important issues. There is a communication system and formal information channels that permit the exploration of issues, goals and objectives; and,

— *Understanding Community* - the collaboration understands the community, including its people, cultures, values and habits.

6

CONSTRUCTION OF TESTS

STUDENT ASSESSMENT AND TESTING

If the purpose of instruction is helping students acquire the learning outcomes, the purpose of testing is to determine if the student was successful. The best time to write the tests the students will take is right after writing the statement of learning outcomes. That way it is likely there will be a high degree of congruence between what was intended and what is measured.

Types of assessment

The classroom test - Of course the most common assessment is the classroom test, and the type of classroom test is most likely related to the number of students in the class and the realities of having to grade them and provide feedback. However, the classroom test many not adequately test the course learning outcomes.

Ideally, the test item would reflect performance on the learning outcome directly. That is, given the learning outcome "Define the following terms: field, record, data file, key field, and data types." Is likely to be measured with a number of multiple choice or matching items. While this is not an exact measure of recall, it does provide some evidence of the student's knowledge of the terms. However, a learning outcome like

"Develop a data table that contains the following fields: SS#, Name, Street, City, State, Zip, and Phone #, using the correct data types," cannot be measured with a multiple choice test. However, testing is always a compromise between accuracy an convenience. Most of the time we have to settle for testing skills that we feel will predict student performance on the higher level skills.

Steps in constructing assessments

— *Step 1. Develop a Testing blueprint:* A blueprint is a plan for testing, it is a description of what types of assessment will be used to assess attainment of the major course objectives. Basically there are only two things you can assess. What do the students know (what can they recall), and what can they do (interpret, discuss, analyze, synthesize, demonstrate, calculate, etc.) The test blueprint can come directly off the course planning worksheet.

— *Step 2 Develop the test*: Depending on the type of test there are guidelines for test development that will help yo develop a more valid and reliable assessment. Linked below are the guidelines for developing the most common types of assessments:

— *Step 3 - Create a scoring key or scoring rubric*: The next step is to create a scoring key. While this seems straight forward for a MC test, it is somewhat more difficult for short answer and essay type questions, since it is the content of the answer, not necessarily the format, that matters.

— *Step 4 - Analyze the test items and student response patterns*: No test is perfect, and sometimes items have to be modified or removed from consideration. How do you do this? What do you look for?

— *Grading* - Now that he test has been taken and scored the score has to be turned into a student grade. Two major considerations are the weight this quiz or test has i determining the student's total grade, and what the points on the test represent as a letter grade.

Testing blueprints

A blueprint is a way to align test items with learning outcomes. The table below the "Know" column list the knowledge and lower-level intellectual skills, the "Do" column lists the application and problem solving skills. Each learning outcome is then paired with a description of the type of item that will be used to assess it. Generally, this also includes the number of questions to be associated with each item.

Know (learning outcomes)

- Be able to define these terms: Table, data types, field, record data file, key field.
- Define or explain these terms: sort, select, query
- Define these terms: form, report.
- List the components and purposes served by each.

Assessment/test description

- Multiple choice or matching (2 questions for each concept).
- Short-answer question asking students to explain the difference between the sorting and selecting operations.
- Short answer. What is the difference between a form and a report? What are the components and purposes of each.

Do (learning outcomes)

- Construct a simple table with the following data fields using SS# as the key field: SS#, Name, Street, City, State, Zip, Work phone, Home phone
- Use commands to sort a table by a single or multiple fields ascending or descending.
- Construct a simple query to select a record or set of records according to a stated criteria
- Using a template, create a data input form, and a simple report for the table constructed in lessons 1 and 2.

Assessment/test description

- Performance test taking the first 10 minutes of class.
- Give each student a set of data with the data fields labeled. Give them 10 minutes to construct a table.
- Course assignment —Download data from the course website and write a query that selects specified records. Sort records ascending or decending
- Have student download a template and create both an input form and an output report.

To determine whether students have met their learning objectives and have acquired the learning outcomes you expected from them, some sort of assessment must be done. The multiple-choice test is one of the most common because of its ease of grading.

Any assessment should measure the learning outcomes you give for the course, the unit, or the day. Review your objectives to see what it is you said the student should be able to do. Then determine what type of assessment to use. Good multiple-choice items should be written directly to assess the student's ability to do what you expected as a learning outcome.

Advantages of objective tests over other forms of testing:

— By definition these testing procedures are more objective than other procedures.

— They are less dependent on opinion than some other forms of testing.

— They can be more reliable than other types of testing.

— Instructors can test a large number of students on a wide range of topics in a shorter time.

CONSTRUCTION OF ACHIEVEMENT TESTS

Achievement tests are well suited to provide educators with objective feedback as to how much students are learning and understanding. Commercially published achievement tests, if used carefully, can provide not only evaluations of the knowledge levels of individual students, but also information about how those students compare with students in other schools. While assessing a wide range of skills, however, commercial achievement tests often provide only limited instructional guidance. They seldom provide feedback on the mastery or non-mastery of the full range of specific skills taught in any given classroom.

The most instructionally-relevant achievement tests are those developed by the individual teacher for use with a particular class. Teachers can tailor tests to emphasize the information they consider important and to match the ability levels of their students. If carefully constructed, classroom achievement tests can provide teachers with accurate and useful information about the knowledge retained by their students.

Step 1. Designing the test

The first step in constructing an effective achievement test is to identify what you want students to learn from a unit of instruction. Consider the relative importance of the objectives and include more questions about the most important learning objectives. If, however, the test focuses on a few objectives to the exclusion of others, students will not have the opportunity to demonstrate their understanding of other aspects of the material and you may not be able to make an accurate assessment of each student's knowledge.

The learning objectives that you want to emphasize will determine not only what material to include on the test, but also the specific form the test will take. For example, if it is important that students be able to do long division problems rapidly, consider giving a speeded test. The types of questions to be used will also depend on the learning objectives. If it is important for students to understand how historical events affected one another, then short answer or essay questions might be appropriate. If it is important that students remember dates, then multiple-choice or fill-in-the-blank questions might be appropriate.

Step 2. Writing the questions

Once you have defined the important learning objectives and have, in the light of these objectives, determined which types of questions and what form of test to use, you are ready to begin the second step in constructing an effective achievement test. This step is writing the questions.

General Principles

While the different types of questions—multiple choice, fill-in-the-blank or short answer, true-false, matching, and essay—are constructed differently, the following principles apply to constructing questions and tests in general.

1. Make the instructions for each type of question simple and brief.
2. Use simple and clear language in the questions. If the language is difficult, students who understand the material but who do not have strong language skills may find it difficult to demonstrate their knowledge. If the language is ambiguous, even a student with strong language skills may answer incorrectly if his or her interpretation of the question differs from the instructor's intended meaning.
3. Write items that require specific understanding or ability developed in that course, not just general intelligence or test-wiseness.
4. Do not suggest the answer to one question in the body of another question. This makes the test less useful, as the test-wise student will have an advantage over the student who has an equal grasp of the material, but who has less skill at taking tests.

5. Do not write questions in the negative. If you must use negatives, highlight them, as they may mislead students into answering incorrectly.

6. Specify the units and precision of answers. For example, will you accept numerical answers that are rounded to the nearest integer?

Multiple choice questions

The most commonly used type of question is the multiple-choice question. Multiple-choice questions are more easily and objectively graded than essay questions and are more difficult to answer correctly without the required knowledge than true-false questions. Multiple-choice questions, however, are probably the most difficult type of question to construct. The following are a few guidelines for multiple-choice question construction.

1. State clearly in the instructions whether you require the correct answer or the best answer to each item.

2. Instead of repeating words in each alternative, include these words in the main body of the question. This will make the question easier to read and the options easier to compare. The grammar or structure of the main part of the question must not contain clues to the correct response, however.

3. Make incorrect alternatives attractive to students who have not achieved the targeted learning objectives.

4. Vary randomly the placement of correct responses.

5. Make all choices exactly parallel. Novice test writers tend to make the correct answer longer and more carefully worded and, by doing so, may provide a clue to the correct answer.

6. Never offer "all of the above" or "none of the above" as an alternative in a best-response multiple-choice question. Whether "none of the above" is chosen as a better

response than one of the other options may depend on what evidence the student considers rather than how well he or she understands the material.

7. Control the difficulty of a question by making the alternatives more or less similar or by making the main part of the question more or less specific. If the alternatives are more similar, the student will have to make finer distinctions among them. If the main part is more specific, the student will be required to draw on more detailed knowledge.

Step 3. Final check

Finally, review the test. Are the instructions straightforward? Are the selected learning objectives represented in appropriate proportions? Are the questions carefully and clearly worded? Special care must be taken not to provide clues to the test-wise student. Poorly constructed questions may actually measure not knowledge, but test-taking ability. For example, if two options on a multiple choice question are redundant, a test-wise student will realize that neither can be the correct answer. By eliminating two choices the student increases his or her chances of answering the question correctly.

Interpreting the test results

If you have carefully constructed an achievement test using the above principles, you can be confident that the test will provide useful information about the students' knowledge of the learning objectives. Considering the questions relating to the various learning objectives as separate subtests, you can develop a profile of each student's knowledge of or skill in the objectives. The scores of the subtests can be a useful supplement to the overall test score, as they can help you identify specific areas which may need attention. A carefully-constructed achievement test can, by helping you know what your students are learning, help you to teach more effectively and, ultimately, help the students to master more of the objectives.

SKILLS NEEDED TO TEST DESIGN

The very process of designing instruction encourages the use of learning targets that serve as a measure of successful learning or, quite simply, a "model of success". This model of success becomes the tool for assessment and forms the test or tests. Thus, if the intent of of some instruction is to teach someone to sharpen a pencil, the model of success, and the test, is a systematic determination as to whether a pencil is properly sharpened. By establishing the test prior to designing the instruction, the designer has the model of success as a benchmark for developing the appropriate instructional materials.

Because the assessment process can involve a range of differing tests, a few guidelines expedite the selection and development.

— Prior to actually designing the instructional materials, establish a model of success, the test or tests.

— Determine when, in the overall curriculum, it will be desirable to test so as to obtain a measure of learner success.

— Assure the learning target or targets are clearly defined.

— Assure the test is consistent with the learning target or targets and provides meaningful feedback to the learners regarding their ability to meet the learning targets.

Depending upon the complexity of the learning task, multiple indicators of performance are often desirable particularly where the learning is of "high stakes"

Be sure to recognize and take into account that that there is typically some measurement error in any test instrument.

With the realization that a test is typically used to measure the success of the process the learner uses, measure the success of the final product, or both the process and product, a vast range of tests are possible but typically can be distinguished as those that fall into the venue of "pencil and paper objective tests" and those that require some sort of rubric to determine the degree to which the learner was successful with the instruction.

Objective tests

The common pencil and paper objective tests, such as multiple choice or matching, are often developed using a "test blueprint" or "table of specifications". There is no prescribed format for the test blueprint. Rather, it is very much an instructor's tool for assuring that the learning targets are recognized and are appropriately addressed in both depth and emphasis for the learners. Instructional emphasis considers the importance of the topic and extent to which the topic will be covered within the instruction and classroom activities. The notion of instructional depth might be described as the thinking skills required to come to a solution. These thinking skills have been well described in several formats, including Bloom's Taxonomy, but may be generalized into two states: those skills requiring the learner to use simple knowledge or comprehension skills to arrive at a conclusion; and those thinking skills requiring the learner to use higher order processes such as the application of learning or having to make value judgments. The test blueprint can also become an important teaching tool, particularly as we emphasize learner centered education, by serving as concise instrument for informing learners as to relative importance of specific instruction.

Sample Target	Test Item	Emphasis	Depth
Describe the purpose of the ISD model.	Describe the purpose for using the ISM approach to instructional design	high	simple

Describe and illustrate the ABCD approach to constructing a learning target.	Define the ABC&D within the context of the learning target.	high	simple
	Construct a learning target indicating the ABC & D.	high	higher order
Describe and provide an example of Bloom's Taxonomy of categories of knowledge, comprehension, application, analysis, synthesis, and evaluation.	Define Bloom's categories of knowledge, comprehension, application, analysis, synthesis, and evaluation.	low	simple
	Provide an example of each of Bloom's categories.	low	higher order

Rubric-based Tests

Rubric oriented tests are inherently more complex than the common pencil and paper objective test but offer greater opportunity to evaluate more complex learning. In its simplest form, a rubric can be thought of as checklist whereby the learner's skills, relative to the learning targets, are being identified. Common tests falling into this domain include essays, portfolios, and performance-based tests. Consistent with learner centered education, the instructor would provide the learners with the rubric thus assuring the learner has a thorough understanding of the instructional expectations.

Sample Test Rubric

Learning Target	Measure	Yes 1/No 0
Insert pencil into sharpener.	Able to properly insert pencil into pencil sharpener.	

Sharpen pencil by applying pressure to the pencil and cranking the sharpener.	Able to apply appropriate pressure to the pencil.	Able to crank the sharpener.
Identify a properly sharpened pencil point.	Able to identify a properly sharpened pencil point by stopping the sharpening process.	
		Total Points

Rubrics can take many forms, but the instructor should recognize the learning targets as foundational to developing the rubric. The rubric should be sufficiently defined so as to minimize bias when scoring learners, and provide learners with worthwhile feedback concerning their successes and weaknesses.

SELECTING TEST ITEMS

When educators construct a test, first and foremost, they must ensure that they are testing what they truly set-out to test (i.e. test validity). In order to accomplish this, the test items educators construct should correspond one to one with the objectives that have been developed. In this regard, the test is an interface between the learning objectives and the instruction that proceeds from these objectives.

Constructing teach-made tests, which are norm-referenced assessments, might include true-false, multiple choice, completion, short-answer, and/or essay items. It may be important to note, however, true-false items are not so consistent in measuring learning. This occurs because it may be difficult to determine the extent of blind guessing. Sax states that...uncertain students can always guess and hope to answer correctly....and teachers will have to construct longer examinations to compensate for guessing. The repercussions on diagnostics, when true-false are used, are substantial. How would we be able to determine if the true-false items were written in confusing terms, too easy, too difficult, or, as stated before, were answered by the learner's guessing? We do not want to leave learning to chance.

WRITING A MULTIPLE CHOICE ITEM

A notable concern of many teachers is that they frequently have the task of constructing tests but have relatively little training or information to rely on in this task. The objective of this section is to set out some conventional wisdom for the construction of multiple-choice tests, which are one of the most common forms of teacher-constructed tests. The comments which follow are applicable mainly to multiple-choice tests covering fairly broad topic areas.

Before proceeding, it will be useful to establish our terms for discussing multiple-choice items. The "stem" is the introductory question or incomplete statement at the beginning of each item and this is followed by the options. The "options" consist of the answer—the correct option—and "distractors"—the incorrect but (we hope) tempting options.

General objectives

As a rule, one is concerned with writing stems that are clear and parsimonious, answers that are unequivocal and chosen by the students who do best on the test, and distractors that are plausible competitors of the answer as evidenced by the frequency with which they are chosen. Lastly, and probably most important, we should adopt the attitude that items need to be developed over time in the light of evidence that can be obtained from the statistical output typically provided by a measurement services office (where tests are machine-scored) and from "expert" editorial review.

Planning

The primary objective in planning a test is to outline the actual course content that the test will cover. A convenient way of accomplishing this is to take 10 minutes following each class to list on an index card the important concepts covered in class and in assigned reading for that day. These cards can then be used later as a source of test items. An even more conscientious approach, of course, would be to construct the test items themselves after each class. The advantage of either of these approaches is that the resulting test is likely to be a better representation of course activity than if the test were constructed before the course or after the course, when we usually have only a fond memory or optimistic syllabus to draw from. When we are satisfied that we have an accurate description of the content areas, then all that remains is to construct items that represent specific content areas. In developing good multiple-choice items, three tasks need to be considered: writing stems, writing options, and ongoing item development. The first two are discussed here.

Writing stems

We will first describe some basic rules for the construction of multiple-choice stems, because they are typically, though not necessarily, written before the options.

1. Before writing the stem, identify the one point to be tested by that item. In general, the stem should not pose more than one problem, although the solution to that problem may require more than one step.

2. Construct the stem to be either an incomplete statement or a direct question, avoiding stereotyped phraseology, as rote responses are usually based on verbal stereotypes. For example, the following stems (with answers in parentheses) illustrate undesirable phraseology:

   "What is the biological theory of recapitulation?

   (Ontogeny repeats phylogeny)"

   "Who was the chief spokesman for the "American System?"

   "(Henry Clay)"

Correctly answering these questions likely depends less on understanding than on recognizing familiar phraseology.

3. Avoid including nonfunctional words that do not contribute to the basis for choosing among the options. Often an introductory statement is included to enhance the appropriateness or significance of an item but does not affect the meaning of the problem in the item. Generally, such superfluous phrases should be excluded. For example, consider:

   "The American flag has three colors. One of them is

   (1) red (2) green (3) black"

   versus

   "One of the colors of the American flag is

   (1) red (2) green (3) black"

   In particular, irrelevant material should not be used to make the answer less obvious. This tends to place too much importance on reading comprehension as a determiner of the correct option.

4. Include as much information in the stem and as little in the options as possible. For example, if the point of an item is to associate a term with its definition, the preferred format would be to present the definition in the stem and several terms as options rather than to present the term in the stem and several definitions as options.

5. Restrict the use of negatives in the stem. Negatives in the stem usually require that the answer be a false statement. Because students are likely in the habit of searching for true statements, this may introduce an unwanted bias.

6. Avoid irrelevant clues to the correct option. Grammatical construction, for example, may lead students to reject options which are grammatically incorrect as the stem is stated. Perhaps more common and subtle, though, is the problem of common elements in the stem and in the answer. Consider the following item:

"What led to the formation of the States' Rights Party?

a. The level of federal taxation

b. The demand of states for the right to make their own laws

c. The industrialization of the South

d. The corruption of federal legislators on the issue of state taxation

One does not need to know U.S. history in order to be attracted to the answer, b.

Other rules that we might list are generally commonsensical, including recommendations for independent and important items and prohibitions against complex, imprecise wording.

Writing options

Following the construction of the item stem, the likely more difficult task of generating options presents itself. The rules we list below are not likely to simplify this task as much as they are intended to guide our creative efforts.

1. Be satisfied with three or four well constructed options. Generally, the minimal improvement to the item due to that hard-to-come-by fifth option is not worth the effort to construct it. Indeed, all else the same, a test of 10 items each with four options is likely a better test than a test with nine items of five options each.

2. Construct distractors that are comparable in length, complexity and grammatical form to the answer, avoiding the use of such words as "always," "never," and "all." Adherence to this rule avoids some of the more common sources of biased cueing. For example, we sometimes find ourselves increasing the length and specificity of the answer (relative to distractors) in order to insure its truthfulness. This, however, becomes an easy-to-spot clue for the testwise student. Related to this issue is the question of

whether or not test writers should take advantage of these types of cues to construct more tempting distractors. Surely not! The number of students choosing a distractor should depend only on deficits in the content area which the item targets and should not depend on cue biases or reading comprehension differences in "favor" of the distractor.

3. Options which read "none of the above," "both a. and e. above," "all of the above," etc., should be avoided when the students have been instructed to choose "the best answer," which implies that the options vary in degree of correctness. On the other hand, "none of the above" is acceptable if the question is factual and is probably desirable if computation yields the answer. "All of the above" is never desirable, as one recognized distractor eliminates it and two recognized answers identify it.

4. After the options are written, vary the location of the answer on as random a basis as possible. A convenient method is to flip two (or three) coins at a time where each possible Head-Tail combination is associated with a particular location for the answer. Furthermore, if the test writer is conscientious enough to randomize the answer locations, students should be informed that the locations are randomized. (Testwise students know that for some instructors the first option is rarely the answer.)

5. If possible, have a colleague with expertise in the content area of the exam review the items for possible ambiguities, redundancies or other structural difficulties. Having completed the items we are typically so relieved that we may be tempted to regard the task as completed and each item in its final and permanent form. Yet, another source of item and test improvement is available to us, namely, statistical analyses of student responses.

Consider the following cautions when crafting multiple choice items.

1) Try to avoid using negatively worded stems.

Example: In the classic Roman play, Menaechmi,the character, Menaechmus,

a) is a kidnapper

b) is from Sicily

c) is not a twin

d) is not married

Notice that the stem options are arranged in alphabetical order.

2) Avoid crafting items concerning personal opinion.

Example: Which of the following extraordinary African-American women writers wrote the most controversial pieces of literature?

a) Alice Walker

b) Bethany Veney

c) Maya Angelou

d) Toni Morrison

3) Avoid using extraneous wording in items.

Example: In a class of fourteen third-graders, there are five children who are considered advanced; they usually score between the 80th and 90th percentiles, on their math tests. Seven of the children fall between the 50th to the 60th percentiles, on all tests. And, three of the children usually score, somewhere between the 40th and 50th percentiles; however, one student is consistently absent on test days and is not ranked. Their scores on a current math test (all students took the same test) were 9,8,9,6, 4,10, 5, 5, 8, 3, 5, 4, 7, and 7. What was the mean score for this class of third-graders on this particular test?

a) 5

b) 6.4

c) 7.2

d) 14

4) Avoid building items that are grammatically incorrect.

Example: Learning is a

a) relatively permanent change in behavior.

b) changes over time.

c) increase in a targeted performance.

Constructing good multiple choice items

— Planning the item – align with your stated learning outcome, determine at what level you want the reply,

— Writing the Stem – The stem is the question or incomplete statement. It is a clearly stated problem and a single problem. Avoid complex questions – keep it simple. If the stem calls for an exception (EXCEPT) or negative (NOT) emphasize that.

— Writing the Alternatives – Alternatives are possible answers. Make them brief. If there are common words put them in the stem. As far as possible, make the alternatives similar in form. Make them grammatically agree with the stem. Avoid any clues. Put in alphabetical or numerical order. Avoid "all of the above" or "none of the above".

— Writing the Distracters – Distracters are alternatives that are incorrect but distract the student who has not learned. Use common errors or common misconceptions.

— Sequencing the items – some sequence is helpful; some tests are sequenced just as the class has been taught. This allows for the natural progression of thought from prerequisite knowledge to broader knowledge or application.

Suggestions for Constructing Multiple-Choice Items

1. Use the stem to present the problem or question as clearly as possible.
2. Use direct questions rather than incomplete statements for the stem.
3. Include as much of the item as possible in the stem so that alternatives can be kept brief.
4. However, when applying definitions, it is recommended you place the terms in the stem and use the definitions as options.
5. List alternatives on separate lines rather than including the options as part of the stem so that all options can be clearly distinguished.
6. Keep all alternatives in a similar format (i.e., all phrases, all sentences, etc.).
7. Make sure that all options are plausible responses to the stem. (Poor alternatives should not be included just for the sake of having more options.)
8. Check to see that all choices are grammatically consistent with the stem.
9. Try to make alternatives for an item approximately the same length. (Making the correct response consistently longer is a common error.)
10. Use misconceptions students have displayed in class or errors commonly made by students in the class as the basis for incorrect alternatives
11. Use "all of the above" and "none of the above" sparingly since students on the basis of incomplete knowledge often choose these alternatives.
12. Use capital letters (A,B,C,D,E) as response signs rather than lower-case letters ("a" gets confused with "d" and "c" with "e" if the quality of the typeface or duplication is poor).

13. Use negatively stated items sparingly. When they are used, it helps to underline or otherwise visually emphasize the negative word. Never use the word "not" in a multiple-choice question.

14. Make sure there is only one best or correct response to the stem.

15. Keep the number of alternatives at five or less. (The more alternatives used, the lower the probability of students getting the correct answer by guessing. Beyond five alternatives, confusion and poor alternatives are likely.)

16. Randomly distribute correct responses among the alternative positions so that there are no discernible patterns to the answer sequence (ABBABBABB, etc.)

17. Try to have a nearly equal proportion of As, Bs, Cs, etc. as the correct answers.

Multiple-Choice Item Writing: Do's and Don'ts.

In this section a few suggestions for item-writing, but only to a limited extent, due to its coverage of other aspects of test development are given. What follows here is a fairly comprehensive list of recommendations for writing multiple choice items. Some of these are backed up by psychometric research; i.e., it has been found that, generally, the resulting scores are more accurate indicators of each student's knowledge when the recommendations are followed than when they are violated. Other recommendations result from logical deduction.

Content

1. Do ask questions that require more than knowledge of facts. For example, a question might require selection of the best answer when all of the options contain elements of correctness. Such questions tend to be more difficult and discriminating than questions that merely ask for a fact. Justifying the "bestness" of the keyed option may be as

challenging to the instructor as the item was to the students, but, after all, isn't challenging students and responding to their challenges a big part of what being a teacher is all about?

2. Don't offer superfluous information as an introduction to a question, for example, "The presence and association of the male seems to have profound effects on female physiology in domestic animals. Research has shown that in cattle presence of a bull has the following effect:" This approach probably represents an unconscious effort to continue teaching while testing and is not likely to be appreciated by the students, who would prefer direct questions and less to read. The stem just quoted could be condensed to "Research has shown that the presence of a bull has which of the following effects on cows?"

Structure

3. Don't ask a question that begins, "Which of the following is true [or false]?" followed by a collection of unrelated options. Each test question should focus on some specific aspect of the course. Therefore, it's OK to use items that begin, "Which of the following is true [or false] concerning X?" followed by options all pertaining to X. However, this construction should be used sparingly if there is a tendency to resort to trivial reasons for falseness or an opposite tendency to offer options that are too obviously true. A few true-false questions (in among the multiple-choice questions) may forestall these problems. The options would be: "1) True 2) False".

4. Don't use items like the following"

   What is (are) the capital(s) of Bolivia?

   A. La Paz

   1) A only

   2) B only

3) C only

Research on this item type has consistently shown it to be easier and less discriminating than items with distinct options. In the example above, one only needs to remember that Bolivia has two capitals to be assured of answering correctly. This problem can be alleviated by offering all possible combinations of the three basic options, namely:

1) A only, 2) B only, 3) C only, 4) A and B, 5) A and C, 6) B and C, 7) A, B, and C, 8) None of the above.

However, due to its complexity, initial use of this adaptation should be limited.

Options

5. Do ask questions with varying numbers of options. There is no psychometric advantage to having a uniform number, especially if doing so results in options that are so implausible that no one or almost no one marks them. In fact, some valid and important questions demand only two or three options, e.g., "If drug X is administered, body temperature will probably: 1) increase, 2) stay about the same, 3) decrease."

6. Don't put negative options following a negative stem. Empirically (or statistically) such items may appear to perform adequately, but this is probably only because brighter students who naturally tend to get higher scores are also better able to cope with the logical complexity of a double negative.

7. Don't use "all of the above." Recognition of one wrong option eliminates "all of the above," and recognition of two right options identifies it as the answer, even if the other options are completely unknown to the student. Probably some instructors use items with "all of the above" as yet another way of extending their teaching into the test (see 2 above). It just seems so good to have the

students affirm, say, all of the major causes of some phenomenon. With this approach, "all of the above" is the answer to almost every item containing it, and the students soon figure this out.

8. Do ask questions with "none of the above" as the final option, especially if the answer requires computation. Its use makes the question harder and more discriminating, because the uncertain student cannot focus on a set of options that must contain the answer. Of course, "none of the above" cannot be used if the question requires selection of the best answer and should not be used following a negative stem. Also, it is important that "none of the above" should be the answer to a reasonable proportion of the questions containing it.

9. Don't include superfluous information in the options. The reasons given for 8 above apply. In addition, as another manifestation of the desire to teach while testing, the additional information is likely to appear on the correct answer: "1) W, 2) X, 3) Y, because ...., 4) Z." Students are very sensitive to this tendency and take advantage of it.

10. Don't use specific determiners in distractors. Sometimes in a desperate effort to produce another, often unneeded, distractor, a statement is made incorrect by the inclusion of words like all or never, e.g., "All humans have 46 chromosomes." Students learn to classify such statements as distractors when otherwise ignorant.

11. Don't repeat wording from the stem in the correct option. Again, an ignorant student will take advantage of this practice.

Errors to Avoid

Most violations of the recommendations given thus far should not be classified as outright errors, but, instead, perhaps, as lapses of judgment. And, as almost all rules have exceptions, there are probably circumstances where some of 1-11 above would not hold. However, there are three not-too-common item-writing/test-preparation errors that represent nothing less than negligence. They are now mentioned to encourage careful preparation and proofreading of tests:

— *Typos.* These are more likely to appear in distractors than in the stem and the correct answer, which get more scrutiny from the test preparer. Students easily become aware of this tendency if it is present.

— *Grammatical inconsistency between stem and options.* Almost always, the stem and the correct answer are grammatically consistent, but distractors, often produced as afterthoughts, may not mesh properly with the stem. Again, students quickly learn to take advantage of this foible.

— *Overlapping distractors.* For example: "Due to budget cutbacks, the university library now subscribes to fewer than (?) periodicals. 1) 25,000 2) 20,000 3) 15,000 4) 10,000"

  Perhaps surprisingly, not all students "catch on" to items like this, but many do. Worse yet, the instructor might indicate option 2 as the correct answer.

— Finally, we consider an item-writing foible reported by Smith. What option would you select among the following (stem omitted)?

  1) Abraham Lincoln 3) Stephen A. Douglas

  2) Robert E. Lee

  The testwise but ignorant student will select Lincoln because it represents the intersection of two categories of prominent nineteenth century people, namely, presidents and men associated with the Civil War. Try this one:

  1) before breakfast

  3) on a full stomach

  2) with meals

Three options have to do with eating, and two with the time of day. Only one relates to both. Unfortunately, some item writers consciously or unconsciously construct items of this type with the intersection invariably the correct answer.

Item Analysis for Multiple-Choice Tests

The statistical behavior of "bad" items is fundamentally different from that of "good" items. Of course, the items have to be administered to students in order to obtain the needed statistics. This fact underscores our point of view that tests can be improved by maintaining and developing a pool of "good" items from which future tests will be drawn in part or in whole. This is particularly true for instructors who teach the same course more than once.

What make an item psychometrically good? In answering this question, it is desirable to restrict our discussion to tests which are written to cover a unified portion of course material such that it is unlikely that a student would do well on one part of a test and poorly on another. If this latter situation is the case, the comments which follow will apply only if the corresponding topics are tested separately. Regardless, this approach would be preferred, because, otherwise, scores would be ambiguous in their reporting of students' achievement.

Once the instructor is satisfied that the test items meet the above criterion and that they are indeed appropriately written, what remains is to evaluate the extent to which they discriminate among students. The degree to which this goal is attained is the basic measure of item quality for almost all multiple-choice tests. For each item the primary indicator of its power to discriminate students is the correlation coefficient reflecting the tendency of students selecting the correct answer to have high scores. This coefficient is reported by typical item analysis programs as the item discrimination coefficient or, equivalently, as the point-biserial correlation between item score and total score. This coefficient should be positive, indicating that students answering correctly tend to have higher scores. Similar coefficients may be provided for the wrong choices. These should be negative, which means that students selecting these choices tend to have lower scores.

Alternatively, some item analysis programs provide the percentages of examinees scoring in the top, middle, and bottom thirds who select each option. In this case, one would hope to find that large proportions of the high scorers answered correctly, while larger proportions of low scorers selected the distractors. The proportion of students answering an item correctly also affects its discrimination power. This point may be summarized by saying that items answered correctly (or incorrectly) by a large proportion of examinees (more than 85%) have markedly reduced power to discriminate. On a good test, most items will be answered correctly by 30% to 80% of the examinees.

A general indicator of test quality is the reliability estimate usually reported on the test scoring/analysis printout. Referred to as KR-20 or Coefficient Alpha, it reflects the extent to which the test would yield the same ranking of examinees if readministered with no effect from the first administration, in other words, its accuracy or power of discrimination. Values of as low as .5 are satisfactory for short tests (10 - 15 items), though tests with over 50 items should yield KR-20 values of .8 or higher (1.0 is the maximum). In any event, important decisions concerning individual students should not be based on a single test score when the corresponding KR-20 is less than .8. Unsatisfactorily low KR-20s are usually due to an excess of very easy (or hard) items, poorly written items that do not discriminate, or violation of the precondition that the items test a unified body of content.

Imporving the ability of Items to Discriminate

The statistics usually provided by a test scoring service provide the information needed to keep a record of each item with respect to its performance. One approach is simply to tape a copy of each item on a 5 x 7 card with the test content area briefly described at the top. In addition, tape the corresponding line from the computer printout for that item each time it is used. Alternatively, item banking programs may provide for inclusion of the proportions marking each option and item discrimination coefficients along with each item's content.

A few basic rules for item development follow:

1. Items that correlate less than .15 with total test score should probably be restructured. One's best guess is that such items do not measure the same skill or ability as does the test on the whole or that they are confusing or misleading to examinees. Generally, a test is better (i.e., more reliable) the more homogeneous the items. Just how to restructure the item depends largely on careful thinking at this level.

2. Distractors that are not chosen by any examinees should be replaced or eliminated. They are not contributing to the test's ability to discriminate the good students from the poor students. One should not be concerned if each distractor is not chosen by the same number of examinees. Different kinds of mistakes may very well be made by different numbers of students. Also, the fact that a majority of students miss an item does not imply that the item should be changed, although such items should be double-checked for their accuracy. One should be suspicious about the correctness of any item in which a single distractor is chosen more often than all other options, including the answer, and especially so if that distractor's correlation with the total score is positive.

3. tems that virtually everyone gets right are useless for discriminating among students and should be replaced by more difficult items. This recommendation is particularly true if you adopt the traditional attitude toward letter grade assignments that letter grades more or less fit a predetermined distribution.

By constructing, recording, and adjusting items in this fashion, teachers can develop a pool of items for specific content areas with conveniently available resources. The suggestions here focus on the development of tests which are homogeneous, that is, tests intended to measure a unified content area. Only for such tests is it reasonable to maximize item-test correlations or, equivalently, KR-20 or Coefficient Alpha (reliability), which is the objective of step 1 above. The extent to which a high average item-test correlation can be achieved depends to some extent on the content area.

It is generally acknowledged that well constructed tests in vocabulary or mathematics are more homogeneous than well constructed tests in social sciences. This circumstance suggests that particular content areas have optimal levels of homogeneity and that these vary from discipline to discipline. Perhaps psychologists should strive for lower test homogeneity than mathematicians because course content is less homogeneous.

A second issue involving test homogeneity is that of the precision of a student's obtained test score as an estimate of that student's "true" score on the skill tested. Precision (reliability) increases as the average item-test correlation increases, all else the same; and precision decreases as the number of items decreases, all else the same.

These two relationships lead to an interesting paradox: often the precision of a test can be increased simply by discarding the items with low item-test correlations. For example, a 30-item multiple-choice test administered by the author resulted in a reliability of .79, and discarding the seven items with item-test correlations below .20 yielded a 23-item test with a reliability of .88! That is, by dropping the worst items from the test, the students' obtained scores on the shorter version are judged to be more precise estimates than the same students' obtained scores on the longer version. The reader may question whether it is ethical to throw out poorly performing questions when some students may have answered them correctly based on their knowledge of course material. Our opinion is that this practice is completely justified. The purpose of testing is to determine each student's rank. Retaining psychometrically unsatisfactory questions is contrary to this goal and degrades the accuracy of the resulting ranking.

CONSTRUCTING ESSAYS AND SHORT ANSWER TEST ITEMS

Essay Items

1) Avoid crafting poorly written essay items.

   Example: Analyze Bentham's hedonistic calculus and think of ways you either agree or disagree with this philosophy by explaining what happens when people consider consequences to their actions.

   To avoid writing items like the one above, create a checklist that asks the following questions:

   1) Does the item reflect the learning target?
   2) Is the item focused?
   3) Does the item present a new or novel situation in which the learner can apply his/her knowledge or skill?
   4) Is the item worded in a way that allows for the learners to interpret correctly what it is you are asking them to do?
   5) Is the level of complexity appropriate for the learner(s)?
   6) From the wording of the item, is the learner clear about the purpose for which they are writing?
   7) Is the item worded so that the learner understand what he/she is required to demonstrate?
   8) In regard to the entire test, have you, the educator, allowed an appropriate amount of time for the student to respond to this item?

Constructing Completion or Short-Answer Items

1) Avoid writing items that are not clear about the expected response.

2) Avoid using more than one blank for each item.

   Using more than one blank causes confusion on the part of the learner.

3) Avoid putting the blank at the beginning of an item. Try placing the blank at the end.

   Putting the blank at the beginning of the item, might cause the learner some confusion as to what he or she is expected to do.

   When writing test items, take into account these caveats. In doing so, you will create more effective, reliable, and valid tests

Advantages of essay and short answer items

Advantages of essay and short answer items include:

— They allow expression of both breadth and depth of learning, and encourage originality, creativity, and divergent thinking.

— Written items offer students the opportunity to use their own judgment, writing styles, and vocabularies.

— They are less time-consuming to prepare than any other item type. (This is misleading. A well thought out discussion question may take more time and actually consist of more parts that just one question.)

The main disadvantages are:

— essay items are difficult and time-consuming to score, and

— they are prone to biased and unreliable scoring.

Suggestions for Constructing Essays and Short Answer Test Items

— Use novel problems or material whenever possible, but only if they relate to class learning.

— Make essay questions comprehensive rather than focused on small units of content.

— Require students to demonstrate command of background information by asking them to provide supporting evidence for claims and assertions.

— Provide clear directions as to the expectations.

— Allow students an appropriate amount of time. (It is helpful to give students some guidelines on how much time to use on each question, as well as the desired length and format of the response, e.g., full sentences, phrases only, outline, and so on.)

— Inform students, in advance, about the proportional value of each item in comparison to the total grade.

— Use a scoring rubric for increasing the reliability of scoring on the exam.

Short answer questions require the construction of a response by students. Common types are completion (fill in the blank, list, etc. and complete sentence short answers.

Short answer are generally considered more valid than mutiple choice because they require the learner to recall the information rather than simply recognize it. Guessing the correct answer is reduced compared to multiple choice. However, they are somewhat more ambiguous, because the reader has to interpret the question (e.g., social reciprocity of apes or humans?)

Rules for constructing short answer questions:

1) Sample enough of the behavior you are testing to have confidence that the student knows it.

2) Tell the student what each item is worth compared to the total test.

3) Avoid, to the extent possible, questions with multiple correct answers.

4) Provide enough of a stem so the answer to the question isn't ambiguous. E.g., _______ _______ disease is caused by a class of _______________ called _______________. is NOT a good question.

5) Remember you won't be able to anticipate the many ways learners will interpret the question. Be prepared to accept answers that were not originally anticipated if the student can tell you why they are correct as they read the question.

TIPS FOR CONSTRUCTING TEST QUESTIONS

True/False Items

— Avoid absolute words like "all," "never," and "always."

— Make sure items are clearly true or false rather than ambiguous.

— Limit true/false questions to ten.

— Consider asking students to make false questions true to encourage higher-order thinking.

Matching Items

— Limit list to between five and ten items.

— Use homogeneous lists. (Don't mix names with dates.)

— Give clear instructions. (Write letter, number, etc.)

— Give more choices that there are questions.

Multiple-Choice Items

— State main idea in the core or stem of the question.

— Use reasonable incorrect choices. (Avoid ridiculous choices.)

— Make options the same length (nothing very long or short).

— Include multiple correct choices (a and b, all of the above).

Completion Items

— Structure a brief, specific answer for each item.

— Avoid passages lifted directly from text (emphasis on memorisation).

— Use blanks of equal length.

— Avoid multiple blanks that sometimes make a sentence too confusing.

Essay Items

— Avoid all-encompassing questions ("Discuss" is ambiguous...tell all you know about a subject).

— Define criteria for evaluation.

— Give point value.

— Use some higher-order thinking verbs like "predict" or "compare and contrast" rather than all recall verbs like "list" and "name."

ITEM BANKING

Various school districts use standardized tests as a way to measure scholastic achievement. Usually, these districts need to revise tests with some frequency to avoid administering the same test year after year. Unfortunately, creating new tests can be a very time consuming endeavor. Not only do test writers need to compose the test items, they also must determine each item's difficulty in order to ensure that a test will neither be too hard nor too easy.

Using item banks, test makers can escape this process. Item banks are files of various suitable test items that are "coded by subject area, instructional level, instructional objective measured, and various pertinent item characteristics (e.g., item difficulty and discriminating power)"

Advantages of Item Banking

The primary advantage of item banking is in test development. Using a item response theory method, such as the Rasch model, items from multiple tests are placed on a common scale, one scale per subject matter. The scale indicates the relative difficulty of the items. Items can be placed on the scale, i.e. into the item bank, without extensive testing. New subtests and tests, with predictable characteristics, can be developed by drawing items from the bank. For example, suppose you are interested in developing a new subtest to cover fractions in seventh grade. You can go to the item bank, identify items related to your objectives and then predict the characteristics of a subtest composed of those items. The effect of including or excluding particular items can also be predicted.

Another advantage of an item bank is that it will permit you to "deposit" additional items to be withdrawn as needed. Depending on the size of the testing program, there can be two practical approaches for making deposits. You can make "large deposits" by merging your item bank with one from another district. You can also make "small deposits" by adding a few locally developed items at a time. The large deposit option will involve purchasing or trading items with another district and then equating their scale to yours. The small deposit option involves piloting a fewer number of items with examinees in several grade levels. This can easily be accomplished by adding a supplemental page containing experimental items to be administered along with a booklet from the school system.

Item banking provides substantial savings of time and energy over conventional test development. In traditional test development, items can only be described relative to the other items within the test and to whom they were given. That is, item characteristics are extremely group and test specific. With item banking, items are described their relative difficulty across grade levels. In order to develop a new test or subtest, one does not need to go through the laborious process of developing a large set of items for piloting and evaluating. Instead, one just draws from the bank. Further, drawing from the bank allows one to make fairly accurate predictions concerning composite test characteristics.

One additional advantage of item banking is that it helps establish a language for discussing curriculum goals and objectives. The items describe individual tasks students are capable or incapable of doing. The location of the items on a calibrated scale allows one to identify the relative difficulty of particular tasks. This provides a way to discuss possible learning hierarchies and ways to better structure curriculum.

Disadvantages of Item Banking

Item banking and item response theory are not cure-alls for measurement problems. Persistence and good judgment must remain vital aspects in any test construction and test usage effort. One must make every possible effort to include only quality items in the item bank. The same care and effort must go into item writing. Items purchased from external sources must be evaluated carefully for match to your curriculum as well as for technical quality. Item banking involves equating various tests and items. It is entirely possible, mathematically, to equate tests which cover entirely different subject matter. At the practical level, this means that it is also possible to equate items which assess subtly, but significantly different skills. In order to avoid this undesirable situation, the item review process must also include a careful evaluation of the skills assessed by each item and tests must be carefully formulated.

The intent of compiling a test using latent trait theory is to be able to make a prediction of the composite test characteristics. While the prediction is often surprisingly accurate, it must be validated. Tests developed using latent trait theory should still be field tested.

While some districts have implemented very successful item banks and Rasch calibrated testing programs without knowing anything about IRT, good practice calls for a staff that is comfortable with and knowledgeable of what they are doing. A district undertaking an item banking project should have full understanding of the practical as well as the mathematical/theoretical aspects of item banking.

An item bank really consists of multiple collections of items with fairly unidimensional content area, such as mathematic computations or vocabulary. Collections of items usually span several grade levels. In order to develop the bank, many tests must be calibrated, linked (or equated), and organized. This requires a great deal of work in terms of preparation and planning and in terms of computer time and expertise. Once the item bank is established, however, test development time, effort, and cost is reduced.

Planning for an item bank

The most crucial step in developing an item bank is planning. This involves the preparation of individuals, the identification of what you have to start an item bank, and the identification of what you hope to accomplish with an item bank.

Everyone on the staff should have enough familiarity with Rasch measurement principles and Item banking to be able to knowledgeably discuss and explain the project. You can formally train your staff by using in-house personnel, bringing in a traveling workshop, or having people attend a pre-session at a research association or conference.

You should have senior level personnel available to answer technical questions that might arise. You should also have computer experts that are capable of doing the following tasks:

1) modifying computer programs,

2) establishing a data base system, and

3) capable of running packaged programs.

If you intend to do any item bank exchanges or purchases, you should have someone on your staff who knows what is available. You need personnel capable of critically evaluating test items for technical quality, curriculum match, unidimensionality, and potential bias. In order to accurately calibrate test items and establish scales, items need to be presented to examinees with a wide range of ability.

In order to link various forms and grade levels within a content area, common anchor items are needed. (These anchor items must be administered along with the items within a given form. The form and anchor items are calibrated together. The anchor item parameter values based on calibration with one form are compared with the anchor item parameter values based on calibration with another form. The difference in parameter values is used to link the forms.) You need to identify for which content areas you have administered overlapping subtests and the number of students responding to the set of items. You may find you will need to gather additional item response data to link forms and grade levels.

Your data processing staff should examine literature and programs on item banking to determine what programs must be developed and what programs can be modified.

As much as possible, you should identify your projected testing needs for the next five years. This would involve identification of which subtests you will need to revise, what additional areas you may need to assess, and how objectives might be differently stressed.

Start-up activities

The start-up activities would mostly involve administrative activities and the data processing staff. Each test would have to be calibrated and equated to the parallel form and adjacent grade levels. The data processing staff would have to adapt existing computer programs to the local system and develop a database system. They would then calibrate each test, equate the tests, and store the equated item parameters and their descriptors in a database system. With a large number of tests and items, this becomes a major undertaking.

Administrative staff would have to coordinate activities to insure that the data requirements are met. During the planning process, a chart can be developed to identify which tests and anchor items have been and will need to be administered to the requisite sample. Working from these charts, testing coordinators will need to organize the administration of tests and subtests needed to calibrate and equate all the items going into the item bank. This involves compiling test booklets, making testing arrangements, collecting response sheets, and preparing data for data processing. Depending on frequency of students taking multiple subtests from different levels and forms, this too can be a major undertaking.

Running the item bank

The item bank will allow you to withdraw items as needed to develop new or even special tests and subtests. There are basically two activities involved in running an item bank—making deposits and withdrawing items to develop a test.

There are two viable options for making deposits to the item bank. The "large deposit" option involves merging an existing item bank with your own. If the existing item bank has been IRT calibrated, then you only need to administer a subset of items (per content area) from the new bank along with items already in your item bank. Remember, each item bank uses its own anchor items and allows you to equate the scales. This part will involve testing with a relatively small group of students. The anchor items from the new item bank can be appended to the present group. Coordination would be similar to that involved in starting your own item bank.

The major task involved in using items from another item bank is a thorough, careful review of the items. All potential entries must be evaluated for technical quality, curriculum match, and potential bias. This would involve your test development experts, curriculum/instructional staff, and coordination between the two.

After an item review, items non-calibrated could be treated like items developed by your staff. "Small deposits" would be made by calibrating and equating a few items at a time. One very efficient approach to collecting the requisite data is to append subtests of new items to original groups. The items within the original group would serve as anchor items for the new subtest(s) of items. In this manner, you can be constantly adding to your item bank.

Once developed and growing, your item bank is ready to provide the advantages discussed above. To develop a new subtest, you would develop a blueprint/table of specifications to outline what you want your new subtest to be like. Curriculum specialists and test development experts would then go to the item bank and identify which items in the bank appear appropriate in terms of content and in terms of their relative difficulty. If they find an insufficient number of items, they can make arrangements to add new items to the bank.

If the bank contains a sufficient number of items of the appropriate nature, the items can be grouped to form a new subtest. Without pilot testing, the characteristics of this new subtest can be predicted. With reasonable accuracy, you will know how much skill an examinee needs to obtain any given total raw score on the new subtest. The prediction should be validated by administering the subtest to students having received appropriate instruction and students not having received such instruction. This can also be accomplished by appending items to the existing forms. This validation would need a sample as large as you used in field testing the original group.

An item bank provides a scale of relative difficulty of tasks that covers multiple grade levels and skills within content areas. As a service to the instructional/curriculum staff, you can provide information on the relative difficulty of different tasks within and across grades levels. For example, you can identify which fraction problems seventh graders find as difficult as certain decimal problems; or you can identify which reading skills taught in fourth grade can be mastered by students in their grade. It could also be used to help organize special programs for gifted and remedial students.

7

Elementary Concept of Normal Distribution Curve and Correlation

NORMAL DISTRIBUTION AND THE NORMAL CURVE

In this chapter we are discussing about a frequency distribution in which the dispersion of the scores is symmetrical about the central mean, that is, in which the frequency of results above the average matches exactly the frequency of results below the average and in which the most frequent result falls at the average. In such a distribution, the high point will be in the middle of the distribution, and each side of the high point will be a mirror image of the other.

For such a distribution, the histogram would be perfectly symmetrical around the centre; in other words, the tallest column will occur exactly in the centre of the diagram and the other columns will fall away on either side of the central value equally on either side. Such a perfectly symmetrical distribution is called a normal distribution (in popular language the shape of this frequency distribution is commonly called a bell curve).

Notice that a normal distribution may come with very different dimensions, but the characteristics mentioned above hold in all cases. In other words, the characteristic bell shape is always present.

Here are a few examples of histograms illustrating normal distribution. These histograms illustrate the probability distribution for success in various coin tosses. The x-axis here indicates the number of heads in a particular sequence of coin tosses; the y-axis represents the theoretical frequency of that result in the given number of fair tosses. The histograms will have different sizes and shapes, because the frequency distribution changes with the number of tosses. But notice that all the histograms are perfectly symmetrical around the centre (the tallest and therefore most frequent value). Remember, once again, that these diagrams represent probability distributions, or the frequency of results theoretically calculated. And since the total of all the probabilities for an event equals 1, the shaded area contained in all the columns equals 1.

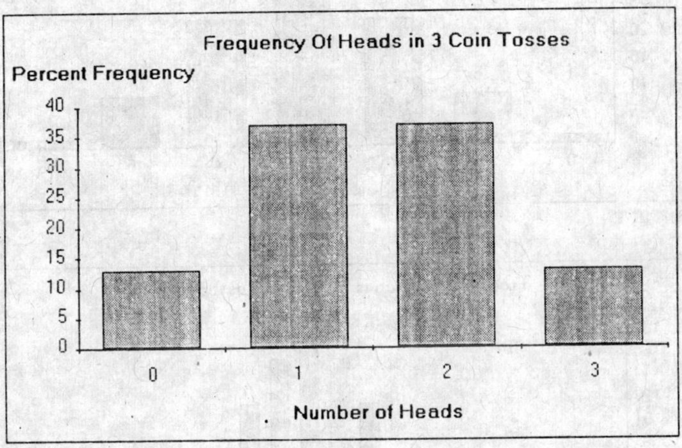

This diagram indicates that in a three coin toss sequence (or three coins tossed simultaneously) there are four possible results: 0 heads, 1 head, 2 heads, and 3 heads (the values on the X-Axis). The percentage frequency of these four possibilities we read off the Y-Axis. We read the following diagrams in the same way. the number of heads on the X-Axis, and the percent probability on the Y-Axis. Notice the perfect symmetry in these distributions.

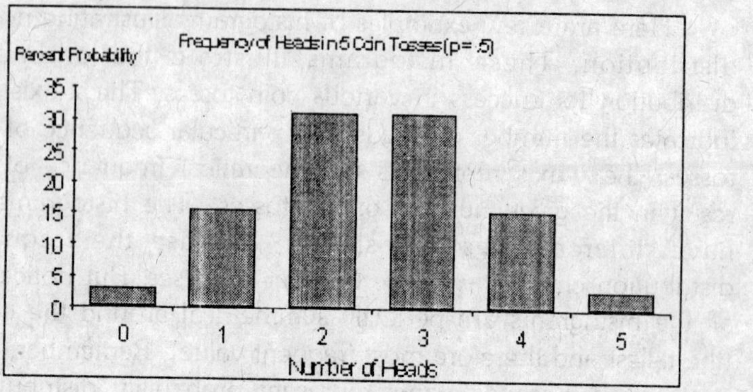

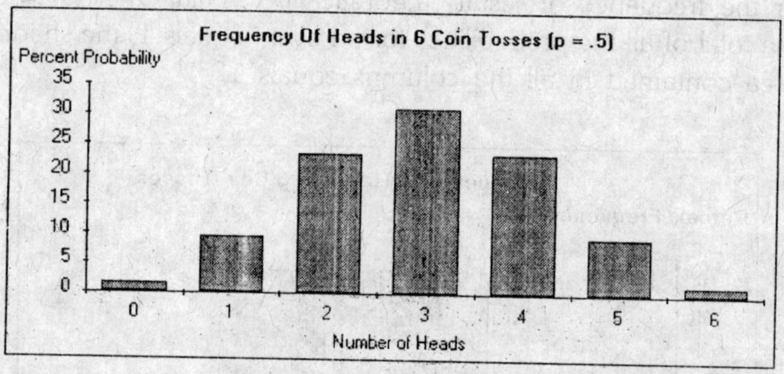

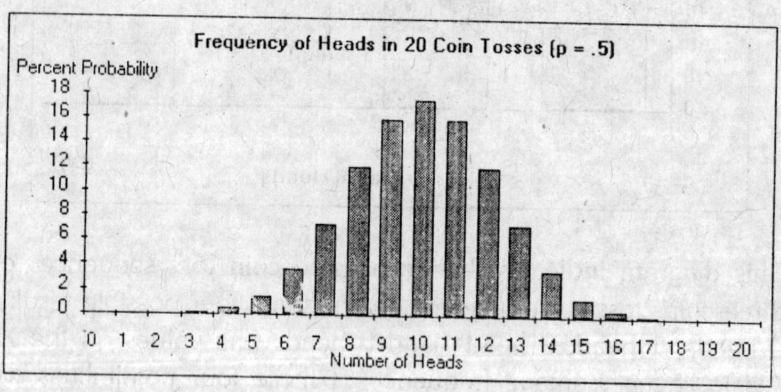

Notice in the above histogram (for 20 coin tosses) how at the extremes (0, 1, 2, 18, 19, 20) the percent probability is so small that the value does not show on the graph. Virtually all the results in a 20 coin-toss sequence will fall between 3 and 17, with the most frequent value in the centre (at 10). The frequencies on either side of 10 are perfectly symmetrical we can see that by the equal heights of 9 and 11, of 8 and 12, of 7 and 13, of 6 and 14, of 5 and 15, or 4 and 16, of 3 and 17.

The Normal Curve

Notice how in the diagrams above, as the number of columns increases, the entire shape of the histogram begins to approximate a curve, with the shaded areas all under the top line. And, in fact, we can readily convert these histograms (using rectangles) to a curve by joining up the central points on the top of each column.

What we have when we do this is exactly the same frequency distribution picture as we had with the columns, except that we have filled in the gaps between columns. Now we do not have the body of the columns, but that does not matter, because the important part of the histogram picture is the line defined by the top centre points of the columns. In such a diagram, the important factor is the area under the curve, for that graphically presents the total frequencies. Equal areas under such a curve will represent equal frequencies.

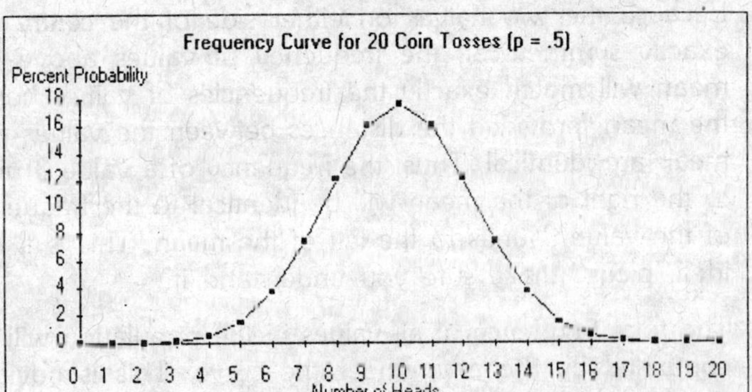

When we join up the columns in the histogram in this way, we produce a particularly useful statistical shape, the normal curve. The normal curve or the normal distribution is an extremely important statistical concept, as important in many areas of enquiry as the right-angle triangle is in Euclidean geometry, and for the remainder of our short study of statistics we shall be dealing only with this frequency distribution. So understand clearly what the normal distribution means.

When we say that a particular population characteristic is normally distributed, we mean the following:

1. The normal frequency curve shows that the highest frequency falls in the centre with an equal and exactly similar curve on either side of that centre. Thus, the most frequent value in a normal distribution is the average, with half the values falling below the average and half above it.

2. The normal curve, often called a bell curve, is perfectly symmetrical. Therefore the median (the arithmetical average), the mode (the most frequent value), and the median (the middle value) will coincide at the centre of the curve (the high point). Make sure you understand this point.

3. The further away any particular value is from the average, the less frequent that value will be.

4. Because the two halves on either side of the centre are exactly symmetrical, the frequency of values above the mean will match exactly the frequencies of values below the mean, provided the distances between the values and mean are identical. Thus, the frequency of a value 3 units to the right of the mean will be identical to the frequency of the value 3 units to the left of the mean. This is a key idea; please make sure you understand it.

5. The total frequency of all values in the population will be contained by the area under the curve. This is obvious

enough, since the total area under the curve represents all the possible occurrences of that characteristic.

6. Various areas under the curve will therefore indicate the percentage of the total frequency. For instance, 50 percent of the area under the curve lies to the left of the mean (i.e., half of all normally distributed results will fall in this area), and 50 percent of the area under the curve lies to the right of the mean. Therefore, 50 percent of all scores will lie to the left and 50 percent to the right of the mean. Equal areas under the curve represent equal numbers in the frequency. Again, please make sure you understand this important idea.

7. Normal curves may have different shapes (i.e., tall and skinny, short and low, and so on). What will determine the overall shape of the symmetrical curve will the value of the mean and the standard deviation in the population (these will define the shape in the same way the centre point and the radius define a circle). But the general characteristics listed above will remain the same.

Please make very sure you understand each one of the above points, because much of what we do from this point on assumes that you are quite familiar with the properties of the normal curve.

Normal distributions are particularly important for a number of reasons not the least of which is that many of the important characteristics we wish to study (including all inherited characteristics) are normally distributed. What that means is that if we gather a very large number of samples of a particular measurement (e.g., height) and construct a frequency distribution, the result will be normal, that is, will manifest the characteristics listed above.

Note carefully that the normal curve is a theoretical depiction of the distribution of frequencies of the values. It does not tell us that in any particular series of measurements of a normally distributed item half must lie above and half below the mean. It indicates that there is a .5 probability that in any series of values, any particular score will lie above or below the mean and that the average will fall in the centre of the distribution. Or, put another way, in any measurement of a heritable characteristic (height, intelligence, weight, and so on) 50 percent of the population will be below the arithmetical average (the mean), because such characteristics are normally distributed. It is not the case that in any distribution exactly 50 percent of the population will fall below the mean—but that must be the case if the frequency distribution is a normal curve.

Not all values are normally distributed (please remember that): for example, the salaries of those working at Malaspina University-College, the responses to a public opinion questionnaire, levels of contaminant in the Georgia Strait. But what makes this particular frequency distribution so important is that a great many things in our world are normally distributed (e.g., population heights, mortality rates, stock market fluctuations, yearly temperature averages, girth of trees, all repeated human measurements of a single natural phenomena, heritable characteristics, and so on). It is an enormously useful and important analytical concept.

Further Properties of The Normal Curve

We have noted above some of the properties of the normal curve (most frequent value is at the centre, symmetry about the central value, diminishing frequency with the distance from the centre). However, there are many more important features.

You may have noticed that the shape of the curve in a normal distribution has a clear point on each side where the slope goes from concave (bulging outward) to concave (bending inwards). If you were walking up the curve you would notice that at first the slope increases, but at a particular point it would begin to decrease as you approach the summit. The point at which this occurs is called the point of inflection.

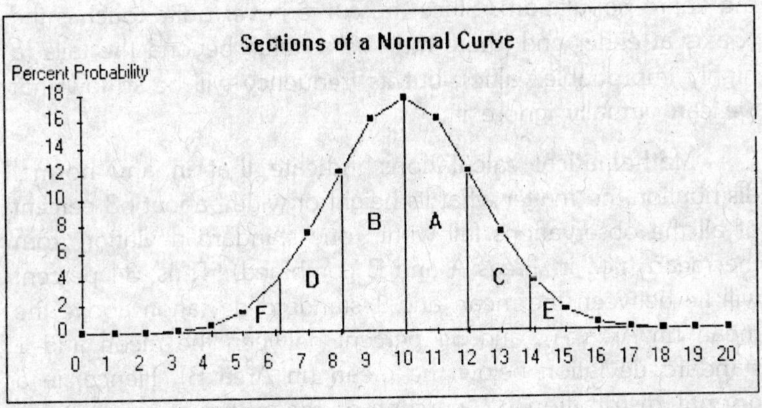

If one draws a perpendicular line from the points of inflection, one on either side of the mean, to the base line (the X-axis) then the distance from that point to the value of the mean on the X-axis (in the centre) is equal to the standard deviation. Make sure you understand this very important property of the normal curve.

Note that these two perpendicular lines drawn from the points of inflection on either side of the mean divide the area under the curve further, so that we now have four separate areas, as follows:

1. The area between the mean and one standard deviation above the mean (Area A);
2. The area between the mean and one standard deviation below the mean (Area B);
3. The area to the right of one standard deviation above the mean (Area C);
4. The area to the left of one standard deviation below the mean (Area D).

Since the normal curve is perfectly symmetrical, Area A will equal Area B, and Area C will equal Area D. And the total of

A, B, C, and D will equal the total area under the curve (i.e., the entire population). Since the curve never quite touches the X-axis at either end, there may be a value beyond the tails (a highly improbable value), but its frequency will be so low that we can virtually ignore it.

Mathematical calculations indicate that in any normal distribution, no matter what its height or width, about 68 percent of all the observations fall within one standard deviation from the mean (i.e., in Areas A and B combined). Thus, 34 percent will lie between the mean and 1 standard deviation above the mean (in Area A), and 34 percent between the mean and 1 standard deviation below the mean (in Area B). Hence, in a normal distribution 32 percent of the observations will fall outside 1 standard deviation, 16 percent on either side (i.e., 16 percent of the population will fall in Area C and 16 percent in area D).

We may express this, more appropriately, in the language of probability, as follows: in any normal distribution, there is approximately a .68 probability that a particular value will fall within 1 standard deviation (SD) of the mean; there is approximately a .34 probability that a particular value will lie between the mean and 1 SD above the mean (in Area A) and approximately a .34 probability that a particular value will lie between the mean and 1 SD below the mean (in Area B). Similarly, there is approximately a .16 probability that a particular value will lie higher than 1 SD from the mean (in Area C), and approximately a .16 probability that a particular value will lie lower than 1 SD below the mean (in Area D).

The diagram below illustrates the areas under the normal curve for one and two standard deviations above and below the mean (i.e., this is the same as the previous diagram, except that the vertical lines indicating two standard deviations from the mean have been added to it, thus creating six areas under the curve).

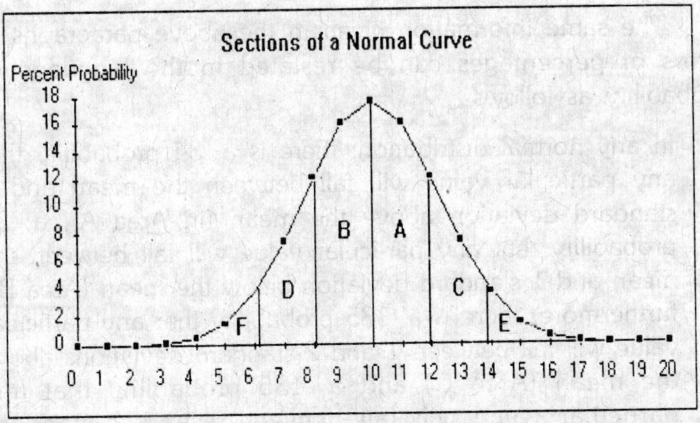

The vertical lines represent the mean (at the centre), and distances of 1 and 2 standard deviations on either side of the mean. As before, Area A and Area B are equal, each defined by the mean and 1 standard deviation on either side of it. Each of these areas (A and B) contains approximately 34 percent of all the values in a normal distribution.

Area C and Area D, which are also equal, are defined by the vertical lines representing 1 and 2 standard deviations from the mean (on either side). Each of these areas will contain approximately 13.5 percent of all the values in a normal distribution.

Areas E and F, at the extreme ends of of the curve are defined as the areas marked off by the vertical line representing 3 standard deviations and the tail ends of the curve. Each of these areas will contain 2.5 percent of all the values in a normal distribution (i.e., in a normal distribution, 5 percent of the population will be beyond 2 standard deviations: 2.5 above the mean, and 2.5 below the mean).

If we continued to draw standard deviation vertical lines to mark off three standard deviations from the mean (not shown on the diagram), we would have two very small areas at the extreme tips of the curve. These areas indicate the values lying more than three standard deviations from the mean, about .3 percent of all the values in the normal distribution.

The same information given in the above paragraphs in terms of percentages can be restated in the language of probability as follows:

1. In any normal distribution, there is a .34 probability that any particular value will fall between the mean and 1 standard deviation above the mean (in Area A), a .34 probability that any particular value will fall between the mean and 1 standard deviation below the mean (Area B); furthermore, there is a .135 probability that any particular value will fall between 1 and 2 standard deviations above the mean (Area C) and a .135 probability that any particular value will fall between 1 and 2 standard deviations below the mean (Area D). Finally, there is a .475 probability that any particular value will fall within 2 standard deviations above the mean (somewhere in Areas A and C) and a .475 probability that any particular value will fall within 2 standard deviations below the mean (somewhere within Areas B and D).
2. Further analysis of the mathematics of normal curves reveals that the area contained by the perpendicular lines representing 3 standard deviations from the mean contains 99.7 percent of the area under the curve and thus represents 99.7 percent of all the scores in the data set. In other words, there is a 99.7 percent chance (or $p = .997$) that in any normal distribution, any particular value will fall within 3 standard deviations from the mean (3).
3. Thus, the areas beyond three standard deviations contain only .30 percent of the total area. This means that in a normally distributed characteristic, the probability of a value lying more than three standard deviations from the mean is .003, or .0015 at the top end (above the mean) and .0015 at the bottom end (below the mean). Thus, it is very rare indeed (but not impossible) for an observed value in a normal distribution to occur more than 3 standard deviations from the mean.

Simple Application of the Properties of the Normal Curve

This mathematical information about a normal curve provides enormously valuable information. For if we know that a population is normally distributed, then if we know the mean of that curve and the standard deviation, we know the probabilities of any particular value falling within specified areas of the curve. We can thus make some important predictions about that population.

For instance, suppose we know that the height of men in a population (say, in Prince George) is normally distributed, that the mean height (from a sample we collect) is 68 in., and the standard deviation is 4 in. We then know the probabilities for the distribution of heights in Prince George, as follows:

Approximately 34 percent of the men will be between 68 in. (the mean) and 72 in. (1 SD above the mean, 68 + 4); approximately 34 percent will be between 68 in. (the mean) and 64 in. (1 SD below the mean, 68 - 4); approximately 13.5 percent will be between 68 in. and 76 in. (between 1 SD above the mean and 2 SD above the mean); and approximately 13.5 percent will be between 64 in. and 60 in. (between 1 SD and 2 SD below the mean); and approximately 2.5 percent will be between 76 in. and 80 in. (between 2 and 3 SD above the mean); and approximately 2.5 percent will be between 60 in. and 56 in. (between 2 SD and 3 SD below the mean).Thus, if a child of yours informs you that she is getting married to some man from Prince George, you already know some important things about your prospective son-in-law, even though you have never met.

There is a .34 probability that his height will be between 68 in. and 72 in.; there is a .34 probability that his height will be between 68 in. and 64 in.; or, putting these two together, that there is a .68 probability that his height is between 64 in. and 72 in. We could obviously continue this analysis to take into account all the percentage frequencies indicated by the normal curve.

Now, this mathematical analysis of the normal curve holds for the frequencies of any value which is normally distributed. Once we know the mean and the standard deviation, we are able to predict the probability of the value for any particular member of the population. And this process is possible, to repeat the point, for any measurable factor whose frequencies are normally distributed. Thus, once we know that a characteristic is normally distributed, what the values are for the mean and the standard deviation, we are in a position to make a number of conclusions about the probable distribution of the entire population.

It is vitally important for an initial understanding of statistics to grasp the point that the features of the normal curve apply to all distribution frequencies of normally distributed items. Normal curves may have many different heights and widths, but in all cases, these characteristics apply:

1. The mean, median, and mode coincide at the high point of the curve and divide the results into two equal and perfectly symmetrical halves.
2. Of all the scores in a perfectly normal distribution, approximately 34 percent will lie between the mean and 1 Standard Deviation above the mean, and approximately 34 percent will lie between the mean and 1 Standard Deviation below the mean.
3. Of all the scores in a perfectly normal distribution, approximately 95 percent will fall between the lines representing 2 Standard Deviations from the mean.
4. Of all the scores, approximately 99 percent will lie between the lines indicating 3 standard deviations from the mean.

Self-Test on Normal Distribution Curve

1. The duration times of a certain brand of battery are normally distributed, with a mean of 80 hours and a standard deviation of 10 hours. As a marketing gimmick,

the manufacturer decides to guarantee to replace any battery which fails prior to a certain time. Approximately how long a guarantee should the company provide so that no more than 2.5 percent of the batteries fail prior to the guaranteed time?

2. You have a contract to make one thousand uniforms for the Canadian navy. The heights of sailors are normally distributed, with a mean of 69 inches and a standard deviation of 2 inches. What percentage of the uniforms will have to fit sailors shorter than 67 inches? What percentage will have to be suitable for sailors taller than 73 inches?

3. Let us assume the results from all large tests are normally distributed. In the final results for Subject A, the mean percentage score is 80 and the Standard Deviation 5. In Subject B, the mean percentage score is 70 and the Standard Deviation 2.5. Suppose you score 75 percent in both courses. What percentage of students received results better than you in Subject A and in Subject B? What is your percentile rank in each subject?

A Normal Distribution and Bernouilli's Theorem

It is important to grasp the point that the bell-like shape of a normal distribution only occurs with a great many samples from normally distributed data. In fact, in any quality normally distributed (e.g., any heritable quality, like height), as Bernouilli's Theorem tells us, the frequency distribution of the results will get closer and closer to the shape of a normal distribution as we increase the number of measurements.

To follow this point more clearly, consider the following diagrams. They represent the frequency distributions of random numbers taken from a population of numbers which is known to be normally distributed. In this case, the mean of the total population is 10 and the standard deviation 3 (chosen arbitrarily).

The first diagram illustrates the frequency distribution for a sample of 100 numbers. You will notice that it does not look very bell-like. The second diagram illustrates the frequency distribution for a sample of 1000 numbers. You can see that the characteristic shape of the normal distribution is beginning to emerge.

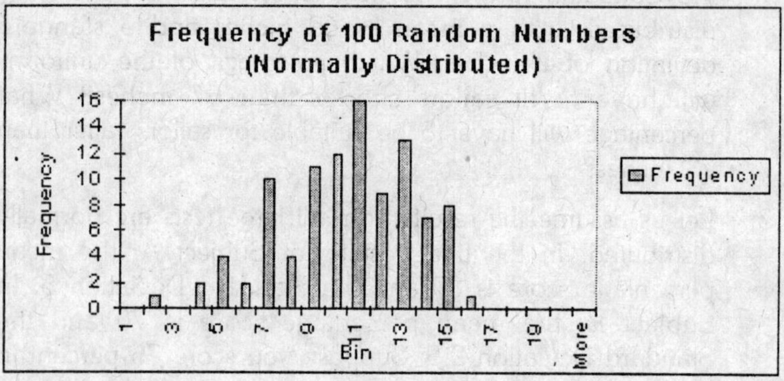

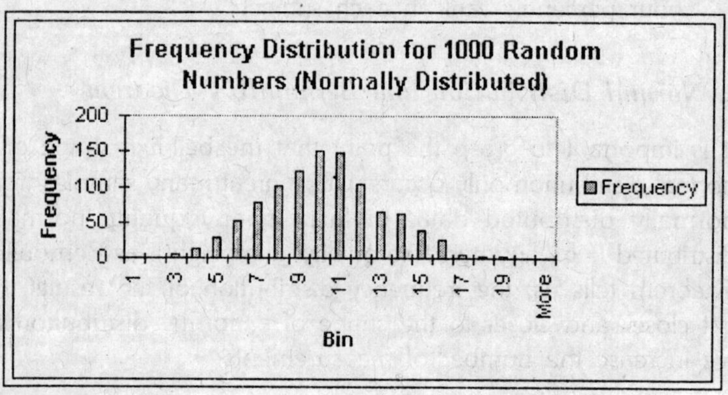

The final two diagrams illustrate the frequency distributions for samples of 2000 and 3000 numbers respectively. Clearly, the final diagram, although still not a perfect bell curve, approximates much more closely than any of the others the characteristic shape of the normal distribution. A larger sample (say, 10,000) would look even closer to the symmetrical bell shape.

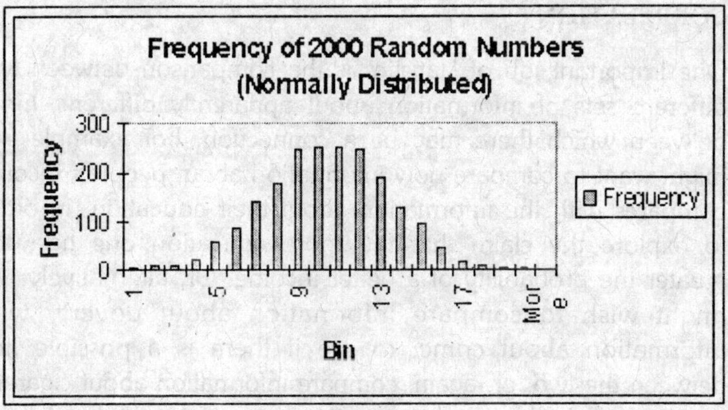

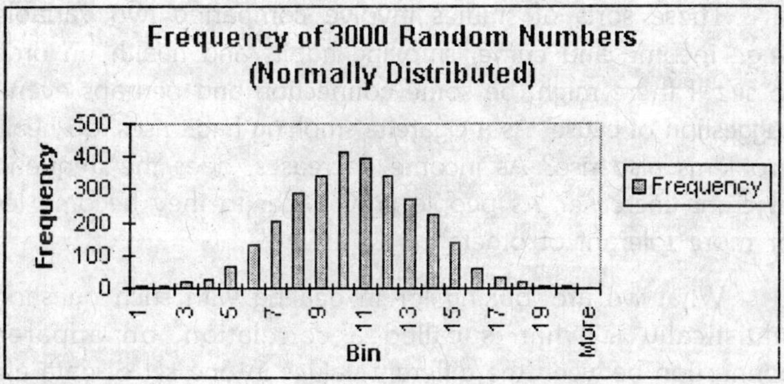

When we are dealing with random number generation from a population which is not normally distributed but which is uniformly random, then increasing the number in the sample is not going to produce more and more closely any clear shape.

Below, for example, are histograms for 1000 and for 2000 numbers between 1 and 400 randomly generated, but this time from a population which is not normally distributed. Notice that there is no emerging bell curve shape as one increases the number of samples from 1000 to 2000.

CORRELATION

One important job of statistics is the comparison between two different sets of information about apparently different things between which there may be a connection. For example, we might want to compare how information about people's income compares with the information about their education, in order to explore the claim that the more education one has, the greater the probability of a better income. Or, alternatively, we might wish to compare information about poverty with information about crime, to see if there is a possible link between the two, or, again, compare information about cigarette smoking habits with information about particular health problems (e.g., heart disease).

These sorts of studies involve comparing two variables (e.g., income and crime, smoking habits and health) in order to see if there might be some connection and perhaps even a suggestion of cause. As a cigarette smoking habit rises, do health problems also rise? As income decreases, does the frequency of crime increase? As people grow older to they become less or more tolerant of others?

What we are looking for in dealing with such questions statistically is what is called a correlation, an apparent connection between the different values in one set of data and in a second set of data, so that as the values in the first set increases, the values in the second set also tend to increase (or, in the case of a negative correlation, to decrease).

Here's a simple example. In an English course, once the instructor has marked a set of class essays, she has a record of the marks, one for each student. Then she assigns a second essay and marks it. Now, she has a record of the marks for two essays written by the same students.

The instructor might wish to know whether the students who did well in the first essay also tended to do quite well in the second essay, whether the students who did well in the first essay tended to do badly in the second essay, or whether there was no apparent connection between the results of the first essay and the results of the second essay (such information would be a useful test of the value of the first essay as a predictor of success in the second). In other words, she might like to see whether there is any significant correlation between the two sets of marks.

Common sense suggests to us that some sets of results should be quite closely correlated. For instance, we would expect the results students received in English 111 to be positively correlated to the results in English 112 (so that students who did well in the first should tend to do well in the second; students who fared poorly in the first course should tend to fare poorly in the second). Similarly, we would expect people who exercise regularly to have a healthier cardiovascular system than those who do not or those who are wealthy to spend more on consumer goods, and so on. But in some cases our common sense expectations may be wrong, and often we may be interested, not just in whether there is a correlation or not, but in how strong that correlation might be.

Positive, Negative, and No Correlation

In considering correlation we recognize three distinct possibilities. The two sets of variables (that is, the two sets of data we are comparing, like exercise and cardiovascular health) may show a positive correlation. That is, as the values in the first set of data rise, the values in the second set of data tend to rise as well (i.e., those who exercise regularly have a greater cardiovascular health). Or the two sets of data may display a negative correlation. That is, those who score higher on the first set of results tend to get lower scores on the second set of results (e.g., the number of alcoholic drinks one has and one's ability to carry out a manual dexterity test).

there may be no correlation: the two sets of data do not appear to have any relationship.

Correlations, as we shall see, can be weak or strong, that is, the relationship between the two sets of values may be really significant or may be slight. A correlation can also be perfect, that is, every change in one set of values may show a exact corresponding change in the second set of values (the paragraphs below contain some examples).

Correlation is an extremely important analytical tool which enables us to begin to sort out claims about important connections, which may or may not be true: the amount of smoking and the incidence of lung cancer, HIV infection and the onset of AIDS, the age of a car and its value, television programming of playoff games and attendance at lectures, poverty and crime, IQ tests and income levels, intelligence and heredity, age and mechanical skills, and so on. People make claims about such matters all the time. The principle of correlation enables us to investigate such claims in order to understand whether they are true or not and, if true, just what the strength of that relationship might be.

Self-Test on Correlation Terms

Indicate for each of the pairs of variables listed below what common sense tells you to expect in the way of an overall correlation between the two sets (positive, negative, perfect, zero):

1. height in centimetres and height in inches;
2. levels of income and amount of spending on consumer goods;
3. the age of a car and its value;
4. two scores thrown on two dice simultaneously;
5. snowstorms and attendance at college classes;
6. ability to see in the dark and the amount of carrots eaten;

prediction that someone with 14 years of formal schooling will probably have about 7.8 as a political participation score. Obviously, this is not a sure-fire guarantee of such a score; it is, however, something of an educated guess. Using the regression line in this manner obviously yields only approximate results, and it may in some cases be misleading if we rely on it too heavily.

A Common Misuse of the Regression Line

It is often very misleading to use the regression line to make predictions outside the range of the data. For instance, I can extrapolate (extend) the straight line, once I have drawn it, and then make predictions well beyond the plotted points. This is often an illegitimate procedure leading to very wrong conclusions. We can draw in a Regression Line by hand, visually estimating where it should come. This is obviously a somewhat subjective procedure, and different people drawing the line will come with slightly different results. Excel, however, will plot the line for us very quickly. Please remember always that a positive correlation does not mean that there will no exceptions to the overall trend. There may be one or more results which do not fit the overall trend of the entire collection of data. Correlation deals with the general tendency of the entire collection of data.

An Example of a Perfect Correlation

Here is another set of measurements. This time the middle column represents the student's scores in percentages for class participation, and the column on the right represents the same score out of 20.

Name of Student	Participation Mark (100)	Participation Mark (20)	Name of Student	Participation Mark (100)	Participation Mark (20)
ab	65	13	hi	72	14.4
bc	90	18	ij	82	16.4
cd	83	16.6	jk	94	18.8

Here is another pair of sets of variables. The first indicates the distance traveled in a new prototype car through the desert at an even speed. The second column indicates the amount of gasoline left in the car's gas tank at each of the inspection points.

Place	Distance from Home (Miles)	Gasoline Left in the Tank (Gallons)	Place	Distance from Home (Miles)	Gasoline Left in the Tank (Gallons)
Home	0	15	Deadman	425	6.5
Podunk	50	14	No Mo Gas	540	4.2
Buzzard Breath	150	12	Last Chance	680	1.4
Paradise	275	9.5	Hope Gone	700	1
Last Hope	350	8	Nowhere Town	750	0

Once again we can illustrate these values in a scatter plot diagram to observe the nature of the correlation:

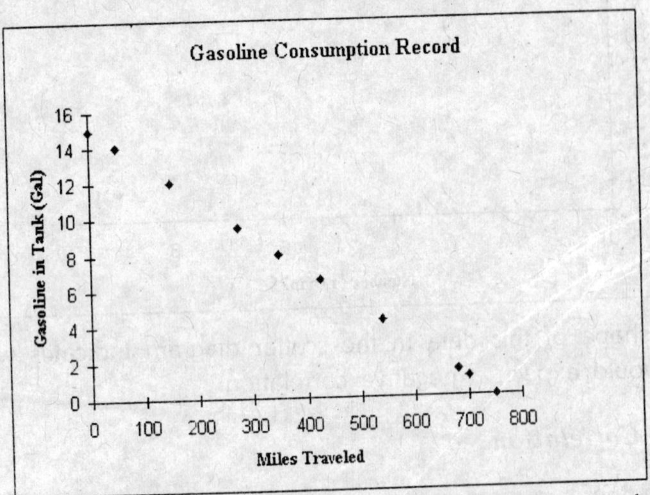

Here we see again that we are dealing with a perfect correlation, because all the plotted points fall on the same straight line. But this time the line slopes downward and to the right. This indicates that the highest values on the Y Axis are associated with the lowest values on the X-Axis, or that as one value

increases the other decreases. This example illustrates a perfect negative correlation. Just as in the first example we can have a positive correlation which is not exact, so we can find a negative correlation which is not exact. In such a case the plotted points will not all fall on the same straight line, but the general shape of the clusterwill slope downward and to the right. For example, if we plotted a set of figures indicating the amount of alcohol consumed against a second set of figures indicating success in a simple test of physical dexterity, we would expect to get a negative correlation: the more drinks consumed, the lower the score in the physical dexterity test. Here is an example of such a scatter plot.

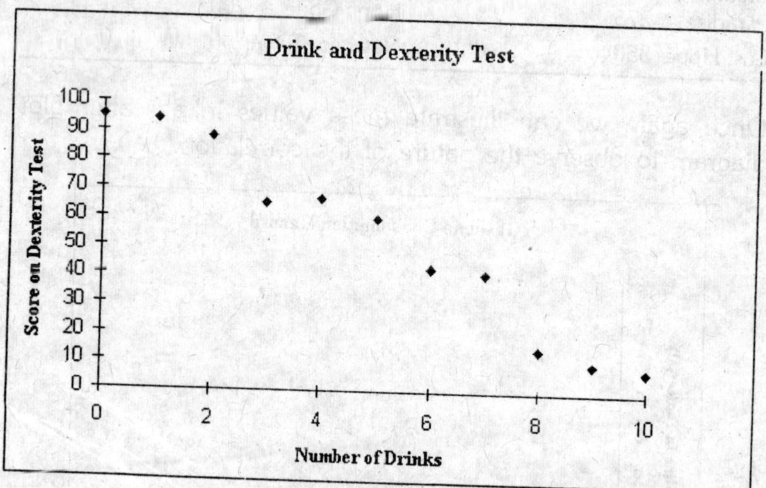

The shape of this data in the scatter diagram indicates what we would expect, a negative correlation.

Zero Correlation

When there is no correlation at all between the two sets of variables, then we will have trouble recognizing an upward or downward overall shape to the plotted data, and the line of best fit will fall somewhere in a horizontal position among the plotted points. For example, here are two sets of variables: the

first lists the number of letters in the name of geographical location in Canada, and the second lists its longitude (approximately). We want to know if there is a correlation between how many letters there are in a Canadian place name and its geographical location. Our common sense suggests that there should not be a correlation, but we just want to check

Name	Number of Letters in the Name	Longitude	Name	Number of Letters in the Name	Longitude
Prince Rupert	12	130	Biggar	6	108
Courtenay	9	125	Pickle Crow	10	90
Kirkland Lake	12	80	Williams Lake	12	122
Brandon	7	100	Yarmouth	8	66
Glace Bay	8	60	Sherbrooke	10	72
Clarenville	11	54	Oba	3	84
Dundas	6	80	Calgary	7	114
Lac Ste Jean	10	72			

If we plot these points on an X-Y graph to produce a scatter diagram, we can then inspect the distribution and draw in a line of best fit. The plotted data looks as follows:

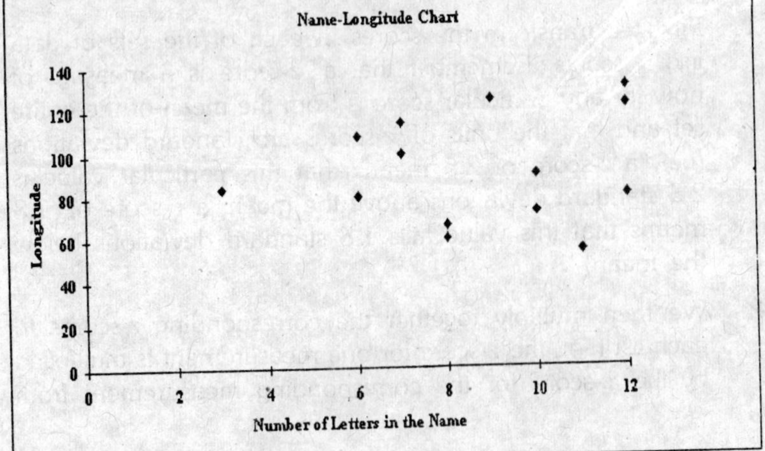

Try to estimate where you would draw the regression line through these plotted points. Notice that one cannot so easily produce one like those we have already drawn, that is, with a distinct slope indicating a positive or negative correlation. And, thus, based on the very small sample we chose, from a visual inspection of the plots, there does not seem to any relationship between the number of letters in a Canadian place name and its approximate longitude.

Mathematical Measure of Correlation: The Correlation Coefficient (r)

The scatter plot diagrams and the regression line give us a general visual idea of what the correlation is between two sets of variables. In many cases, however, we require a more accurate measure, so that we can compare one correlation with another. In other words, knowing that a correlation exists is valuable; more valuable, however, is to know the size of that correlation. Such a mathematical measure of the correlation between two sets of variables is called the Correlation Coefficient. It is most commonly symbolized by the letter *r*.

The following paragraph outlines how the Correlation Coefficient is calculated. However, this method is something Excel will do for us, once the data is entered. The method is listed here for interest:

1. First we transform the scores in each of the sets of data into *z*-scores. Remember that a *z*-score is a measure of how far any particular score is from the mean of the entire set and that the units of *z*-scores are standard deviations (i.e., a z-score of 2.5 means that this particular value is 2.5 standard deviations above the mean; a *z*-score of -1.8 means that this value falls 1.8 standard deviations below the mean)
2. We then multiply together the corresponding *z*-scores in each list (i.e., the *z*-score for one measurement is multiplied by the *z*-score for the corresponding measurement from

the other set of data. Remember that a positive number multiplied by a negative number produces a negative result; a negative number multiplied by a negative number produces a positive result.

3. Then, we add up all the results produced by Step 2 above.
4. Finally, we divide the figure obtained in Step 3 by the total number of pairs of scores (i.e., get the average of figures derived in Step 2.This process will always produce a number between -1.00 and +1.00. This number is called the correlation coefficient (symbolized by the letter r). If $r = -1$, then the correlation is a perfect negative correlation; if $r = 1$, then the correlation is a perfect positive correlation. If $r = 0$, then the correlation is zero (no relationship between the variables).

Strength and Significance of a Correlation Coefficient

Now that we have a mathematical value for our correlation coefficient ($r = 0.31$), how are we to interpret that? Does this mean that our diagnostic test is a good one, that we can rely on it?

The strongest positive correlation is 1.0, and the closer our r value is to 1.0 the stronger the correlation between the two sets of values we are analyzing. The closer to 0 our r value, the weaker the correlation. The following general categories indicate a quick way of interpreting our calculated *r* value:

— 0.0 to 0.2 Very weak to negligible correlation

— 0.2 to 0.4 Weak, low correlation (not very significant)

— 0.4 to 0.7 Moderate correlation

— 0.7 to 0.9 Strong, high correlation

— 0.9 to 1.0 Very strong correlation

Our result of 0.31 is thus very weak or low; as an evaluative tool our diagnostic test is not all that useful, since the results

on it do not reveal very much about the future results in the final marks. There is some positive correlation, but not enough to make the diagnostic reliable as a predictor.

One useful rule of thumb for estimating the importance of the r value is to calculate the square the correlation coefficient (i.e., calculate $r2$). This squared result will give us a rough percentage for the amount of variation in the final result which is directly attributable to the other variable.

For example, suppose our diagnostic test was a good measure of writing ability. The correlation between that writing test and the final marks is 0.31. If we square this value, we get the value 0.096, or 96 in 1000 or 9.6 percent. On the basis of this, we can claim that 9.6 percent of the students' success in the course is attributable to the writing skills they had at the very start of it (i.e., what we measured in the our diagnostic test). We would then have to conclude that success is this course is not very dependent upon the writing skills the students have upon entry.

Suppose now we administer another diagnostic test at the very start of the course, this time measuring reading ability. And we discover when the course is over that the correlation between the results of that diagnostic test and the final marks for the course is 0.8 ($r = 0.8$). If we square 0.8, we get 0.64 or 64 percent. We can then claim that 64 percent of the students' success in the course is directly attributable to the reading skills they possessed when they started. Obviously, this conclusion assumes that the diagnostic test is an excellent measure of the students' reading ability.

It will be apparent that correlation analysis is a very useful tool for investigating all sorts of claims. We may often think that one particular skill, quality, or value has a direct and important effect upon another. Correlation analysis enables us to test such claims and to provide some quantifiable measure to them.

de	74	14.8	kl	50	10
ef	84	16.8	lm	75	15
fg	78	15.6	mn	58	11.6
gh	60	12			

If we plot these points on a scatter diagram as before, putting the Participation Mark (100) on the X-axis and the Participation Mark (25) on the Y-axis, then we get the following diagram:

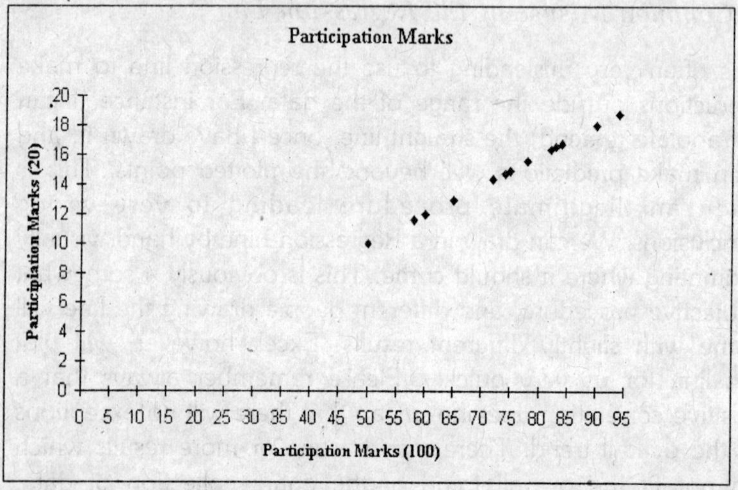

Notice here that the general shape of the plotted points moves upward and to the right—indicating once more a positive correlation. In this example, there is an added observation: the data we plotted forms a perfect straight line, with every plotted point from the data we collected falling exactly on the same straight line. Clearly, if we wanted to draw a line of best fit here, it would coincide exactly with all the data. Such a result produces what we call a perfect positive correlation: every increase in the value of the X-axis brings about an exactly corresponding increase in the Y-axis value. We would expect this result, of course, because the values are basically the same measurement. A similar result would occur if, for example, we plotted the weight of ten students in grams against the weight of the same students in pounds or a range of temperature readings in Celsius against the same readings in Fahrenheit.

7. daily cigarette consumption and cardiovascular health;
8. heights and weights of elementary school children;
9. weekly consumption of calories in food and drink and body weight;
10. age and physical strength in senior citizens.

Working with an Example

Suppose we wish to explore the claim that people's political participation increases with the number of years they spend in school. We think this claim is true, but we wish to substantiate it. In other words, we wish to see whether there is a correlation between the participation in the political process and years of formal education.

First, we collect data from each person in the study. We devise a test to measure a person's participation in the political process; we have people provide the appropriate information on this variable, and we ask them the tell us their years of formal schooling. This collection yields the following information:

Respondent	Political Participation Score	Years of Formal Schooling	Respondent	Political Participation Score	Years of Formal Schooling
A	1	5	K	7	13
B	2	8	L	8	14
C	2	7	M	8	15
D	3	9	N	9	15
E	3	10	O	7	13
F	4	11	P	10	16
G	5	11	Q	9	16
H	6	11	R	8	14
I	5	12	S	9	13
J	6	12	T	9	14

From a glance at the figures, we might conclude that there seems to be some relationship, for the higher scores in the middle column appear to be accompanied, in general, by higher scores in the right-hand column. However, we want to be sure about this point and not simply rely upon visual impressions from such a table.

Creating a Scatter Diagram in Excel

One standard way visually to express the correlation between two sets of variables is to draw a diagram in which each result is plotted on a standard X-Y graph. The X-Axis represents the value of one variable and the Y-Axis the value of the other variable. Each score in the set (in our example from Respondent A to Respondent T) is plotted on the graph, so that a distinct point is located for each member in the data set according to the two numerical values associated with each respondent.For example, for the above data, we can construct a graph in which the value for the Years in School is plotted on the X-Axis and the value for Political Participation is plotted on the Y-Axis. Thus, we can locate each respondent's position exactly on the graph. We will come up with twenty points.

The following chart (created by Excel) illustrates the results. Notice that there are 20 points plotted and that each corresponds to a particular Respondent's scores in the two columns of the table above.

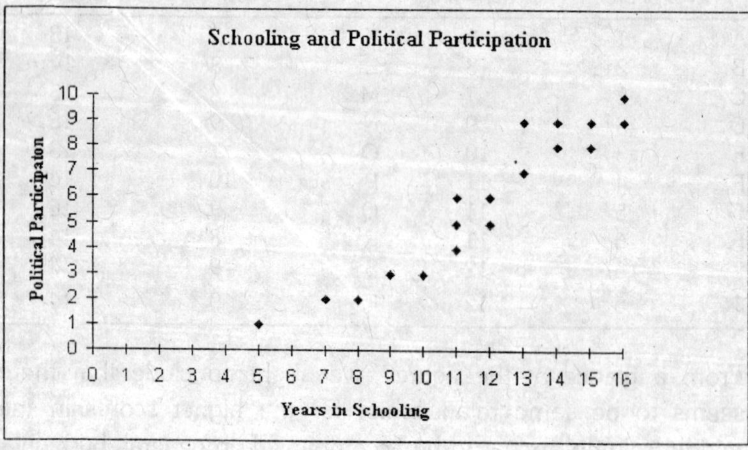

Notice that two people have 16 years of formal schooling (two values on the vertical line drawn through 16 on the X-Axis). Four respondents are shown on the graph with a Political Participation Score of 9, two with a Political Participation Score of 8, two with a Political Participation Score of 2, and so on. We call such an illustration a scatter diagram or scatter plot. Make sure you are familiar with what this graph represents and how to read it. Do not proceed until you feel very comfortable with this visual presentation of information.

Look for a moment at the overall shape of all the points in the chart. It seems to be characterized by a generally linear cluster which rises upward and to the right. This shape suggests strongly that as the Y values rise (i.e., go vertically upward), the X values increase also (i.e., move to the right). This point is not true for every single point in the cluster, of course, but as an observation about the overall general shape of all the points, that claim seems to hold. Thus, these results seem to show a positive correlation: the higher the value for the years of formal schooling, the higher the score on the Political Participation test—that seems to be the general trend of the entire range of respondents (even if some of the plotted points do not follow that overall trend).

The Line of Best Fit (Regression Line)

One way to emphasize the overall orientation of all the plotted points in the scatter diagram is to draw through the plotted data a straight line which comes as close as possible to all of the plotted points. Such a line is called the line of best fit (or the regression line). If we do that for the above graph (and Excel will draw such a line for us), we can recognize Immediately the overall orientation of the results as sloping upward and to the right.

Notice that this chart presents the same data as the last chart, except that there is a plotted straight line (of square points) through the points plotted from the data we collected from the respondents (the diamond shaped points). This line, which is derived from the plotted points, is the straight line which comes closest to all the points which correspond to the measured data. It is called the line of best fit or the regression line.

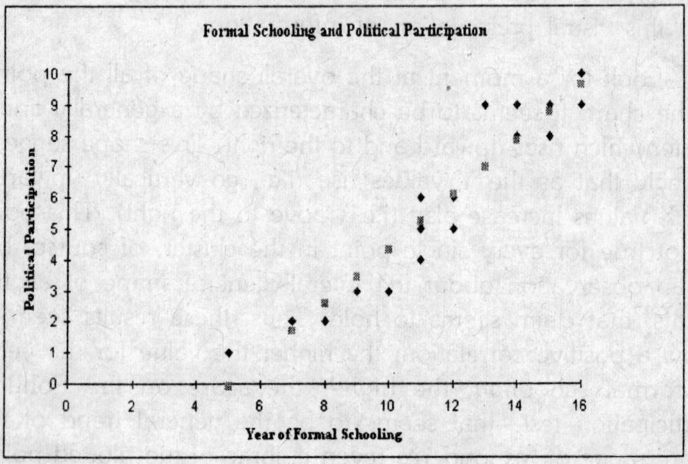

We can see from this line of best fit that it very clearly slopes upward and to the right. This confirms our sense from the overall shape of the cluster that it indicates a positive correlation: an upward slope clearly demonstrates that as the Y values increase the X values tend to increase.

We can use the regression line, once we have drawn it, as a general predictor. That is, with the line in place, we can use it to read off values for cases not included in the study. For example, if we want to know what this data reveals about the probable political participation score someone with 14 years of formal schooling, we can read directly up from the value 14 on the X-axis, see where it meets the regression line, and read horizontally across to the Y-axis. That value in this chart is (about) 7.8. Thus, on the basis of this study, we can offer a

8

STATISTICAL ANALYSIS

The mean, median and mode are measures of the central tendency of a variable but they do not provide any information of how much the measurements vary or are spread.

MEASURES OF DISPERSION

Range

The RANGE of a set of measurements is the difference between the smallest and the largest measurement. For example, if the weights of 7 pregnant women were 40, 41, 42, 43, 44, 47 and 72 kg, the range would be 72 − 40 = 32 kg. Although simple to calculate, the range does not tell us anything about the distribution of the values between the two extreme ones.

If the weights of 7 other pregnant women were 40, 46, 50, 55, 60, 65 and 72 kg the range would also be 72 − 40 = 32 kg, although the values are very different from those of the previous example.

Percentiles

A second way of describing the variation or dispersion of a set of measurements is to divide the distribution into percentiles. As a matter of fact the concept of percentiles is just an extension of the concept of the median, which may also be called the 50th percentile.

Percentiles are points that divide all the measurements into 100 equal parts. The 3rd percentile (P3) is the value below which 3% of the measurements lie. The 50th percentile (P50), or the median, is the value below which 50% of the measurements lie. To determine percentiles, the observations should be first listed from the lowest to the highest just like when finding the median.

The concept of percentiles is used by nutritionists to develop standard growth charts for specific countries from a representative sample of children whose weight and height are measured according to their age in months.

Standard deviation

To determine how much our measurements differ from the mean value there is a measure that we use when applying statistical tests. This measure is called the standard deviation. The Standard deviation is a measure that describes how much individual measurements differ, on the average, from the mean. To obtain the standard deviation of a set of measurements you have to complete the following steps:

— Calculate the mean of all the measurements.

— Calculate the difference between each individual measurement and the mean.

— Square all these differences.

— Take the sum of all squared differences.

— Divide this sum by the number of measurements minus one.

— Finally (since the differences from the mean have been squared), take the square root of the value obtained (in order to get back to the same unit of measurement).

Example 1:

11 children of 3 years of age were weighed and the following weights were obtained:

13, 14, 14, 15, 16, 16, 16, 17, 17, 18 and 20 kg

The number of measurements (n) is 11.

To calculate the standard deviation:

(1) We first calculate the mean: the mean value is 16 kg.

(2) Next, we calculate the distance of each measurement from the mean (16-13 = 3; 16-14 = 2; etc.):

3, 2, 2, 1, 0, 0, 0, 1, 1, 2, 4

(3) These values are then squared (3 x 3 = 9; 2 x 2 = 4; etc.):

9, 4, 4, 1, 0, 0, 0, 1, 1, 4, 16

(4) The sum of these squared differences (9 + 4 + ...) is 40.

(5) This sum is divided by the total number of measurements (n) minus one (n – 1 = 10):

40

10 = 40

(6) Finally, we take the square root to obtain the standard deviation from the mean:

$\sqrt{4}$ = 2kg

A large standard deviation shows that there is a wide scatter of measured values around the mean, while a small standard deviation shows that the individual values are concentrated around the mean with little variation among them.

For instance, if the weights in Example 1 were

10, 11, 12, 14, 16, 16, 16, 18, 20, 21 and 22 kg,

the mean weight would still have been 16 kg. However, the standard deviation would have been 4 kg, indicating a much larger variation in the observations.

THE NORMAL DISTRIBUTION

Many variables such as height, weight and age have a normal distribution. This distribution is a bell shaped curve with most of the values clustered near the mean and a few values out near the tails. The normal distribution is symmetrical around the mean. The mean, the median and the mode of a normal distribution have the same value.

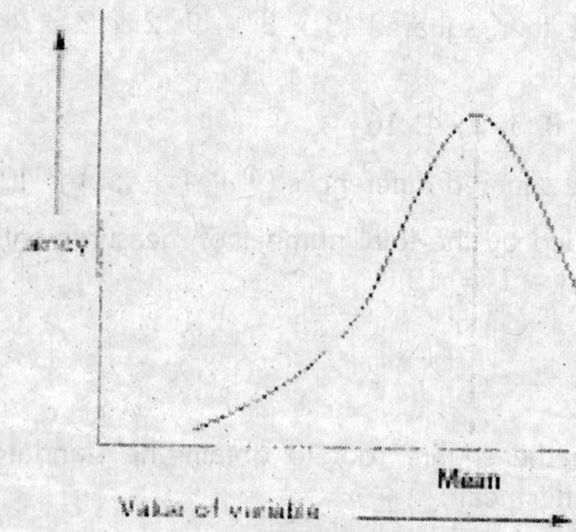

Figure 1. Normal distribution curve

In Figure 2 a histogram of the heights of pregnant women attending an antenatal clinic is shown, with the normal curve drawn over it.

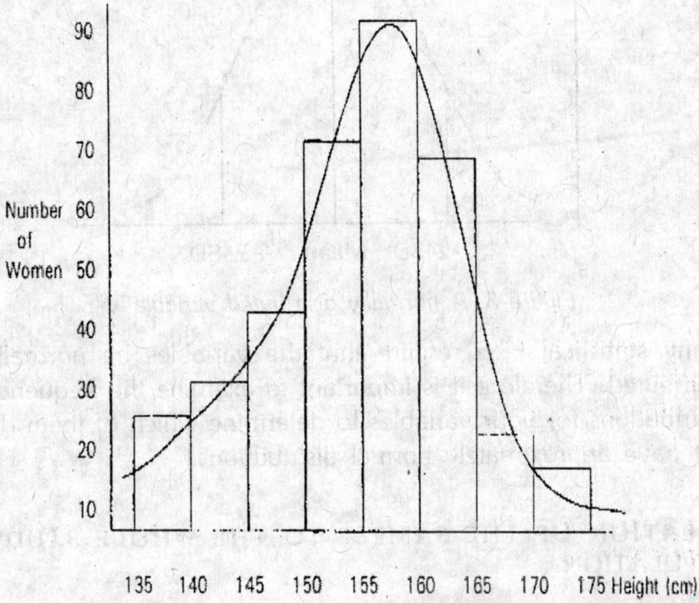

Figure 2. Heights of pregnant women attending an antenatal clinic

An important characteristic of a normally distributed variable is that 95% of the measurements have values that are approximately within 2 standard deviations (S.D.) of the mean. This is shown in the figure below.

Example 2:

If the mean height of a group of 120 women is 158 cm and the standard deviation is 3 cm, it means that about 95% of the women are between 152 and 164 cm (assuming that the heights are normally distributed). In other words, 2.5% of the women (which in this case corresponds to 3 women) are shorter than 152 cm and 2.5% (or 3 women) are taller than 164 cm.

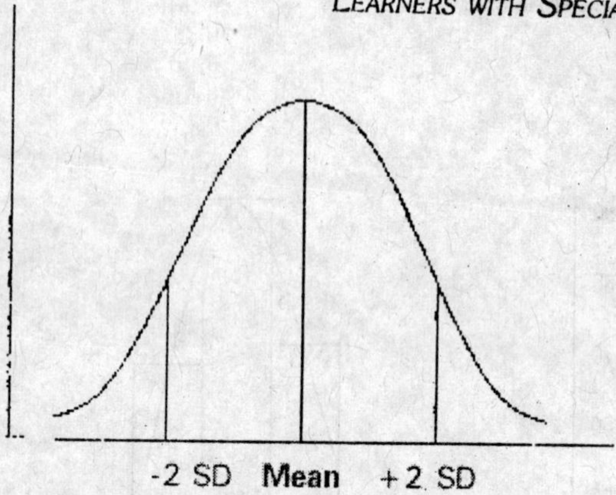

Figure 3. A normally distributed variable

Many statistical tests require that the variables be normally distributed. Therefore it is important to examine the frequency distributions for your variables to determine which of them do not have approximately normal distributions.

RELATION OF THE SAMPLE TO THE WHOLE STUDY POPULATION

When you undertake a study it is usually necessary to draw a sample from your study population(s). You will then describe each population on the basis of the information collected from the sample. In other words, you will try to generalise the findings from the sample to the larger study population. Obviously, this can only be done if the sample is selected in such a way that it can be considered representative of the whole study population. Any value of a variable obtained from the sample (e.g., a sample mean) can then be considered as an estimate of the corresponding study population value (population mean).

For example, if 158 cm is the calculated mean height of a sample of 120 women in a certain town you hope it is a good approximation of the mean height of the whole population of women in that town.

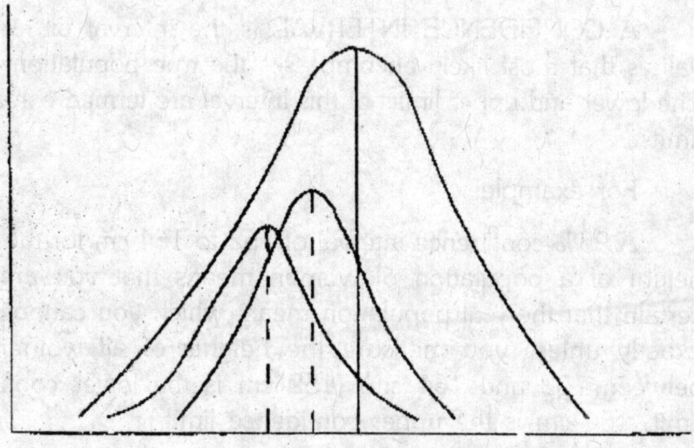

Figure 4. A frequency distribution curve and two sample curves for a variable that is normally distributed

However, the sample mean is not likely to be identical to the population mean. If you draw another sample of 120 mothers, you might find a mean of 157 cm, which is not identical to the first sample mean. It probably also differs from the true mean height of the total population from which the sample was drawn. This phenomenon is called SAMPLING VARIATION. Figure 4 shows a frequency distribution curve of a population with the curves of two different samples inside it. Note that any representative sample will have a distribution curve similarly shaped to the population curve, but it can fall anywhere within the population curve.

How to Determine the Extent to Which the Findings in the Sample are Representative for the Study Population

To find out to what extent a particular sample value deviates from the population value, a range or an interval around the sample value can be worked out which will most probably contain the population value. This range or interval is called the CONFIDENCE INTERVAL.

A CONFIDENCE INTERVAL is the interval or range ot values that most likely encompasses the true population value. The lower and upper limits of this interval are termed confidence limits.

For example:

A 95% confidence interval of 152 to 164 cm for the mean height of a population of women means that you are 95% certain that the real population mean, which you cannot know exactly unless you measure the heights of all women, lies between 152 and 164 cm. (152 cm is the lower confidence limit, 164 cm is the upper confidence limit.)

The calculation of a confidence interval takes into account the STANDARD ERROR. The standard error gives an estimate of the degree to which the sample mean varies from the population mean. It is computed on the basis of the standard deviation. We will now discuss how to calculate:

— the standard error and the 95% confidence interval of a mean (for numerical data), and

— the standard error and the 95% confidence interval of a percentage (for categorical data).

How to calculate the standard error and 95% confidence interval of a mean

When dealing with numerical data you may wish to estimate to what degree the sample mean varies from the population mean. The standard error for the mean is calculated by dividing the standard deviation by the square root of the sample size:

$$SE = \frac{\text{standard deviation}}{\sqrt{\text{sample size}}} \text{ or } \frac{SD}{\sqrt{n}}$$

It can be assumed, for a normally distributed variable, that approximately 95% of all possible sample means lie within two standard errors of the population mean. In other words, we can be 95% sure that the population mean, of which we want to have the best possible estimate, lies within two standard errors of our sample mean.

When describing variables statistically you usually present the calculated sample mean plus or minus two standard errors. This is then called the 95% CONFIDENCE INTERVAL. It means that you are about 95% certain that the true population mean is within this interval.

In Example 1 the weights of a random sample of 11 three-year-old children were taken in a village. The sample mean was 16 kg and the standard deviation of the sample was 2 kg. The standard error is:

$$\frac{2}{\sqrt{11}} = 0.6 \text{ kg}$$

The 95% confidence interval is:

$$16 \pm (2 \times 0.6) = 14.8 \text{ to } 17.2 \text{ kg}$$

This means that we are approximately 95% certain that the mean weight of all three-year-old children in your population lies between 14.8 and 17.2 kg.

Note that the larger the sample size, the smaller the standard error and the narrower the confidence interval (or the margin of error, sample size) will be. Thus the advantage of having a sufficiently large sample is that the sample mean will be a better estimate of the population mean. However, at a certain point increases in sample size demand vast investments in time and money, whereas the confidence interval only marginally decreases. In the above example an increase in sample size would clearly increase the reliability of the calculation.

With a sample size of 20 (instead of 11), the standard error would have been:

$$SE = \frac{2}{\sqrt{20}} = 0.45 \text{ kg}$$

and the 95% confidence interval for the mean weight would have been from 15.1 to 16.9 kg.

How to calculate the standard error and 95% confidence interval of a percentage

In the previous section we calculated the standard error and the 95% confidence interval of a sample mean, starting with numerical data. We will now do the same for a percentage that was calculated from categorical data.

Example 3:

Among a sample of 120 TB patients, which was drawn from the total population of TB patients in the country, it was found that 28 (or 23.3%) did not comply with their out-patient treatment. The other 92 (or 76.7%) exhibited a satisfactory degree of compliance. We now want to calculate the standard error of the percentage of non-compliance (23.3%). This is done as follows.

If p represents one of the percentages (23.3%) and 100 – p represents the other (76.7%), then the standard error of the percentage is obtained by multiplying them, dividing the result by the number in the sample and taking the square root. The formula for the standard error of a percentage is:

$$SE = \sqrt{\frac{p(100-p)}{n}}$$

In the example this is:

$$\sqrt{\frac{23.2 \times 76.7}{120}} = 3.9$$

We now also want to calculate the confidence interval for the percentage of non-compliance in the whole country.

The 95% confidence interval is

$$23.3\% \pm (2 \times 3.9)$$

which is between 15.5% and 31.1%.

This means that we are 95% confident that in the population of all TB patients in the country from which the sample of 120 was drawn, 15.5% to 31.1% do not comply with their out-patient treatment.

Note that instead of percentages we can use proportions, which can take on any value between 0 and 1. The formula for the standard error would then be:

$$\sqrt{\frac{p(1-p)}{n}}$$

In the example this is:

$$SE = \sqrt{\frac{0.233 \times 0.767}{120}} = 0.039$$

The 95% confidence interval would be between 0.155 and 0.311, or between 15.5 and 31.1%.

USE OF MEANS AND MEDIANS

Sometimes, data have outliers, which are values that are much bigger or much smaller than most of the values in the data set. Outliers affect the mean, but not the median. The median does not contain as much information as the mean because it does not take all values into consideration. The mean takes into consideration all data in the set.

It is good to know both so that we can have a piece of information that summarises information from all data (mean) and so that we can detect the presence of outliers as well.

Median, mean and mode can be used to highlight points of view. For example, when the owner of a football team talks about his club's expenses, he will like to use the mean of footballer's salaries because it takes into consideration the wages of all players. The mean in this case is not representative of the majority of the footballer's salaries because there are some few players who earn much more than the rest of their colleagues . Someone representing the footballer's party would use the median as an example of a typical footballer's salary: half of the players earn more than the median and half less than the median.

— If data have outliers in the upper end of the histogram or distribution, we say that it is skewed to the right. It has a positive skew. The mode<median<mean.

— If data have outliers in the lower end of the histogram or distribution, it is skewed to the left. It has a negative skew. The mean<median<mode.

— If the distribution is bell-shaped, data are symmetric. Mean=median=mode.

— Refer to the textbook in order to see graphic examples of skew and symmetry.

Standard deviation

It can be defined as the average distance from the average. It is the typical distance from any point in the data set to the centre. Letter s stands for the standard deviation for samples and s (Greek sigma) for the standard deviation of populations. How to calculate the standard deviation:

1. Find the mean of the data set.
2. Take each value (X) and subtract the mean from it.
3. Square each of the differences
4. Add up all the results from step 3.
5. Divide the sum of squares found in step 4 by the number of values in the data set minus one (n-1).

Interpreting the standard deviation

A small standard deviation means that data or values are closer to the mean, on average, while a large standard deviation means that results are farther away from the mean, on average.

Properties of the standard deviation

— It can never be a negative number

— Its smallest possible number is 0, which means that all the values in the data set are exactly the same.

— It is affected by outliers.

— It has the same units as the original data (Kg, minutes, etc)

The range

The range is the difference between the highest and the lowest value in the data set, after having put all values in ascending order. It is sometimes used as a measure of variability of the data, but this is not very meaningful. It is better to use the standard deviation.

Percentiles

Percentiles report the relative standing of data. It reports the percentage of data in the set below a certain datum. Calculating percentiles:

1. Put all the values in the data set in ascending order.
2. Multiply k percent times the total number of values, n.
3. Take the result and round it up the nearest whole number
4. Count the values from the smallest to the largest until you reach the value from step 3.

By taking into consideration the data of our last example (standard deviation) we are going to calculate the 90th percentile. The data are already in ascending order. We multiply n=10 times 90/100, we obtain 9. We don't need to round it up, since it's a whole number. The 90th percentile is the 9th value of the set, which is 9. This means that 90% of the grades obtained are below 9. Note that the 50th percentile is the median.

9

STANDARDISED AND TEACHER-MADE TESTS

STANDARDISED TESTS

Standardised tests, are measuring instruments which have been through a rigorous process of development and testing and will have available published data on the reliability and validity of the instrument. Normative data, i.e. data collected using the instrument, usually from a variety of different samples of the relevant population, will also be available.

The process of developing standardised tests is not very dissimilar to that involved in the development of questionnaires and attitude scales. Certainly the wording of items and the general construction of the scale will be similar to these other types of measure. Similarly the standardised test will have been subjected to item and factor analysis to identify the discriminatory items and to produce a measure of internal reliability or consistency, i.e. to demonstrate that all the items are contributing to the construct being measured. It is also likely that factor analysis, a statistical procedure, may have been used in the development of the standardised test. This allows the test constructor to examine the structure of the test, is the construct being measured unidimensional or are there more than one dimensions to the construct. For example the Eysenck Personality Inventory is a standardised test which measures the personality construct in terms of two dimensions - Extraversion and Psychoticism. The Multidimensional Locus of Control scale measures three dimensions of health belief, i.e. Internal beliefs, Chance beliefs, and beliefs in Powerful Others. Although in developing the scale the author may suspect a particular dimensional structure to the scale, factor analysis allows this to be confirmed or rejected.

The process of standardisation is essentially iterative. The researcher continues to refine the instrument through repeated testing during which the items used in the test will be "tweaked", the wording may be adjusted, items removed, others added, but most importantly the reliability and validity of the test will be examined and confirmed. An instrument must be reliable and valid if it is to have general application and researchers can be confident in using the instrument.

There are a great many standardised tests available to the health sciences researcher, both of a clinical nature and others designed to measure the psychosocial aspects of health care. Researchers new to a field should always try to use a standardised test wherever possible. It is not an easy task to develop standardised tests, and new researchers should not take on this task lightly, but if you must, then please look at the section on constructing standardised scales. Unfortunately, because these tests superficially appear simple, researchers will attempt to carry out studies with their own test instruments. This results in research being published in which tests are used, but no indication of the reliability and validity of the tests, nor details of the population on which the test may have been standardised, is presented. At best this is bad research, at worst it could lead to totally inappropriate conclusions being reached.

Standard Scores

To determine how well a student did in a test or to compare scores from different tests, you need to interpret the scores in terms of the means and standard deviations of the respective distributions. Essentially, each score must be evaluated in terms of its relative standing, or position, in the distribution; then these relative standings must be compared.

A score alone cannot tell how well a student did. For exmple, is 90 a good score? Well, perhaps the majority gets above 95 and 90 is considered an F! Is 65 a poor score? If the mean is 40, then 65 may be an A! Because the first test score may be 1 standard deviation below the mean and the second score is 1.5 standard deviations above the mean. Doing this for each score in its respective distribution gives us measures of relative standing called Z scores.

Formula for Z Scores

To find out how many standard deviations a score is from the mean, subtract the mean from the score and divide by the standard deviation. So Z scores are defined by...

$$Z = \frac{X - \bar{X}}{SD}$$

A general verbal formula for a Z score is a score minus its mean divided by its standard deviation. This formula is appropriate for describing the relative position of an original raw score in a sample and can be used to compare two or more scores from the same or different distributions. For example, you can compare your score on the first quiz in a given course to another person's score on that quiz or to your performance on the second quiz. So Z scores computed for each raw score allow you to compare relative performances. To describe a score in a population, the following formula would be used:

$$Z = \frac{X - \mu}{\sigma}$$

Characteristics of Z score

Notice that Z scores are expressed in terms of standard deviation units. In other words, standard deviations are the units of measure for Z scores. For an IQ score with Z=1.5, the score is 1.5 standard deviation units above the mean. For a person's height which has Z=2.7, the height is 2.7 standard deviations above the mean. Notice that Z scores not only give the distance of the score from the mean in standard deviation units, but also the direction of the score from the mean by using the sign of the Z score.

The mean of a set of Z scores is 0 and the variance and standard deviation of a set of Z scores are 1.

A final characteristic of z scores is that the transformation to z scores does not change the shape of the distribution from that found for X. If the distribution of X is positively skewed, then the distribution of z scores computed from the X scores is also positively skewed. Whatever the shape of the distribution of X, the distribution of z will have the same shape.

Standard Normal Distribution

Normal Distributions are:

— symmetric

— continuous

— unimodal

— bell-shaped

— asymtotic

— the mean, median, and mode are all equal.

Normal distributions are important in statistics because of their wide range of applicability. They serve as good approximations for two types of distributions: the distributions of some variables, such as IQ and height, and the sampling distributions of some statistics, such as means. Also, normal distributions play an important role as the assumed distributions for scores used in some statistics and for errors in measurement theory.

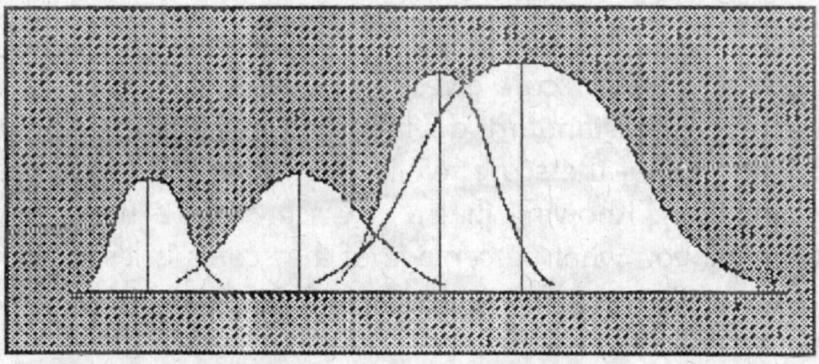

Family of Curves (vertical lines show the values of means)

Now, with these infinitely many normal distributions, how do we find the proportations of cases in any one distribution? To solve this problem, there would have to be infinitely many tables that display the proportations, or would there have to be some transformations which would not change the shape of the distribution but would give a known mean and variance. The answer is the transformation from raw to z scores. Since we are transforming any normal distribution to a standard distribution, the normal distribution with mean=0 and variance=1 is called the standard normal·distribution. The standard normal distribution is available in table form and is the distribution used to find proportions of cases for any normal distribution.

In working with the standard normal distribution, it will be helpful to think of the proportion of cases and area under the curve as interchangeable concepts. The total area under the curve is 1, and the total of all proportions is 1, because area and proportion of cases are the same for theoretical distributions such as a normal distribution. Since a proportion is a relative number, it must be greater than or equal to 0 and less than or equal to 1. Relating proportions to area, we cannot have negative area, but we can have zero or any area up to the total of 1.

Percentiles

Although a standard score gives the position of a score relative to the mean in standard deviation units, it does not give information about the score relative to the rest of the scores in the distribution. Knowing that a raw score of 12 has $z = 1.1$ does not tell you what percentage of the scores is less than 12. The percentile rank of a score is the percentage of the distribution which lies below the score and gives direct information about position relative to the rest of the scores. As shown in the following table, the 50 percentile is the mean. A score at the 62 percentile is equivalent to a B or a C.

MAKING THE MOST OF STANDARDIZED TESTS

Improving Test Scores

Odds are your child will have to take at least one standardized test each academic year and, considering the bills in the U.S. Congress, standardized tests will become high-stakes tests. A high-stakes test is a standardized test tied to a major education decision, such as whether a student will advance to the next grade, enter a preferred program, or receive a high school diploma. High-stakes tests could also be tied to district or school funding, and teachers' and administrators' salaries.

Whether or not you find a particular standardized test appropriate, your child still needs to perform at his or her best. Consider the following test-taking suggestions from the U.S. Department of Education's Educational Resources Information Center on Assessment and Evaluation:

— Talk to your child's teacher often to monitor his or her progress and to find out what activities you can do at home that may help your child's test performance.

— Be aware of your child's test performance and be sure that you can interpret the results when they become available.

— Make sure your child is well-rested and eats a well-rounded diet.

— Encourage your child to listen carefully to test-taking directions and ask questions about any instructions that are unclear.

— Don't be overly anxious about test scores, but encourage your child to take tests seriously.

— Tell your child that the best way to prepare for tests — whether they're teacher-made or standardized — is to study and know the subjects.

ALTERNATIVES TO STANDARDIZED TESTS

The use of standardized tests by schools is commonly criticized. The tests do not necessarily test what students have learned. They do not reveal what the student has achieved.

Critics have further suggested that alternatives to standardized tests be developed and used for more effective student evaluation. Such alternatives have included criterion-referenced tests, teacher-made tests, contract grading, interviews with students and their parents, and detailed documentation of a student's accomplishments. Each of these alternatives is described briefly below.

Criterion-referenced tests

Criterion-referenced tests are designed to evaluate the accomplishment of specifically stated instructional objectives. They may resemble norm-referenced tests in format and in type of administration and scoring. They differ in the way they are interpreted: on a criterion-referenced test, a student's performance is evaluated in terms of the performance of the other students taking the test. In this way, criterion-referenced tests can be more useful to teachers in identifying and planning remedial instruction in the areas in which an individual student of the entire class has demonstrated weaknesses.

Teacher-made tests

Teacher-made tests are advocated because they can be tailored to specific curricula or specific needs for information about students. Generally, teacher-made tests are criterion-referenced and are designed to measure students' mastery of the material being taught. They can provide information on small units of instruction not covered by standardized tests. For best results, teachers require opportunities for training in the development and use of tests.

Contract grading

In a contract grading system, the teacher and student agree at the beginning of a unit on particular course objectives to be fulfilled by the student, on the support to be provided by the instructor, and on how the results will be evaluated. The contract provides a form of record keeping that documents student achievement in relation to specified objectives. Upon completion of a contract, teacher and student cooperatively evaluate the work, choose new assignments, and seek to clarify previous or newly stated objectives. One caution is in order: a contract should be used as a process for learning rather than merely an instrument for getting a job done.

Interviews

Interviews with students and parents can also yield information useful in evaluating the student's progress. An interview with a student can be as specific as a teacher sitting with a child and asking him or her to share information about how to solve particular mathematics problems. Or it may be broad and probe classroom activities, student-peer interaction, classroom problems, and teacher and school goals. Parent interviews may yield unique ways of looking at their child's progress and promote a renewed interest in their child's learning.

Documentation

Documentation of students and their work should include examples of the child's work (such as drawings or photos), the child's. journal, the child's notebook or written work, the teacher's weekly records and assessment of the child's work, the teacher's reports to the parents, and sociograms. Extensive descriptions of the child's total involvement in the learning process should be included. Analysis of such documentation can provide meaningful evaluation of children's learning.

TEACHER-MADE TESTS

Test scores may be used for a portion of the students mark When teachers make up tests, some of the following suggestions may be helpful:

Tests should be balanced among the following:

— short answer/paragraph answer

— words/pictures/maps/diagrams/etc.

— easy/difficult questions

— factual knowledge/application of knowledge

— knowledge/skills

As much as possible, test questions should be given within a meaningful context.

Rather than:	Try this:
Name the continents and oceans.	Name the continents and oceans as shown on the map. (Provide a clear, uncluttered map with continents and oceans

	numbered.)
Define the following:	Read the following sentences. Tell what axis each underlined word means. You may use sentences, phrases, examples or diagrams. The earth rotates on its axis.
Mark the following true or false.	Mark the following true or false. For the false statements, rewrite them so they are true.
Answer the following questions: or Describe how you have improved in a skill while doing this unit. or List 3 things you have learned, what you enjoyed most, etc.	Write 2 questions that you have about the following topics:

Students should not be penalized with a low mark in Social Studies because they are weak in reading or writing. These students may be assisted in one of several ways.

— The teacher might go over the test beforehand and read and explain each question.

— Tests could be done in small groups or with a partner.

— The teacher might form a small group during the test and quietly read each question with the group, allowing time for students to write their answers or give them orally.

— In some cases it may be appropriate for some students to

have a tutor coach them beforehand.

The teacher might choose to use a format dfferent from the conventional test. For example:

— Make up a test that has as many questions (or groups of questions) as there are students in the class. Tape or place each question on a student!s desk. The students are given 30 seconds (?) at each desk to answer the questions and rotate at a signal given by the teacher. The studenti' responses are written on a sheet of foolscap that has beei. clearly numbered beforehand. (Students should be reminded during the test to double check the numbers of their questions.)

— A variation of this is the use of testing stations where a variety of materials are set up, and a group of students would answer a set of questions or respond to some directions.

This type of test has a number of advantages:

— It allows a teacher to use pictures, news articles, special maps, artifacts, library books, etc.

— The students all finish at the same time.

— If the answers are straight forward, it could be marked by the students immediately after the test. Answers could then be discussed along with the maps, artifacts, etc. that were used.

— It may be advantageous when testing for attainment (e.g using an index, locating a book in a drawer from the card catalogue, accessing on-line information, interpreting a legend on a map, etc)

- The students enjoy the change.

Students may be given the option to earn marks in alternate ways. This particular r the students and teachers curriculum, fo example, would be conducive to having design and carry out various long-term projects.

Test questions should test only the knowledge, skills and understandings that have actually been taught.

There should be no surprises when it comes to student evaluation.

— Students should always be aware of evaluation criteria and procedures.

— They should have a role in the evaluation process.

— They should receive regular feedback as to "how they are doing.

Even though parents and the media value published test scores, most teachers do not rely on standardized tests to tell them what their students know and don't know. Standardized tests occur so infrequently that one aggregate score is not very helpful in determining future instructional goals. Teacher-made tests, however, allow teachers to make decisions that keep instruction moving. Teachers can make changes immediately to meet the needs of their students.

The key to teacher-made tests is to make them a part of instruction—not separate from it. Tests should be instructional and ongoing. Rather than being "after-the-fact" to find out what students did not learn, they should be more "before-the-fact" to target essential standards.

Teachers also need to make adjustments in their tests for the various learning styles, multiple intelligences and learning problems of the students in their classes. It would be impossible to address every student's needs on every test, but efforts should be made to construct tests that motivate students to learn, provide choices and make allowances for individual differences.

How can we design better teacher-made tests?

Most teachers will not have time to rewrite all their tests to conform to the guidelines suggested below. However, it is important to make sure new tests are designed to meet student needs—and truly reflect learning.

Guidelines for teacher-made tests

1. Create the test before beginning the unit.
2. Make sure the test is correlated to course objectives or learning standards and benchmarks.
3. Give clear directions for each section of the test.
4. Arrange the questions from simple to complex.
5. Give point values for each section (e.g., true/false count for two points each).
6. Vary the question types (true/false, fill-in-the-blank, multiple choice, essay, matching). Limit to 10 questions per type.
7. Group question types together.
8. Type or print clearly. (Leave space between questions to facilitate easy reading and writing.)
9. Make sure appropriate reading level is used.
10. Include a variety of visual, oral and kinesthetic tasks.
11. Make allowances for students with special needs.
12. Give students some choice in the questions they select (e.g., a choice of graphic organizers or essay questions).
13. Vary levels of questions (gathering, processing and application questions).
14. Provide a grading scale so students know what score constitutes a certain grade.
15. Give sufficient time for all students to finish

Comparison of Standardized and Teacher-made Tests

	Standardized	Teacher-Made
Learning Outcomes	Measurement general outcomes and content appropriate to the majority of schools in the U.S. They are tests of general skills and understanding tend not to reflect specific or unique emphases of local curricula.	Well adapted to the specific and unqiue outcomes and contents of a local curriculum; they are adaptable to various sizes of work units, but tend to neglect complex learning outcomes.
Quality of test items	Qualty of items generally is high. Items are written by specialists, pretested, and selected on the basis of the results of a quantitative item analysis.	Quality of items is often unknown. Quality is typically lower than that of standardized tests due to the limited time of the teacher.
Reliability	Reliability is high, commonly between .80 and .95, and frequently above .90.	Reliability is usually unknown, but can be high if items are carefully constructed.
Administration and scoring	Procedures are standardized; specific instructions are provided.	Uniform procedures are possible, but usually are flexible and unwritten.
Interpretation of scores	Scores can be compared to norm groups.Test manual and other guides aid interpretation and use.	Score comparisons and interpretations are limited to local class or school situation. Few, if any, guidelines are available for interpretation and use.

INDEX

Adolescent Sexuality 122
Amputation 6
Arthrogryposis 8

Bernouilli's Theorem 245

Career Planning Process 186
Cerebral Palsy 9
Chronic illnesses 5
Cognitive Development, Theory of 100
Cognitive skills 88
Collaboration Checklist 188
Contract grading system 284
Contract grading 284
Conventional test 287
Counseling Programmes 76
Criterion-referenced tests 283
Cystic fibrosis 4

Data collection 177
Defence Mechanisms 119
Developmental competencies, 77
Documentation 285

Early childhood stimulation programs 90
Educational programs 79

Fraud's theory 82
Frequency distribution 232

Guidance and Counseling Programmes 76
Guidance curriculum 77

Hospitalization 87, 95

Instructional process 180
Interchangeable concepts 281
Interest Inventories 186
Interval recording 185
Interviews 284
Invisible Handicaps 4

Juvenile Rheumatoid Arthritis (JRA) 16

Learning styles, 288

Margaret Mead 84
Measurement theory 281
Mental Retardation 13
Mobility Disabilities 6
Multidimensional Locus of Control scale 278
Muscular Dystrophy (M.D.) 17
Myers-Briggs Type Indicator(MBTI) 187

Non verbal clues 75
Non-verbal messages 105
Normal Curve 235

Normal Distribution 232

Observable behaviors 181
Occupational exploration 81
Oral communication skills 174
Oral examination 172

Perceptual Disorder 13
Personal adjustment 111
Personality Inventory 277
Physical disability 1
Physical impairment 89
Psychosocial Development 82

Recording rates 184

Scatter Diagram 252
Self Assessment 186
Self Concept 105
Simple Application 243
Situational problems 76
Special skills 171
Spina Bifida 18
Spiritual dimension 75
Standard deviation units 282
Standard Normal Distribution 280
Standardisation, process of 278
Standardised Tests 277
Student performance 179

Teacher-made tests 284, 288
Time sampling 186

Value Inventories 186

Zero Correlation 258